Library and Society

M Ram

RANDOM

RANDOM PUBLICATIONS
NEW DELHI (INDIA)

Library and Society

ISBN 978-93-5111-946-3

Published in 2016 in India by

RANDOM PUBLICATIONS

4376-A/4B, Gali Murari Lal, Ansari Road
New Delhi-110 002
Phone : +9111-43580356, 011-23289044, 011-43142548
e-mail: sales@randompublications.com,
info@randompublications.com, randomexports@gmail.com
Reprint 2021

Type Setting by : Friends Media, Delhi-110089
Digitally Printed at : Replika Press Pvt. Ltd.

Preface

A library is organized for use and maintained by a public body, an institution, a corporation, or a private individual. Public and institutional collections and services may be intended for use by people who choose not to—or cannot afford to—purchase an extensive collection themselves, who need material no individual can reasonably be expected to have, or who require professional assistance with their research.

Information is power and we live in a world where the boundaries of that power are rapidly shifting. The nature of the new society and the role to be played by libraries is shaping up into one of the great debates of the information age, for most countries now recognize the importance of information as a vast resource.

Public libraries typically provide services free of charge to anyone who wishes to use them, although lending is often restricted to residents of the locality. Many provide literacy programmes, reader development promotions and act as an information point for the availability of local public services. Typically they collect and preserve a wide range of materials relating to the history and development of the locality. Special services have been developed to serve the needs of particular groups such as children (including storytelling programmes), housebound people, and the visually impaired. Public libraries in particular strive to serve all sections of their communities without discrimination.

Prosperity and the development of society and of individuals are fundamental human values. They will only be attained through the ability of well-informed citizens to exercise their democratic rights and to play an active role in society. Constructive participation and the development of democracy depend on satisfactory education as well as on free and unlimited access to knowledge, thought, culture and information. The public library, the local gateway to knowledge, provides a basic condition for lifelong learning, independent decision- making and cultural development of the individual and social groups.

It is hoped that this book shall find its place with anyone who is interested to know and learn more about the basics of library and information science. Not only the students, but the teachers of library and information science can derive equal benefit from this series. The books are equally suited to librarianship, library science students and library staff seeking to upgrade their skills.

– Author

Contents

1

Digital Libraries and Society

INTRODUCTION

Digital libraries are large, organized collections of information objects. Whereas standard library automation systems provide a computerized version of thc catalog—a gateway into the treasure-house of information stored in the library—digital libraries incorporate the treasure itself, namely the information objects that constitute the library's collection. Whereas standard libraries are, of necessity, ponderous and substantial institutions, with large buildings and significant funding requirements, even large digital libraries can be lightweight.

Whereas standard libraries, whose mandate includes preservation as well as access, are "conservative" by definition, with institutional infrastructure to match, digital libraries are nimble: they emphasize access and evolve rapidly.

The five stages in this part provide an excellent illustration of the huge variety of interesting issues in digital library research that impacts the Asia Pacific region. Unlike the New World, where most of the research on technological aspects of digital libraries originates, Asia has an exceptionally rich cultural heritage. This manifests itself in a huge legacy of documents, in various forms—from paper to palm leaves—and in various different conditions.

The need to preserve this legacy is particularly pressing in today's world, where political instability is rife and climate change is beginning to have an effect. As recent events have shown, disasters, both manmade and natural, can have a devastating effect on fragile cultural artifacts.

S.M. Shafi from the University of Kashmir, India, surveys the many issues involved with digital archiving of medieval manuscripts in Asia. Libraries are pillars of education, and it is natural to expect that digital libraries will provide new opportunities for innovative educational practices.

These will be particularly relevant to the Asia Pacific region because of the huge disparities in access to education between the different communities there. Peer-to-peer learning has always been a crucial factor in personal development, although it is frequently ignored in educational studies.

Natalie Lee-San from Nanyang Technological University, Singapore, describes her studies of how digital libraries can provide an innovative, perhaps revolutionary, environment for peer-to-peer learning amongst youths. She touches on many practical issues: gender differences, different learning styles, different levels of media and computer literacy, and age-related differences.

Many economies in the Asia Pacific region are agricul-turally-based. Modern agriculture is a knowledge-based activity that can benefit greatly from digital libraries. Mila Ramos from the International Rice Research Institute in the Philippines describes a large-scale digital library system designed to support the growth, nurturing, harvesting, and distribution of that most Asian of staples, rice.

This digital library supports an institute whose goal is to improve the well-being of present and future generations of rice farmers and consumers, particularly those with low incomes. The institute's library houses the world's most comprehensive collection of technical literature on rice, and provides a widely-used international reference service.

As in many specialized libraries, digital library technology is seen to have special advantages in a world of shrinking library budgets. Intellectual property issues are a central driving force behind the market in information of which libraries are a part. And the questions become more complex as the nature of today's information shifts from a primarily book-based culture to one that embraces all types of multimedia objects, and large, carefully-curated, collections of such objects.

The stage on *"Multimedia digital library as intellectual property"* by Hideyasu Sasaki and Yasujshi Kiyoki at Keio University in Japan clarify the copyright situation as it affects multimedia collections and compilations. They go on to discuss the patentability of particular retrieval mechanisms, an essential component of digital libraries. The fifth stage in this part on how digital library research impacts the Asia Pacific region is the present one, on digital libraries in society.

Most existing digital library projects, being research-oriented, are predicated on state-of-the-art equipment and interfaces, academic and research institutions, special collections. In contrast: digital library technology can and should be available to everyone, on all platforms, in all countries; and it can and should enable ordinary people to exercise their creative powers to conceive, assemble, build, and disseminate new information collections that are designed not just for western academics but for a wide diversity of different audiences throughout the world. Though less glamorous, this may, in the end, be a more important goal for society.

Digital libraries pose an inherent tension between the technologist's desire for advanced solutions that use the latest and greatest hardware and software, and the librarian's desire for wide, crossplatform availability and long-term preser-vation—as epitomized by the sustained success of paper as a delivery medium.

To achieve universal access for both information consumers and collection-builders is really a problem for HCI. We examine the social need for digital libraries, particularly in developing countries, by briefly sketching some trends in commercial publishing and contrasting them with a growing international perspective of information as a public good. We draw out the implications for the user interface, which is the principal bottleneck in allowing non-specialist people to make public information available in focused collections that are universally usable.

Then we introduce digital library technology and illustrate it with a particular example, the Greenstone digital library software, which is designed for a broad user base and is in widespread use in many corners of the world—from Uganda to the US, Kazakhstan to Canada, Nepal to New Zealand. Following that, we review a project that is applying digital library technology to the distribution of humanitarian information in the developing world, a context that is both innovative and socially motivated.

Next we discuss issues of universal access and illustrate them with reference to the Greenstone software. We include a brief demonstration of a prototype system that is intended to allow anyone to build and disseminate information collections, and illustrates some human interface challenges that arise when providing necessarily complex functionality to a non-computer-oriented user base. We close with the hope that future digital libraries will find a new role to play in helping to reduce the social inequity that haunts today's world, both within our own countries and between nations.

BOOKS, LIBRARIES, AND THE SOCIALLY DISADVANTAGED

Today, the long-standing three-way tension between the commercial interests of publishers, the needs of society and information users, and the social mandate of public libraries, is being pulled and stretched as never before. First, the very notion of a "book" is evolving in many different directions: books become more interactive; publishers rent content; books are distributed under restrictive conditions that mechanically prohibit sharing.

While it would be premature to make specific predictions, it seems likely that these trends will further disadvantage the disadvantaged—particularly those in poorer countries who have yet to benefit from ready access to ordinary books. Second, a huge body of information is becoming freely available on the Internet.

Much is of questionable quality, but some is very good indeed. In many cases the information is provided for the "public good" rather than for commercial profit, and the redistribution of such information is likely to be encouraged, rather than prohibited, by those who make it available.

Initiatives like UNESCO's "Information for all" programme and the upcoming World Summit on the Information Society highlight the importance of public information; they are founded on the belief that information literacy will help alleviate many of the problems confronting human societies.

Third, the implications for libraries are mixed. Whereas new controls by publishers over how the content they own may be used presents libraries with significant problems, the ready availability of "public good" information meshes well with library philosophy.

A new role is emerging for information professionals who can select material, index it, add appropriate metadata, and redistribute it in added-value form for the good of society. Suitable technological infrastructure is being provided by the open source movement, which is making available high-quality software for repackaging and distribution of information (and not just on computer networks).

Books

What future has the book in the digital world? The question is a complex one that is being widely aired. Authors and publishers ask how many copies of a work will be sold if networked digital libraries enable worldwide access to an electronic copy of it.

Their nightmare is that the answer is *one*: how many books will be published online if the entire market can be extinguished by the sale of one electronic copy to a public library? To counter this threat, the entertainment industry is promoting new *"digital rights management"* (DRM) schemes that permit a degree of control over what users can do that goes far beyond the traditional legal bounds of copyright.

Indeed, the acronym is more aptly expanded as "digital restrictions management" because it is concerned solely with content owners rights and not at all with user's rights. It is, in effect, a "private governance system in which computer systems regulate which acts users are and are not authorized to perform".

Anticircumvention rules are sanctioned by the *Digital Millennium Copyright Act* (DMCA) in the US. The DMCA has been used, for example, to prosecute a Norwegian teenager for writing software to play a DVD that he had purchased on a computer for which no commercial playback systems exist. Can DRM be applied to books? The motion picture industry can compel manufacturers to incorporate encryption into their products because it holds key patents on DVD players. Commercial book publishers are promoting e-book readers that, if adopted on a wide scale, would allow the same kind of control to be exerted over reading material.

Basic rights that we take for granted—such as the ability to lend a book to a friend, resell it on the second-hand market, keep it indefinitely, continue to use it when your e-book reader breaks down, donate it to charity, preserve it for your grandchildren, copy excerpts without resorting to a handwritten transcription—are in jeopardy.

DRM allows such rights to be controlled, monitored, and withdrawn instantly, and DMCA legislation makes it illegal for users to seek redress by taking matters into their own hands. Fortunately, perhaps, lack of standardization and compatibility issues are delaying consumer adoption of e-books.

In the realm of scholarly publishing, digital rights management is more advanced. Academic libraries license access to content in electronic form, often in tandem with purchase of print versions too. They have been able to negotiate reasonable conditions with publishers—probably because they represent the lion's share of the scholarly market.

However, the extent of libraries' power in the consumer book market is moot. One can envisage a scenario where publishers establish a system of commercial, pay-per-view, libraries for e-books and refuse public libraries access to books in a form that can be circulated. These new directions present our society with puzzling challenges, and it would be rash to predict what society's response will be. But one thing is certain: they will surely increase the degree of disenfranchisement of those who do not have access to the technology.

Public Information

In parallel with publishers' moves to reposition books as technological artifacts with refined and flexible control over how they can be used, an opposing trend has emerged: the ready availability of free information on the Internet. Of course, the world-wide web is an unreliable source of enlightenment, and undiscriminating use is dangerous—and widespread.

As early as 1996 complaints arose that the Web's contents are largely unattributed, undated, unannotated, unreliable; information about author and publisher is unavailable or incomplete; far too many resource catalogues are chasing far too few original or non-trivial documents—complaints that are very familiar today. But one thing has changed: search engines and other portals have enormously increased our ability to locate information that is at least ostensibly relevant to any given question.

Teachers complain bitterly that students view the Web as a replacement for the library, harvesting information indiscriminately to provide answers to assignments that are at best shallow and at worst incoherent and incorrect. One consolation is that the very same search facilities can be used to detect plagiarism.

Nevertheless, the Web abounds with accessible, high-quality information. Many social groups, non-profit societies and charities make it their business to create sites and collect and organize information there. To take a single example at random, a Google search for *diabetes* returns three national diabetes associations in the top ten hits, and of course many more exist.

Each of these sites offers a cornucopia of valuable information on the disease, which is not commercial and provided for the public good. Widespread use is strongly encouraged, and it seems likely that arrangements could be made for re-distribution of the material presented there, particularly it was intended as a not-for-profit service and appropriate acknowledgement was made.

One of the key problems with information distribution via the Web is that it disenfranchises developing countries. Although the Web does not extend into the homes of the socially disadvantaged in developed countries either, various national programmes are working to provide access.

But network access varies enormously across the world. Whereas in 1998 more than a quarter of the US population were surfing the Internet, the figures for Latin America and the Caribbean was 0.8 per cent, for Sub-Saharan Africa 0.1 per cent, and for South Asia 0.04 per cent. Schools and hospitals in developing countries are poorly connected.

Even in South Africa, the bestconnected African country, many hospitals and 75 per cent of schools have no telephone line. Universities are better equipped, but even there up to 1,000 people can depend on just one terminal. The Internet "is failing the developing world".

Prompted by this inequity, the importance of information, and particularly public information, is today being highlighted by prominent international bodies. For example, UNESCO's "Information for all" programme was established in 2001 to foster debate on the political, ethical and societal challenges of the emerging global knowledge society and to carry out projects promoting equitable access to information.

It reflects a growing awareness that information is playing an increasing role in generating wealth and human capital, and that participation in the "global knowledge society" is essential for social and individual development.

Information literacy is described as "a new frontier" by the Director of UNESCO's Information Society Division. The Inter-national Telecommunications Union has established a World Summit on the Information Society, held in Geneva in December 2003 and Tunis in 2005, to promote a global discussion of the fundamental changes that are being brought about in our lives by the transformation from an industrial to an information society, and to confront the extreme disparities of access to information between the industrialized countries and the developing world.

CO-USAGE OF DOCUMENTS IN A LARGE DIGITAL LIBRARY

Creating relationships between similar documents is an activity that has a long distinguished history in Information Retrieval. In his textbook on the subject Korfhage (1997) writes "Probably the single key concept behind information storage and retrieval is document similarity". A practical motivation for the search for similarity is to improve information retrieval. When users have found one document they can be directed to similar documents that may be worth their attention.

A more theoretical motivation is the discovery of patterns of thought within a body of knowledge that is dispersed across a collection of documents. There are, of course, many ways in which similarity between documents can be assessed. One way is to use the judgement of an expert.

This is typically done by classifying documents according to a subject classification. This is a tried and trusted method. However, it requires human expertise and labour. These do not come cheap these days.

Therefore many collections have no classification data. Within the collection of documents that we study in this paper, three in four documents do not have a subject classification. Other classic measures of relationship between academic papers are the strengths of co-citation and bibliographic coupling. Such an analysis presumes that a citation index for the papers is available. Producing one manually is even more expensive than subject classification.

It is possible to use recently available software for autonomous citation indexing. Barrueco Cruz and Krichel report on on recent effort s using the same digital library that we study here. In this paper, we introduce a completely new concept of similarity that is user-centered.

We start with the idea that two documents are similar if they respond to the same information need. Thus roughly speaking we can think of two document as similar, if many users will withdraw the papers together while they are working on the system. Provided that we have a digital library with a long log of usage, we can find which papers have frequently been used together. This is what we will refer to as "co-usage" in the following. We are not aware of a study that has developed and tested this concept within a digital library context. We are, of course, aware that commercial systems use a related concept. Amazon.com, for example, suggests to a customer who is considering to purchase an item x that other people who bought x also bought item y. But since users are anonymous in our digital library, within the scope of our collection, the evidence on common usage is more difficult to gather.

MEASURING CO-USAGE

Our dataset comes from logs of the usage of the RePEc digital library. We have built this library over many years. RePEc is the largest free distributed academic digital library in the world. It is a pioneering effort in three respects.

First, RePEc pioneered the business model of the Open Archives Initiative distinction between data providers and service providers. RePEc has grown over 200 archives that are used in 10 different user services.

Second, RePEc is more than a collection of data about documents. RePEc offers a comprehensive picture of academic output by describing collection of documents, persons that are involved as authors of documents or editors of collections, and the institutions to which they belong in a relational database scheme.

Third, RePEc is essentially volunteer driven and has no owner. It is a public good much like the Internet. The data that we examine comes from the WoPEc user service. This service, founded in 1993 is available on the web at three locations since 1994.

These are Hitotsubashi University in Tokyo, Japan, Manchester Computing in the UK, and Washington University in St. Louis in the USA. The web site has static pages for each paper. In addition, there are a number of pages that link different papers together.

There are pages that list papers that have been issued within same series, and there are pages that group papers with the same subject classification. The log data also contains indication about what searches users have been making. However, as far as we are concerned, only the access to the description of the individual papers is relevant.

To begin with, recall that WoPEc is a non-commercial service. WoPEc does not enter into a contractual arrangement with a customer, with or without an exchange of money. Contractual arrangements with customers are expensive to arrange because they involve complicated negotiations, privacy issues etc. On the other hand contractual arrangement—even without exchange of money—generate customer data. The customer data itself has considerable value, see Shapiro and Varian for an illuminating discussion.

In the period that we examine, cookies have not been used. Therefore we need to wade through the log to find traces of usage by the same persons. All that the log offers is a trace to the Internet address (*i.e.* IP number) of the client machine, a file or action performed, and a time when this happened. Over recent years, the Internet is more and more accessed through personal computers rather than through multi-user systems.

However, we can not be completely sure that an IP number corresponds to the machine of an individual user, because there are caching sites. Therefore we must be watchful of IP addresses that appear particularly frequently. Let us for the moment make the assumption that the usage data from one single machine comes from one single user. We are then in the happy situation that we have identified the user.

However, to be able to claim that papers that are appearing together are joined together because they correspond to the same user need, we still have to assume that the information need of the user remains the same throughout the period of observation. This is problematic. Typically users will regard WoPEc as a reference source, and therefore naturally turn to it with different information needs. Therefore it is likely that the log contains material that corresponds to different information needs, even if they are expressed by the same user.

Therefore, we have chosen to think of users using the system within sessions. We typically think of a session as an academic, using a web browser on a desktop machine, going to the WoPEc site, make a few searches and look at a few results. Or we can think of it as a student, walking into a computer lab, uses a search engine, finds a page on the WoPEc service and navigates it for further data.

Technically, we define a session as a subset of the total log that comes from the same IP address within a certain time frame. In fact we assume that there must not be more than one hour between two consecutive log entries for them to qualify to be within the same session. In addition, we do not consider repeat access to the same paper as two different accesses to that paper. Such access is likely to occur mainly for technical reasons, such as that the user did not have time to read the article at the first discovery.

Under these restrictions it appears to be convenient to model sessions as sets of papers. We can now proceed to a formal definition of co-usage. Let D be the set documents in the library and S be the set of sessions. Each session s contains a subset of the set of documents, *i.e.* s Ì D. Introduce | · | as as notation for the number of elements in a set. Let there be two documents di and dj. Let u(di, dj) be the set of all sessions that contain both di and dj. For convenience of notation, write u(di) = u(di, di). Then we propose to call the co-usage coefficient c(di, dj) as follows

$$c\left(d_1,d_j\right)=\frac{\left|u\left(d_i,d_j\right)\right|}{\left|u\left(d_i\right)\right|\left|u\left(d_j\right)\right|}.$$

The motivation for introducing the product in the denominator is to ensure that we do not have situations where one paper appears frequently with another by the sheer size of its own usage. It also leads c(di, dj) to gain the attractive properties that 0 <= c(di, dj) <= 1 and that c(di, di) = 1. It is clear that the measure that we propose here is an intuitive one. It is not a scientifically developed metric of the likelihood that, whatever size the session is, we will see the two papers appearing together in the session.

It is possible to evaluate that probability. However that calculation is not attempted here. It is left for future work. Even if we can theoretically ascertain how to calculate the probability, we can not in practice calculate it for all possible document couples, because of the amount of calculations that would have to be made within a large digital library as ours.

Results

We ran a programme to search for co-usage on a log for three years 1999–2001. There are 102551867 lines in the log. We discarded 24836221 requests for images, 401614 requests for CSS files, and 9315 contained another error. 3164598 requests contained a 404 error and were omitted. Most of them went to robots.txt. 3966837 distinct hosts accessed the system. We exclude all accesses from hosts that accessed robots.txt. In addition, there are cache and proxy sites that we would like to remove as well. This is a more difficult terrain. The rule that we chose was to look at each day's log, and detect all hosts that issued more than 100 requests. In total, we detected 23068 such hosts, and discarded 17484961 lines because they were made by these hosts. This left us with 23413849 to analyzed. We detected 5251337 sessions.

We limited ourselves to sessions that had more than 3 accesses and less than 100, and that included at least one search. There were 69179 sessions that remained for analysis. We can not make the results available here, for obvious reasons of space. Therefore we have placed them at http://openlib.org/home/krichel/kumegawa/report.htm. We print the top couples that have the highest co-usage, up to a rounded coefficient of 50 per cent. The following results appear when we look through the data.

First, papers in the same series seem to be much more prone to co-usage than papers from different series. It is often papers by the same authors, over different periods of time, available in the same working paper series or journal that appeared to be co-used a lot. This observation suggests that the original split of the data in different series does not only provide an organizational layer to the data, but also a semantic one. Second, from reading through the related couples, it appears that a key concept that appears in the title immediately explains the co-usage. Thus, it should be possible to gain insights into key concepts that are of user interest by looking at the title data of papers that are co-used, and find the common words. This would be an interesting subject for further research.

This paper has introduced co-usage as a means to make document to document relationships. The concept of co-usage has been found to lead to excellent empirical results. Our results suggests that the concept of co-usage is a valid and interesting one.

Any remaining problems that we are experiencing to make it work in practice are consequences of poor measurement of usage, rather than flaws in the underlying theoretical reasoning. Just in the case of co-citation and bibliographic coupling, there will be a debate on how useful co-usage analysis really is. We have opened that debate with this paper.

There are two further consequences from this paper. In the short run, we intend to incorporate co-usage similarity into future developments of WoPEc, to build links from the description of one paper to the description of another as suggested by co-usage analysis.

In the longer run, we believe that our work can be seen as simple, but pioneering step towards information retrieval systems that are learning. Instead of having a system that has a fixed procedure that is applicable whatever the query an the collection, we can imagine that future information systems will learn from past user behaviour to better serve the present user. Co-usage appears as a key concept to move things forward in that direction.

SORTING SEARCH RESULTS OF LITERATURE DIGITAL LIBRARIES

An OLDL (Online Literature Digital Library) is a library in which collections, *i.e.*, publications from one or more domains of study, are stored in digital formats and accessible by users through the Internet.

Examples of well-known OLDLs are:

- IEEE Xplore
- CiteSeer
- Google Scholar
- PubMed

Digital libraries are rapidly growing in popularity. For instance, ScienceDirect, the world's leading scientific, technical and medical information resource celebrated its billionth article download in November'06 since, launched in 1999. Besides usage, digital libraries are also rapidly growing in terms of size and diversity of topics.

For instance:

- In Computer Science, ACM Digital Library has close to one million full-text publications collected over 50 years, to search and download.
- In Electrical Engineering and Computer Science, IEEE Xplore, another OLDL, provides users with on-line access to more than 1,700 selected conferences proceedings.

These high growth rates introduced several challenges facing the information access capability of OLDLs. Next we list few challenges that probably guides future research related to LDLs.

CHALLENGE 1: LARGE SIZES AND TOPIC DIVERSITY OF SEARCH OUTPUT RESULTS

Search outputs of OLDLs tend to suffer from the 'topic diffusion' problem, where commonly, keyword-based searches produce a large number of publications over a large number of topics, where not all topics are of interest to the user. One way to solve this problem is to assign scores to search results. Assigning scores to publications helps OLDLs to present the most important relevant publications to the user first, Citation-based publication score measures are commonly used for ranking publications. At the present time, OLDLs lack effective and accurate publication ranking.

CHALLENGE 2: LACK OF EFFECTIVE SCORING FUNCTIONS FOR PUBLICATIONS

At the present time, OLDLs lack effective and accurate publication rankings. Providing accurate publication scores can help users in reducing the time spent in searching OLDLs, and thus enhances the scalability of OLDL usage as users can quickly identify important relevant publications to their topic of interest.

CHALLENGE 3: LACK OF EFFECTIVE SCORING FUNCTIONS FOR SEARCH OUTPUTS

In the field of literature digital libraries, citation analysis is employed to order digital library search outputs. Examples of citation-based measures are citation-count and PageRank. However, as noticed by, citation-based measures compute popularity of publications based on the 'current' state of a citation graph that continuously changes and evolves.

Thus PageRank is effective in capturing the popularity of publications based on the current citation-graph inhand. We show that PageRank may assign inaccurate popularity scores for both old and recent publications. And thus PageRank cannot be used to rank OLDL search outputs. We therefore need effective techniques to order search results based on their importance and relevance to users' interests.

EVALUATING PUBLICATION SCORING FUNCTIONS IN DIGITAL LIBRARIES

This section deals with the issues of defining score functions for publications in digital libraries, and evaluating how good they are.

Presently, digital libraries do not assign scores to publications, even though they are potentially useful for:

- Providing comparative assessment, or 'importance', of papers; and
- Anking papers returned in search outputs.

Using social networks or bibliometrics, one can define a number of publication score functions. Existing citation-based publication score functions are all based on the notion of prestige in social networks and bibliometry. The well-known PageRank algorithm determines the importance of a publication by the number and importances of publications with links to it. The Hyperlink Induced Topic Search (HITS) algorithm is similar to the PageRank algorithm in that HITS involves computing two scores for each publication; hub and authority scores. Authorities represent high-prestige publications, whereas hubs are publications that have links to authorities.

Other citation-based score functions can be derived as follows:

- Use normalised citation count as the basis for a score function.
- Revise the score of a paper using the score of its publication venue.
- Add weights to citations, *e.g.*, citations by an 'important' author's work are more significant.
- Revise the score of a paper using temporal distributions of citations; *e.g.*, citations in the last 10 years are more significant than earlier citations.

- Revise a paper score using the score of its citation venue; that is, capture the notion of a hub or an authority, *e.g.*, survey journal represents a hub, whereas a research paper represents an authority.
- Revise a paper score by the score of its author.

Citation-based Publication Score Functions

PageRank

Importance of papers that cite a particular paper determines its importance. PageRank and HITS were designed based on this assumption. PageRank scores is computed recursively using the formula

$$P_{i+1} = (1-d)M^T P_i + E$$

Where *Pi* and *Pi+1* are the current and next iteration PageRank vectors respectively. *M* is a matrix derived from the citation matrix *C* by normalising all row-sums in *C* to *1*. *C*, in turn, is the adjacency matrix of the graph *G* formed as follows; the papers represent the graph nodes, and the citation relationships between these papers represent the edges. *C* is of size *NxN*, where *N* is the total number of papers in the system. Finally, *d* and *(1-d)* are the future citation probability. Given that an author *A* who is writing a new paper and already cited paper *u* which in turn cites paper *v*, and let *w* be a paper in AnthP selected randomly. The parameter *d* represents the probability that A will cite *w*, and *(1-d)* is the probability that *A* will cite *v*. To guarantee the algorithm convergence, it is assumed to have a hidden link between each pair of the graph nodes. This link is represented by the user-defined parameter *E*. A variation of *E* is simply *E1=d*. Another variation of E that is used in is,

$$E_2 = d / N[1_N]P_i.$$

Hubs and Authorities

Authority score of paper *P* is computed by summing up the hub scores of the papers citing *P*. Hub score of *P* is computed by summing up the authority scores of the papers that *P* cites. Computation is recursive until results converge after a number of iterations. One difference between HITS and PageRank is that the first one works on papers in the result set of a query, while the latter considers all the papers independent of the query.

Citation Count

A paper, normally, does not cite another paper unless the cited paper is relevant. And, large number of citations to a paper gives an indication that the paper is important. Based on this fact, one can use citation count as a measure for paper importance. For a given paper *P*, let CitationCount (*P*) be the number of times paper *P* is cited by other papers. Using the number of citations, paper

P is as important as those papers that have the same number of citations and more important than those papers that have fewer citations. As suggested, refer to this paper ranking measure as PCitation_Count.

Evaluating Publication Score Functions

Figure shows the three score functions, namely, PageRank (PPgRank), Authorities scores of HITS (PAuth) and, the Citation-count (PCitCnt). As it is clear from the figure the three functions are highly skewed, and do not separate scores well over the interval. This figure is based on the AnthP digital collection from the field of data management. In the author observed the skewness and inseparability of these functions independently in computer science and life sciences publications as well. And, it is shown that distributions of citation-based score functions are also highly skewed and decay very fast. Studies show that the cause is topic diffusion since, scores are computed with respect to the full publication set.

In the authors compared and evaluated several publication score functions, including PageRank and Authorities scores, both adopted from the www search domain, and citation-count scores from the bibliometrics domain. The authors observed the separability problem with all of these functions which is that none of these scoring functions assigns scores that distribute well over a given scale, *e.g.* Instead, distributions of existing publication score functions are highly skewed, and decay very fast resulting in a much less useful comparative publication assessment capability for users.

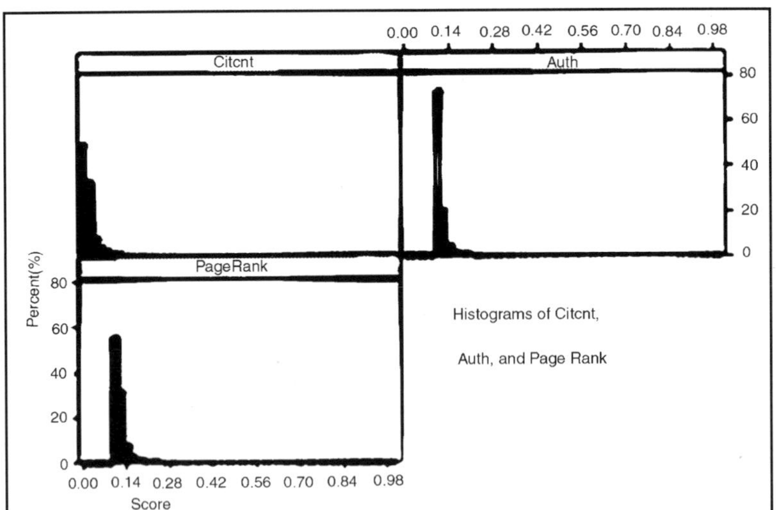

Fig. Skewness of Score Distribution of the Three Main Citation-based Publication Score Functions.

This lack of separability is caused by the 'rich gets richer' phenomena, *i.e.*, a very small number of publications with relatively high numbers of in-citations have even higher chances of receiving new citations. Yet, these scoring functions are still not very accurate, probably caused by topic diffusion in search outputs. In the following section, and by using the research-pyramid model proposed in, the authors in normalise scores of publications within their own research pyramids, which allows for a fair comparative assessment of publications as publications are compared to their peers in their own research pyramids.

IMPROVED PUBLICATION SCORES VIA RESEARCH PYRAMIDS

Providing accurate publication scores for search results and ranking publications returned as search results accurately can help users in reducing the time spent in searching OLDLs. And, better publication rankings are also useful for comparative assessments of publication venues and scientists as well. At the present time, OLDLs lack effective and accurate publication rankings. For instance, ACM Digital Library returns rankings of publication search results that are unexplained and not useful to users.

Moreover, search outputs of OLDLs tend to suffer from the 'topic diffusion' problem, where commonly, keyword-based searches produce a large number of publications over a large number of topics, thereby producing scores that are non-specific to topics. The research evolution model proposed in suggests that citation relationships between research publications produce multiple, small pyramid-like structures, where each pyramid represents publications related to a highly specific research topic. A research pyramid is defined as a set of publications that represent a highly specific research topic, and usually has a pyramid-like structure in terms of its citation graph.

Publications within an individual research pyramid are:

- Motivated by earlier publications in the topic area is motivated in part by citations; and
- Use techniques proposed in publications from other research pyramids in part uses some of the techniques presented in citations.

Other 'reasons' for citations may also be observed. In this section, our goals are to:

- Provide a solution to the OLDL search output ranking problem due to the topic diffusion problem, by grouping search outputs at the most-specific topic level and without identifying the topics themselves;
- Eliminate the low separability problem of score functions; and
- Improve the accuracy of three score functions, namely, PageRank, Authorities and Citation Count score functions.

The research pyramid (RP) model is used to improve the separability and accuracy of publication scores, and is based on normalising publication scores within a limited scope, namely, within individual research pyramids. These improvements come from the fact that publications are now compared to their peers within their peer groups, namely, their own research pyramid publications that are on the same topic. In two approaches to identify research pyramids are presented and evaualted. The first, called LB-IdentifyRP, uses Link-Based Research Pyramid identification, which captures research pyramids by identifying pyramid-like structures from the citation graph of the publication set. The second approach, called PB-IdentifyRP, uses Proximity-Based Research Pyramid identification, utilises a graph-based proximity measure, namely SimRank to compute similarities between publications, and then restructures the k-most-similar publications into a research pyramid.

Properties of Research Pyramid Model

In the authors have observed three properties of research publications in three separate data sets, namely, ACM Anthology which is a collection of 15,000 publications and computer sciences and life sciences publication sets, each with 70,000 publications. These properties are utilised in the identification of research pyramids.

Property 1 (Maximum Citation Age)

In OLDLs, most publications receive most of their incitations within a fixed number of years after their publication dates. We refer to this value as the Maximum Citation Age, and denote it by CAgeMax. It has been observed in that, in the AnthP, CSSet and the LSSet datasets, most publications receive 90 per cent of their in-citations in 10 years, *i.e.*, CAgeMax=10.

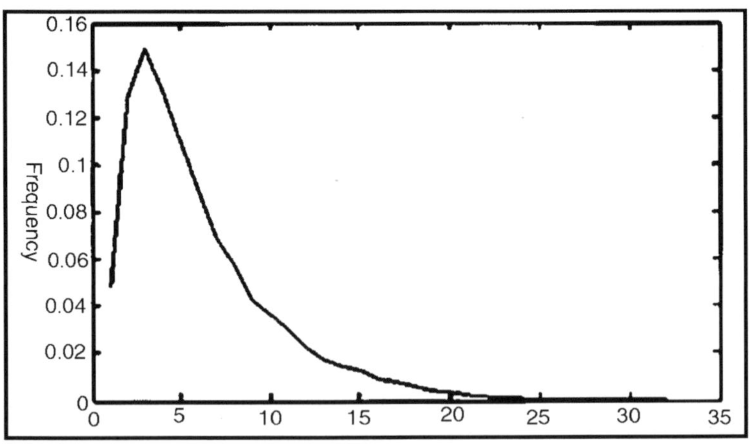

Fig. Citation Age Distribution Curve of AnthP

Figure presents the citation age distributions in AnthP. We give a tighter bound for citation age within which topical similarity within an RP is maintained between citing and cited publications. In rare cases, publications may cite works older than CAgeMax.

It is found that a great proportion of these citations are for historical reasons, which we interpret as: old cited works:

- Have coarse similarity to citing papers; and
- Do not belong in the RP of the citing publication.

Property 2 (Topic Specificity Over Time)

Scientific research publications quickly become very topic-specific over time, usually referable via a highly specific topic.

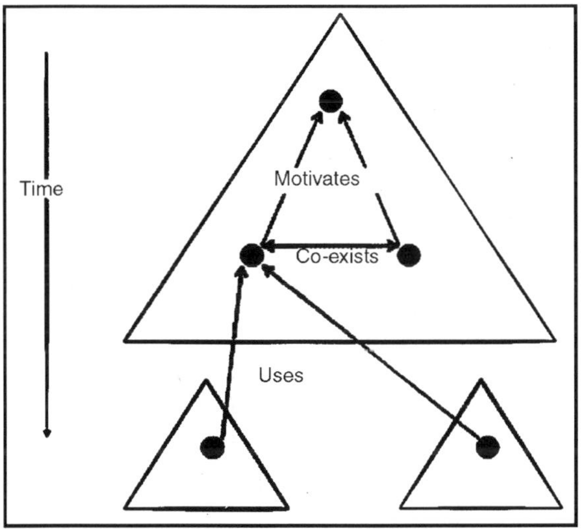

Fig. The RP-based Model.

As illustrated in figure, an old research pyramid that covers a certain research topic leads to instantiations of new research topics, and thus to creations of new RPs, that use techniques proposed in the publications of parent RP(s). Again, such old citations carry topical similarity between the citing and cited publication at a coarse granularity level. Possible citation exchanges between different RPs also occur and are of type 'uses', *i.e.*, the citing paper uses techniques proposed by the cited paper.

Example

Codd's paper E. F. Codd, 'A Relational Model of Data for Large Shared Data Banks', Commun. ACM 13(6): 377-387 is about the topic relational model, and cited around 580 times. A new and more specific topic of 2000's say, rank-aware join algorithms, is coarsely related to the more general topic relational model in that, a publication P in the RP of rank-aware join algorithms and citing Codd's paper 'uses' the techniques proposed in the RP of the relational model.

Property 3 (Topic Similarity Decay Over Citation Path)

After very small citation path distances, topical similarity between papers decays significantly. From figure, after a citation path of length 3, the topical similarity, as measured by SimRank, significantly decays. We refer to this value by LMax-TopicDecay. This observation led the authors in to build RPs of height at most 3 in the experimental results section.

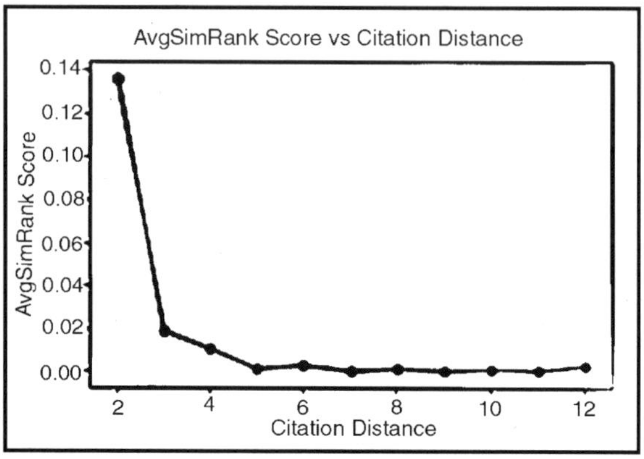

Fig. SimRank Scoer Change with Citation Distance.

Property 4 (Topic Similarity Decay Over Citation Age)

After a certain citation age, topical similarity between the citing and the cited papers significantly decays. From figure, in the AnthP set, after a citation age of about 5 years, the topic similarity between the citing and cited papers decays significantly. We refer to this value by CAgeMax-TopicDecay. This observation led the authors in to build RPs in the experimental results section such that the maximum citation age within an RP is 5 years. The two characteristics that identify a research pyramid RP are.

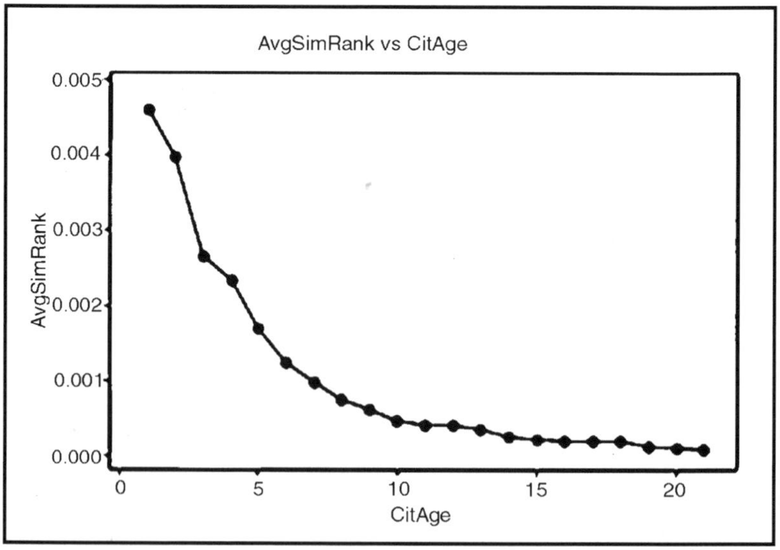

Fig. SimRank Score Change with Citation Age.

RP-Property 1 (High Topic Specificity)

An RP, usually organisable into a pyramid, is a set of publications that represent a highly specific research topic. We maintain high topic specificity of RPs by applying properties 3 and 4, and keeping the height of research pyramids low. Note that we make no attempts to identify the topic associated with an RP, as our approach does not need the topics explicitly. But, in interactive environments, providing topics to users is useful.

RP-Property 2 (Research Pyramid Construction)

RPs are arranged into pyramid structures either directly by using citation graphs (*i.e.*, the link-based approach) or indirectly using the publication times and close proximity of papers.

Research Pyramid Identification Procedures

Based on the properties of publications and characteristics of RPs, next we propose two offline research pyramid identification procedures, namely, the link-based (LB) and the proximity-based (PB) RP identification procedures. Both procedures start by choosing a candidate root node for an RP, called the cornerstone paper. The paper that is located at the root of a research pyramid receives more citations than others as other publications within the research pyramid are 'motivated' by it, and directly or indirectly cite it. Thus, our approach is to identify papers with high in-citations as cornerstone papers (*i.e.*, the roots) of RPs to be constructed. The link-based procedure locates research pyramids by identifying pyramid-like structures in the citation graph of the publication set. In summary, within an individual RP, publications are topically related and motivated by each other and we use the four properties to identify citations within RPs—as summarised next. In AnthP, the average number of citations to a paper, denoted by CI, is 2.066. Note that, in our experiments, we consider only the AnthP citations that are completely within AnthP; any citation from a paper within AnthP to a paper that is not in AnthP is removed. Using Property 3 and RP-Property 1, we limit RP heights to 3. Thus, the expected number of papers within a research pyramid RPP with paper P as the root and with height 3 is |RPP| = 1 + CI + CI2 + CI3 H' 15. Of course, the actual identified RP sizes vary.

Some RPs may deal with active research topics, and, in such cases, the number of in-citations of publications are noticeably higher than CI, leading to noticeably higher RP sizes as well. Figure presents the link-based LB-IdentifyRP procedure. The proximity-based PBIdentifyRP is similar, except that the function call to LB-FormRP is replaced by the function call PB-FormRP.

The procedure LB-IdentifyRP:

a. Selects a cornerstone paper P from the existing publication set as an RP root, by simply picking the current most-cited publication;

b. Calls LB-FormRP to locate the RP set RPP of P; and

c. Eliminates RPP from the current publication set CurrAnthP, and repeats (a)-(c) again, until no more publications are left in CurrAnthP.

Note that our approach in this chapter is to create distinct and non-overlapping research pyramids. An alternative approach, not reported here due to space limitations, is to allow overlapping research pyramids as follows: Do not to eliminate any papers from the original publication set; instead, simply colour each selected publication, and continue until all publications are coloured, meaning that, when the algorithm ends, each paper belongs to at least one RP set, and possibly more.

The two main functions of the link-based LB-IdentifyRP procedure are ChooseRoot and LB-FormRP. ChooseRoot chooses publications that are cornerstone papers, or roots of research pyramids. The function LB-FormRP forms the RPP of a root publication P by adding direct citers of P into RPP, and indirect citers of P at a level up to the LMax; in experiments, we choose LMax as 3, by following the property 3. The function Citers(P, l, CAgeMax-Topic-Decay) returns the set of publications that cite P at a level l (which is at most LMax) where the citation age of the citing paper with respect to P is less than the maximum citation age CAgeMax-Topic-Decay. In more detail,

- Paper-id pidP of root P along with its level 0 is inserted into RPP and the queue Q, which holds paper-ids for future expansions and their distances to the root paper P.
- Two-tuple <Pi, A > in Q is dequeued, and expanded by locating direct or indirect citers of Pi so long as their levels with respect to P is at most LMax-TopicDecay and their citation age with respect to P is less than the maximum citation age CAgeMax-TopicDecay. All expanded publications and their level info with respect to P are inserted into the queue Q.
- The above two steps are repeated until Q is empty; then RPP is returned.

```
proc LB-IdentifyRP(AnthP, RP-Sets)
{
RP-Sets:= Ø;
CurrAnthP:= AnthP;
while (CurrentAnthP = Ø)
{Root:=ChooseRoot(CurrAnthP);
RPRoot:=LB-FormRP(Root,LMax-TopicDecay);
RP-Sets:=RP-Sets U RPRoot;
CurrAnthP:=CurrAnthP-RPRoot;
}
}
```

(a) Procedure LB-IdentifyRP

```
funct ChooseRoot(CurrAnthP)
return TopCitedTopicDecay(CurrAnthP);
(b) Function ChooseRoot
funct LB-FormRP(P, LMax)
{Set RPP:={P}; Queue Q;
Q.Enqueue({P},0);
while(Q is not empty)
{<Pi, A>:=Q.Dequeue;
if(A<LMax)then
{CiterSet=Citers(Pi, A, CAgeMax-TopicDecay);
Q.Enqueue(CiterSet,(A+1));
RPP = RPP +CiterSet;
}}}
Return RPP}
(c) Function LB-FormRP()
Funct PB-FormRP(P, LMax)
{Set RPP={P}; Queue Q;
Q.Enqueue(P,0);
while(Q is not empty)
{<Pi, A>:=Q.Dequeue;
if(A<LMax) then
{CiterSet(Pi):=Citers(Pi, A, CAgeMax-TopicDecay)
TopSimSet:=TopSim(Pi,|CiterSet(Pi)|, CAgeMax-TopicDecay);
Q.Enqueue(TopSimSet, A +1);
RPP= RPP+TopSimSet;
}}
Return RPP}
(d) Function PB-FormRP()
```

Fig. Functions of LB-and PB-IdentifyRP Algorithms

The function PB-FormRP of the proximity-based approach utilises a graphbased proximity measure, namely SimRank to compute similarities between publications.

It captures RPP of the root publication by locating publications that are most similar to P and yet:

- Are linked to P with a citation path length of at most LMax-TopicDecay; and
- Have a citation time distance less than CAgeMax-TopicDecay. SimRank iteratively computes similarity scores between nodes in a graph G following the rule that "two nodes are similar if they are linked with similar nodes".

In other words, the SimRank similarity between two nodes a and b, S is iteratively computed using the formula:

$$S(a,b) = \left[C/|I(a)|\ |I(b)\ |\right] * \sum_{i=1}^{|I(a)|} \sum_{j=1}^{|I(b)|} S\left(I_i(a), I_j(b)\right)$$

where I(a) and I(b) are sources of in-links of a and b, respectively. C is the decay factor between 0 and 1. We choose C=0.8. If | I(a) | or | I(b) | = 0 then S(a, b)=0 by definition, in the case where a=b, S(a, b)=1. The space complexity of the naive SimRank algorithm is O(N2) where N is the graph size. We prune as in by considering node pairs that are near each other in the range of radius r. We choose r=6, which is twice the value of the expected research pyramid height.

PB-FormRP receives as input the root P, the maximum level LMax from root, and utilises the maximum citation age CAgeMax-TopicDecay and returns the RP set RPP of publication P following the same main steps of LB-FormRP with one main difference: the way the twotuple <Pi, t > dequeued from Q is expanded, as follows:

- Top | Citers Pi, A,CAgeMax-TopicDecay | similar papers, based on SimRank, to Pi are identified. The number of citers of Pi is used to capture the density of the RP being identified, and thus to expand RP at Pi accordingly;
- The identified similar papers are added to RPP and also enqueued to Q for further expansion, this time with the level increased by 1. Similar to LB-FormRP a maximum level of LMax-TopicDecay is employed.

Advantage of PB-FormRP over LB-FormRP is that it successfully captures co-existing members of RP as well as those that are not reachable through any citation path from RP's root. We give an example.

Example

Figure shows two RPs; RP1 and RP2. RP1 contains two co-existing roots A and B. Such a case occurs when two researchers work on the same problem simultaneously.

At some point of our RP identification process, A will probably be recognised as a root of a new RP, say RP3, as it has more in-citations than B. And, since, B is not reachable through any path from A, LB-FormRP will fail to identify B as a member of RP3. PB-FormRP will succeed to place both A and B into RP3 in this case as B is very similar to A.

A similar problem will be observed with paper C that is not reachable through any path from the root. Furthermore, LB-FormRP may incorrectly identify F, that probably 'uses' a technique proposed in A, as a member of RP3 when F is really a member of RP2 which co-exists with RP3. PB-FormRP successfully repels F from RP3 as F is not similar to A or any of RP3's members, based on SimRank. We observe here that PB-FormRP may capture pyramid-like structures, but not exactly pyramid structures.

SimRank computes similarity between two papers P1 and P2 by averaging the similarity of the citers of both. However, note that similar papers to a member of an RP will be the other members of the same RP since, members of an RP are usually cited by each other.

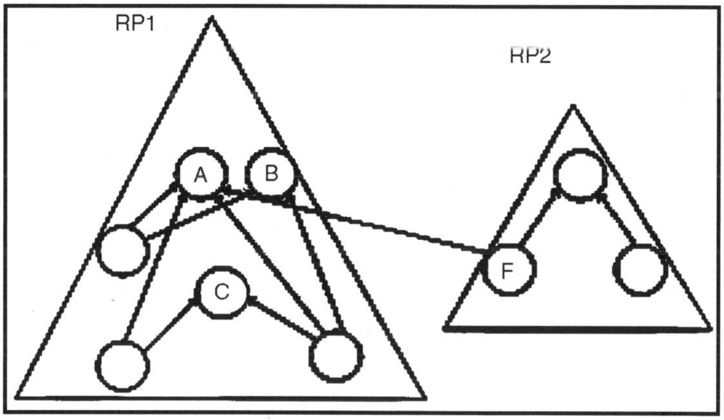

Fig. Examples where PB-FormRP is more Successful than LB-FormRP.

HUMANITARIAN INFORMATION USING DIGITAL LIBRARIES

Digital libraries provide perhaps the first really compelling *raison d'être* for computing technology in the developing world. Priorities in these countries include health, agriculture, nutrition, hygiene, sanitation, and safe drinking water.

Though computers *per se* are not a priority, simple, reliable access to practical information relevant to these basic needs certainly is.

In an article entitled *"The promise of digital libraries in developing countries"* Witten mention ten information collections, available on the Web and CD-ROM, from organizations ranging from UN agencies to small NGOs, in which Greenstone is being used to deliver humanitarian and related information in developing countries.

For example, the Humanity Development Library described is a compendium of practical information aimed at helping reduce poverty, increasing human potential, and giving a practical and useful education. We describe four new ones that have been created recently, and distributed in the same way.

Fig A Selection of Recent Humanitarian Digital Library Collections on CD-ROM.

The Researching Education Development library is a project of the *Department for International Development* (DFID), a British government department responsible for promoting develop-ment. Its central focus is a commitment to an internationally agreed target of halving the proportion of people living in extreme poverty by 2015.

Associated targets include ensuring universal primary education, gender equality in schooling, and skills development. It works in partnership with other governments and multilateral institutions, with business and the private sector, with civil society and the research community. It has created a CD-ROM library containing many education research papers and other documents.

Each one represents a study or piece of commissioned research on some aspect of education and training in developing countries. The Energy for Sustainable Development library was initiated as part of the outreach phase of the World Energy Assessment, which was initiated jointly by the *United Nations Development Programme* (UNDP), the *United Nations Department of Economic and Social Affairs* (UNDESA), and the *World Energy Council* (WEC), along with funding from the United Nations Foundation. This library contains a broad and valuable collection of 350 documents from UNDP, UNDESA, WEC and many other organizations.

It includes titles that all these organizations have published on the subjects of energy for sustainable development—technical guidelines, journals and newsletters, case studies, manuals, reports, and other training material. The documents are in English, Spanish and French, and one document has Arabic, Russian and Chinese translations as well.

The UNAIDS Library contains publications in the "Best Practice" collection which form a unique resource for those working in planning and practice. It is produced by the Joint United Nations Programme on HIV/AIDS, whose global mission is to lead, strengthen and support a response to the AIDS epidemic that will prevent the spread of HIV, provide care and support for those infected by the disease, reduce the vulnerability of individuals and communities to HIV/AIDS, and alleviate the socioeconomic and human impact of the epidemic.

The Health Library for Disasters is the result of a collaboration between the emergency and disaster programmes of the *World Health Organization* (WHO) and the *Pan American Health Organization* (PAHO), with the participation of many other organizations: the *United Nations High Commissioner for Refugees* (UNHCR), the *United Nations Children's Fund* (UNICEF), the International Strategy for Disaster Reduction (EIRD); the Red Cross Movement (ICRC and IFRC); the SPHERE Project; non-governmental organizations such as OXFAM; and national organizations such as the National Emergency Commission of Costa Rica.

It contains more that 300 technical and scientific documents on disaster reduction and public health issues related to emergencies and humanitarian assistance. A follow-up to the Spanish-language Biblioteca Virtual de Desastres discussed by Witten *et al.*, it includes technical guidelines, field guidelines, case studies, emergency kits, manuals, disaster reports, and other training materials.

UNIVERSAL ACCESS

Universal access to digital libraries presents huge challenges to software engineers and HCI practitioners. The Greenstone digital library software allows us to glimpse some of the issues, although it certainly does not yet effectively address them all.

Platforms and Distribution

Most digital libraries are accessed over the web, using any web browser. However, in many environments, particularly in developing countries, web access is insufficient and the system must run locally. And if people are to build and control their own libraries, a centralized solution is inadequate: the software must run on their own computers.

Thus digital library systems intended for broad access should run on a wide variety of computer systems, particularly low-end ones. Developed under Linux, the Greenstone server runs on any Windows, Unix, or MacOS/X system. All versions of Windows are supported, from 3.1 up.

Supporting primitive platforms poses substantial challenges of a rather mundane nature: for example, Microsoft compilers no longer support Windows 3.1 and it is necessary to acquire obsolete versions. Under Windows, pre-built collections can be viewed on any system with at least 8 Mb RAM, but collections cannot be built under Windows 3.1/3.11—for this at least a Pentium processor is generally required, except for very small collections.

The fact that Greenstone does not run on early Macintosh systems is a serious drawback in certain environments. In an international cooperative effort established in August 2000 with UNESCO and the Belgium-based Human Info NGO, Greenstone is being distributed widely in developing countries with the aim of empowering users, particularly in universities, libraries, and other public service institutions, to build their own digital libraries.

UNESCO recognizes that digital libraries are radically reforming how information is acquired and disseminated in its partner communities and institutions in the fields of education, science and culture around the world, and particularly in developing countries. Their hope is that this software will encourage the effective deployment of digital libraries to share information and place it in the public domain.

The UNESCO distribution of Greenstone is a CD-ROM that contains the full source code and executable binaries for Windows and Linux, along with all necessary associated software. Full documentation and five demonstration collections are included.

The current CD-ROM is trilingual, with complete interfaces, instructions, and documentation in English, French and Spanish. For those with Web access, the same package is also available for download from the Greenstone Web site, often in a form that is slightly ahead of the CD-ROM version—for example, many other language interfaces are included and full documentation is available in Russian and Kazakh too.

Providing accessibility in different languages is more difficult than one might at first realise. As well as the manuals, installation instructions and installation prompts, the licensing agreement, and the readme files have to be translated too.

Access for Readers

Greenstone collections like the Humanity Development Library can be published as standalone collections on removable media such as CD-ROM, or presented on the Web. CD-ROM is a very practical format in developing countries. Any Greenstone collection can be converted into a self-contained Windows CD-ROM that includes the Greenstone server software itself and an integrated installation package. The installation procedure has been thoroughly honed to ensure that only the most basic of computer skills are needed to install and run a collection under Windows.

Even standalone Greenstone users interact through a Web browser: Netscape is supplied on each CD-ROM for those who do not already have a browser. In standalone mode the software runs locally but incorporates a Web server so that if the system happens to be connected to a network—say a hospital or school intranet—information is available to other machines that may not possess CD drives.

This happens automatically: no special configuration is necessary. Another difficult engineering challenge is checking for the existence of a network. While installed network software is easily detected, it is hard to determine non-intrusively whether it is operational. Incorrectly installed or configured software is endemic in developing countries, because computers there are often cast-offs whose software is inappropriate to their present environment, yet system support to rectify the problems is unavailable.

It is essential for universal access that such problems are addressed properly and solved satisfactorily without involving the user, even though they are mundane and timeconsuming. Greenstone provides some support for the visually impaired by incorporating a "textual" mode of access that replaces all images by textual prompts. This output is suitable for users with speech synthesizers or other specialized access devices. However, the facility is not well advanced: in particular, we have not yet refined it through usability testing and interface improvement.

Building New Collections

Effective human development blossoms from empowerment rather than gifting. As the Chinese proverb says, "Give a man a fish and he will eat for a day; teach him to fish and he will eat for the rest of his days." Disseminating information originating in the developed world, like the Humanity Development Library, is a useful activity for developing countries. But a more effective strategy for sustained long-term human development is to disseminate the capability of creating information collections, rather than the collections themselves. This will allow developing countries to participate actively in our information society, rather than observing it from outside.

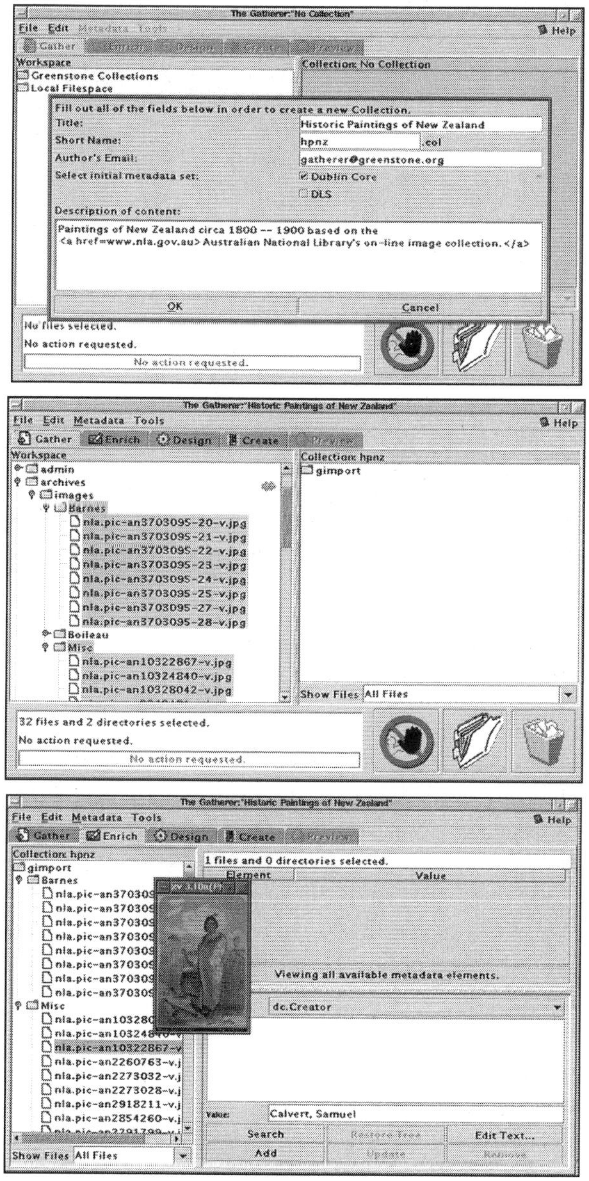

Fig. (Contd.)

Fig. Building a Collection with the Gatherer.

It will stimulate the creation of new industry. And it will help ensure that intellectual property remains where it belongs, in the hands of those who produce it. Users whose skills resemble those of librarians rather than computer specialists should be able to build and distribute their own digital library collections. As an initial step in this direction, Greenstone includes an interface called the "Collector" that is intended to help people build their own library collections. Collections may be built and served locally from the user's own web server, or remotely on a shared digital library host. End users can build new collections styled after existing ones from material on the Web or from their local files—or both, and collections can be updated and new ones brought on-line at any time.

The interface, which is intended for non-professional end users, is modeled after widely used commercial software installation packages, frequently called software "wizards"—a term we deprecate because of its appeal to mysticism and connotations of utter inexplicability. We chose this interaction style because it simplifies the choices and presents them very clearly.

Figure 1.3 shows a new Greenstone librarian interface, currently undergoing beta testing by UNESCO at sites in Argentina, India, Kazakhstan, Mexico, and South Africa, which builds on lessons learned from the Collector. It incorporates a great deal of additional functionality, particularly the ability for users to associate metadata with any item or group of items, and to reuse metadata elements without retyping them.

In figure, it is being used to collate a selection of images for a digital library collection, augment these source documents with textual metadata and then build and view the collection. From here, it is a matter of a few further clicks to produce a self-installing CD-ROM version of the collection.

In this illustration the user is developing a digital library collection of historic paintings of New Zealand. The user creates a new collection using the file menu, and a resulting popup window prompts for some general information about the collection. Once the user has filled out this form the main window becomes active. A series of panels guide the user through the processes required to build the collection.

The left-hand pane of the *Gather* panel shows the file system and the right-hand one represents the contents of the collection, initially empty, which the user populates by dragging and dropping files. In figure, the user has moved to the *Enrich* panel and is adding textual metadata to the selected documents. The next two panels, *Design*, *Create*, help the user structure the collection, control its appearance, and build it.

On completion the result is viewed in the *Preview* panel. Figure shows a page from the newly built collection, in which source documents are alphabetically listed by artist. Shown alongside each thumbnail are the artist's name, its catalog number, image dimensions, and its download size.

The full-size image is shown by clicking on the thumbnail. The user may skip backwards and forwards through the panels using them to augment and enhance the collection, perhaps adding further source documents, editing metadata values, and altering the collection's appearance.

Customization

An important component of access is allowing people to control the appearance of the collections they create. Many who build digital libraries want to brand them to ensure that they with an appropriate personal, institutional, or corporate image, and some can only contemplate software solutions that allow them to do so.

Although Greenstone comes with the standard appearance shown in figure—a distinctive bar down the side of all pages except those that show documents in the library, a green access bar with yellow buttons, etc.—the interface is highly configurable. Greenstone creates all pages that appear on the screen on the fly: none are stored in advance. They are generated using macros, written in a simple language specially designed for the job, that perform textual replacement.

One reason is that Greenstone accommodates a large number of different interface languages and macros help cope with this. All text fragments are couched as macro definitions. To add a new language, just the macro contents need to be translated—no web pages need be reworked.

Every page displayed by the system is passed through a macro interpreter that expands all the macros on the page. The interpreter checks a language variable and uses the macro definitions pertaining to it, which loads the page in the appropriate language.

Macros can have parameters. In this case, the parameter is the language variable: it causes the appropriate text fragment to be used for the macro's expansion. If there is no Arabic version for a particular macro, the interpreter will automatically substitute the default version.

This lets system developers experiment with the interface without having to worry about translating every little bit of new text immediately. Defaulting to English is not ideal—it reflects an Anglo-centric mindset—but it seems better than displaying nothing. Macros are also used to deal with display variables. Whenever a web page contains information that is not known in advance—like the number of documents returned by a search, or the value of a particular metadata item, or the content of a document page—a macro name is used in the page description.

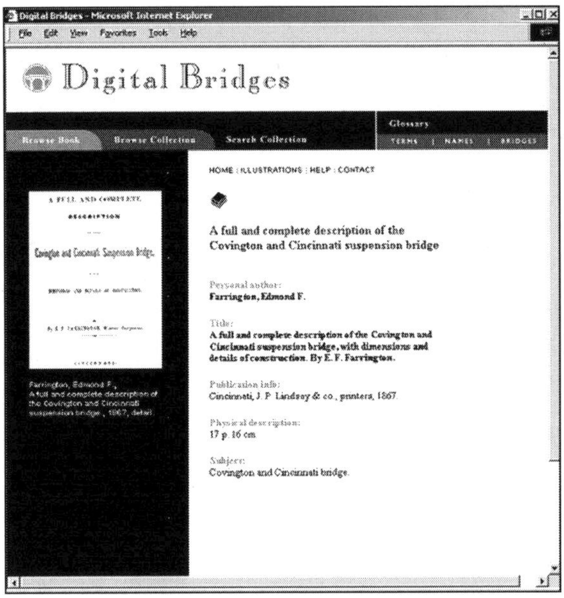

Fig. A Customised Interface to Greenstone.

Unlike language macros, these macros are *dynamic*: their content is not stored in advance but generated by the system in accordance with the value of the variable in question. Users can completely alter the form of the user interface by rewriting the macro files—or even by writing their own web pages which embed the dynamic macros that generate bits of Greenstone output.

Figure 1.4 shows a Greenstone interface that has been heavily customised by Lehigh University Library, Pennsylvania. The standard Greenstone appearance has been completely obliterated in favour of an in-house style, yet all the Greenstone functionality is available. Figure shows a thumbnail of a book cover on the left, and full bibliographic information on the right. Entering a book displays facsimile images of its pages.

Internationalization

The international Unicode character set is used throughout Greenstone, and documents in any Unicode-supported language and character encoding can be imported. Collections of documents in Arabic, Chinese, Cyrillic, English, French, Spanish, German, Hindi, and Maori are publicly available.

The New Zealand Digital Library Web site hosts many of these, and the Greenstone Web site links to sites that contain further examples. It makes little sense to have a collection whose content is in Chinese or Russian, but whose supporting text—instructions, navigation buttons, labels, images, help text, and so on—are in English.

Consequently, the entire Greenstone interface has been translated into a range of languages, and the interface language can be changed by the user as they browse from the *Preferences* page. All the language fragments in the interface are stored in macro files. These have been translated by Greenstone users in other parts of the world and contributed back to the project.

Figure 1.5 shows an example: a Russian collection. Currently, interfaces are available in Arabic, Czech, Chinese, Dutch, French, Galician, German, Hebrew, Indonesian, Italian, Kazakh, Maori, Portuguese, Russian, Spanish, Turkish, and English. Managing the organizational and software complexity of any comprehensive and evolving open source software system presents a significant challenge.

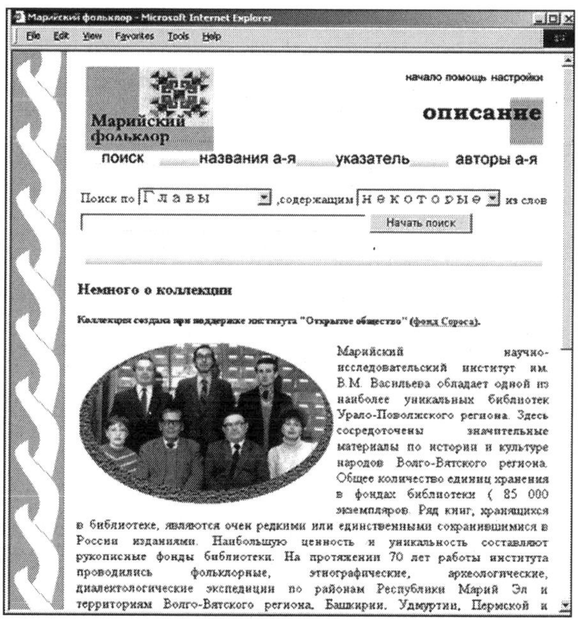

Fig. A Russian Digital Library Collection.

However, the challenge is greatly magnified when the interface is available in different languages, for enhancements to the software and changes to the interface must be faithfully reflected in each language version. No single person knows all interface languages; no single person knows about all modifications to the software—indeed there is likely no overlap at all between those who translate the interface and those who build the software. Currently, Greenstone has about twenty interface languages and there are around 600 linguistic fragments in each interface, ranging from single words like *search*, through short phrases like *search for*, *which contain*, *of the words*, to sentences like *More than... documents matched the query*, to complete paragraphs like those in the on-line help text.

Maintaining the interface in many different languages is a logistic nightmare. The solution adopted by Greenstone is to incorporate a language translation facility, which allows authorized people to update the interface in specified languages. A standard version control system is used to manage software change, and from this the system automatically determines which language fragments need updating and presents them to the human translator.

LIBRARIES AND THEIR ROLE

What is the librarian to make of all this? The mandate of today's public libraries, in sharp contrast to that of publishers, is to facilitate the open distribution of knowledge. Librarians strive to enable the free flow of information. Their traditions are liberal, founded on the belief that libraries should serve democracy.

To help fulfil their mission as resource centers for citizens, public libraries maintain collections of records, policy statements, government documents, and so on. A recent promotional video from the American Librarian's Association exults that "the library is democracy's place of worship".

Clearly, the impending redefinition of the book as a digital artifact that is licensed rather than sold, tied to a particular replay device, with restrictions that are clearly laid out and mechanically enforced, is an innovation that goes right to the heart of libraries.

The changing nature of the book may make it hard, or even impossible, for libraries to fulfill their mandate by providing quality information to readers. And on the other hand, the emergence of a vast storehouse of information on the Internet poses a different kind of conundrum. Librarians, the traditional gatekeepers of knowledge, are in danger of being bypassed, their skills ignored, their advice unsought.

Search engines send users straight to the information they require—or so users think—without any need for an inter-mediary to classify, catalogue, cross-reference, advise on sources. The ready availability of information on the Internet, and its widespread use, really presents librarians with an opportunity, not a threat.

Savvy users realise they need help, which librarians can provide. A good example is Infomine, a cooperative project of the University of California and California State University. Infomine contains descriptions and links to a wealth of scholarly and educational Internet resources, each of which has been selected and described by a professional academic librarian who is a specialist in the subject and in resource description generally.

Participating librarians see this as an important expenditure of effort for their users, a natural evolution of their traditional task of collecting and organizing information in print. What kind of technical infrastructure is needed to support and promote this kind of work?

Open source software is a powerful ally for librarians who wish to extend liberal traditions of information access. These systems make the source code freely available for others to view, modify, and adapt; and the very nature of the licensing agreement prevents the software from being appropriated by proprietary vendors. But the open-source movement is more than just a vehicle for librarians to use: its link with library traditions goes much deeper.

Public libraries and open source software both enshrine the same philosophy: to promote learning and understanding through the dissemination of knowledge. Both are pervaded by a sense of community, on the one hand the kind of inter-institutional cooperation exemplified by interlibrary loan and on the other teams of designers and programmers that frequently cross national boundaries.

New trends in information access present librarians in developed countries with difficult and conflicting challenges. Meanwhile, however, the situation in the developing world is dire. Here, traditional publishing and distribution mechanisms have failed tragically.

For example, whereas a US medical library subscribes to about 5,000 journals, the Nairobi University Medical School Library, long regarded as a flagship center in East Africa, last year received just 20 journals. In Brazzaville, Congo, the university has only 40 medical books and a dozen journals, all from before 1993, and the library in a large district hospital consisted of a single bookshelf filled mostly with novels.

Digital Libraries and the Challenge for HCI

Traditional libraries are substantial institutions that occupy physical space, present a physical appearance, and exhibit tangible physical organization. When standing on the threshold of a large bricks-and-mortar library you gain a sense of presence and permanence that reflects the care taken in building and maintaining the collection inside. Digital libraries, in contrast, are lightweight. But they provide potentially far greater accessibility, which means that they will have even greater social effects.

Once created, they can, without significant institutional support, continue to serve users. They can be distributed throughout most of the developed world over the Internet. In developing countries and remote corners of the developed world they can be circulated on removable media—CD-ROM, DVD, or 100 Gb disk units the size of videocassettes—and updated over radio. Issues of copyright pose difficult problems, but they are manageable. For example, there is plenty of non-copyright material, or material whose owners are prepared to donate copyright for socially useful purposes, and trends towards more open access to academic and humanitarian information are visible. Not everyone sees digital rights management and the DMCA as the way forward, and in the longer term publishers, to remain viable, will have to investigate alternative revenue models for the information they own.

No wonder international organizations such as the United Nations, along with many smaller *non-government organizations* (NGOs), are keenly interested in digital library technology. Advances in digital library technology are radically lowering the bar for the design and production of richly-organized, coherent, focused collections of information.

Now, anyone with access to sufficient source material can use public-domain software to build large, fullysearchable, collections the size of traditional personal or institutional libraries—in minutes. Let the minutes stretch to hours and the collection can be polished, organized, branded, distributed. It can include fully-illustrated text, images, video, music.

It can present attractively-designed pages with consistent use of icons. Keywords, key phrases, even acronyms and their definitions, can be extracted—automatically—and used to underpin novel means of access. Let the hours stretch to days and metadata can be manually added that permits further levels of organization. Given access to programming skills, creative new facilities that stretch the imagination can be rapidly integrated into the system. All this, one might say, can be done with ordinary Web sites: there is no need for digital library technology.

However, bitter experience has shown that all but the most rudimentary sites do require significant institutional support—for organization and maintenance. The Web is littered with incomplete, unfinished, unmaintained, out-dated, inconsistently-organized, useless information collections.

Just as traditional library cataloging procedures integrate new works into existing collections with minimal overhead so that they immediately become first-class members of the collection, so digital libraries allow new documents to be added completely automatically.

In the case of traditional libraries this is done through the small but non-negligible overhead of generating a new catalog entry. With ordinary Web sites it requires inserting links manually into index pages and the like, and may involve adding links not only into the new document but also into existing ones that ought to reference it—it's like rewriting the book, and maybe revising all other books in the library too!

In contrast, digital libraries bring access structures instantly and effortlessly up to date whenever new documents are added. The challenge for HCI is to design and build digital library systems that fulfill the potential of digital libraries as a "killer app" for computers in developing countries, which will bring concomitant benefits in almost every other sphere of application.

For the information consumer we need access to information that is guaranteed across space, time, and culture. We need flexible distribution mechanisms for documents, and for information objects of all types, that can be accessed on all computer platforms—including the lowliest. We need a choice of distribution over the Web or on removable media such as CD-ROM or DVD.

Digital libraries can incorporate flexible presentation that caters to individual differences, such as large-font displays or spoken output for the visually impaired. Libraries are places where information is preserved, not rendered obsolete, and digital libraries must instill confidence that information prepared today can be accessed next week, next decade, next century—regardless of technological changes.

An important aspect of digital libraries is their ability to work in local languages, promoting pluralism and reducing the risks of homogeneity. Because language is the vehicle of thought, communication, and cultural identity, this will encourage diversity and strengthen individual cultures. But there is a long way to go: even Unicode is woefully incomplete in certain areas, such as African languages. Naturally, today's digital library systems focus principally on the reader: the consumer of the material stored in the library's treasure-house. But digital libraries make a more radical, and perhaps ultimately more important, contribution by empowering ordinary users to conceive, assemble, build, and disseminate new information collections themselves.

In principle, modest computing resources are quite sufficient to enable users to build new collections by gathering together material in local files or on the Web; augmenting it with appropriate metadata that supports convenient search and browsing operations; incorporating advanced features like key-phrase extraction, document summarization, and metadata extraction; designing an attractive and functional interface; and publishing the collection on a variety of different media that are suitable for the intended readership.

The HCI challenge is to realise this potential for users—such as most librarians—who have a strong understanding of information and its organization, but no more interest in computers than they have in papermaking technology, last millennium's vehicle for information dissemination.

AN ORGANIZED COLLECTION OF INFORMATION IN DIGITAL LIBRARIES

A digital library is an organized collection of information:

A focused collection of digital objects, including text, video, and audio, along with methods for access and retrieval, and for selection, organization, and maintenance of the collection.

This definition deliberately accords equal weight to user and librarian. The latter functions are often overlooked by digital library proponents, who often work from a technology perspective rather than from the viewpoint of library or information science, but it is precisely these aspects that allow digital libraries to be used to democratize information dissemination.

As a concrete example, consider the Humanity Development Library, a collection of some 1200 authoritative books and periodicals, produced by many disparate organizations—UN agencies and other international organizations—on various areas of human development, from agricultural practice to economic policies, from water and sanitation to society and culture, from education to manufacturing, from disaster mitigation to micro-enterprises.

It contains 160,000 pages and 30,000 images, which if printed would weigh 340 kg, cost $20,000, and occupy a small library book stack.

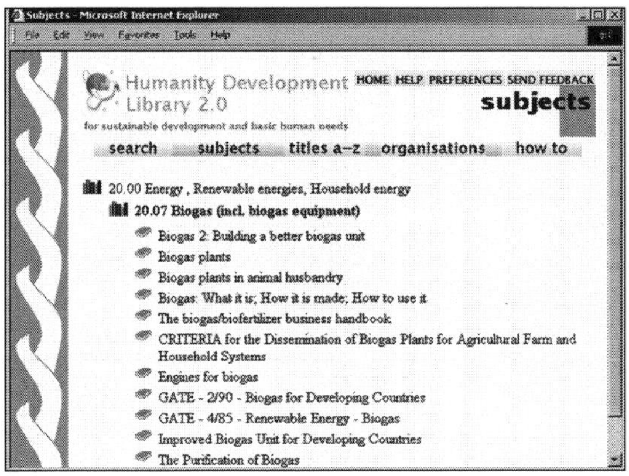

(a)

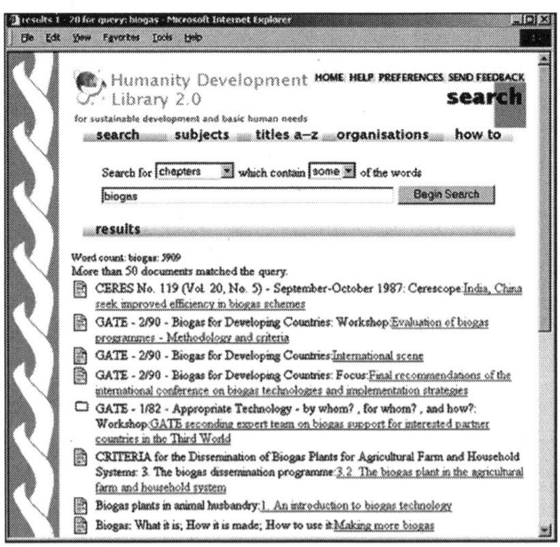

(b)

Fig. (Contd.)

Instead, it takes the form of a digital library and is distributed on a CD-ROM throughout the developing world at essentially no cost. The Humanity Development Library is produced using the Greenstone software, a freelydistributed open-source project whose aim is to create novel digital library technologies and make them available for others to use. Greenstone digital libraries are arranged in *collections*. A collection comprises several documents, and a library may include several collections, each organized differently. Collections built with Greenstone offer simple but effective searching and browsing facilities based on metadata and the full text of electronic documents. Each collection is individually designed to take advantage of whatever metadata is available.

All collections support full-text searching and most provide several different browsing options, although they differ depending on the collection design and the metadata available. Typically you can search for particular words that appear in the text, or within a section of a document, or within a title or section heading. A variety of interfaces exist for browsing collections by *title*, *subject*, *date*, or any other metadata chosen by the collection designer.

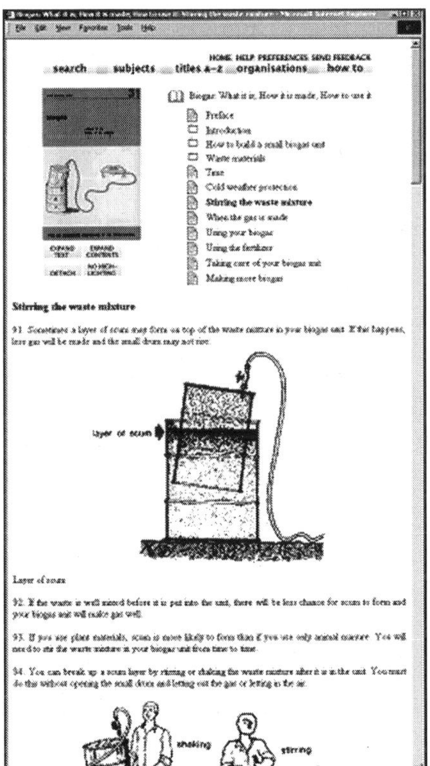

Fig. The Humanity Development Library: (a) Searching for *Biogas*; (b) Browsing by Subject; (c) Reading a Document.

Figure shows snapshots of the Humanity Development Library. In figure documents are being searched for stages containing the word *biogas*. In figure the collection is being browsed by subject: *Energy, Renewable energies, Household energy*. Pursuing an interest in energy from biogas, the user selects a book by clicking on its book icon. All the icons in the screenshots of figure are clickable.

The navigation bar beneath gives access to the searching and browsing facilities, which differ from one collection to another. This particular collection can be searched by book, chapter, or section, and browsed by subject, title, organization, and "how to" metadata as indicated by the navigation bar. Documents are presented as Web pages generated by Greenstone from the source material.

In figure, the book's cover is displayed as a graphic on the left, and an automatically constructed table of contents appears at the start of the document. The current focus, *Stirring the waste mixture*, is written in bold in the table of contents; its text starts further down the page.

Incidentally, the material in this collection on building household biogas plans is fascinating, though it is not directly relevant to this chapter. Greenstone collections present documents as automatically-generated Web pages.

This allows documents in different source formats to be presented in a consistent manner, and lets users view the entire collection with a standard Web browser—no special viewing applications are required. However, the collection maintainer may choose to present the original source document instead of, or as well as, the HTML version, and rely on the user's web browser to select a suitable application to display the document. In general, Greenstone deals well with documents and metadata in a wide variety of different formats.

2

Information Society in Library

First, the general development of the information society is pushing to re-evaluation of all the institutions which work with information, data, and knowledge-indirectly also with culture. In this connection the roles of education and media have been discussed already quite largely also in the European Union. But libraries — as well as other memory institutions like archives and museums-have not been considered. Still, there is a clear need in the information society to maintain an institution which is concentrating in collecting and organizing information and offering general access to it.

Until now, this work has been underestimated, but I argue the situation will change! Libraries are especially important now when the whole idea of education is stressing more and more independent learning and acting. All citizens must be able to find and use information. It is the key raw material-but it is a zero resource, if there are no access points to it and if documents are in chaotic order.

Here we can see libraries enter the stage:

- The unique function of libraries is to acquire, organize, offer for use and preserve publicly available material irrespective of the form in which it is packaged in such a way that, when it is needed, it can be found and put to use. No other institution carries out this long-term, systematic work.

Culture must be nominated especially: it has an important and unique role in mobilizing resources of human beings. It has been described: *T*o some extent, culture makes its influence felt more indirectly than knowledge, but it is impossible to imagine how people's creative powers could be fully activated without the impact of culture, which extends into the depths of the mind. The challenge to modern societies is that the basic resource, knowledge, is developing from information in very individual, capricious and unpredictable process. It cannot be commanded.

Still, societies can support this development, *e.g.* by offering acces to cultural and knowledge treasures. This can even be translated into economic language: to get out the best from the human resources in Europe, this resource must be feeded up with rich and various cultural and information contents! I would like to stress especially the idea of organising information by libraries. It is often shadowed by the second important side of library work: offering access. But in the life-long learning and new technology context just all forms of organising documents are getting more to the focus. This is clear to anybody who has tried to find something from not-so-often-used Internet web sites.

NEW LINES IN THE EU AND IN THE UNITED STATES

In accordance with these phenomenons, there are new political lines in the European Union (EU): The Maastricht Treaty in 1992 launched the cultural aspects. This was only after a long discussion, which made it clear that we have to remember to separate the national view and the European view. The Amster-dam Treaty in 1997 declared citizenship as an impor-tant theme. A significant part of this are a.o. granting infor-mation skills and access to information to every European.

In addition to this, the European future strategies need to meet the democratic aspects of the information society development. One of the crucial points is again general access to information. Libraries, especially public libraries, are a good tool in all of these new areas. But the European union does not support whichever cultural or citizen concentrated projects in Europe. In the interests of the European Union there is always to find the European element.

So, what can be done in library policy on the European level, taking in account that libraries are primarily a part of national education and cultural policies?:

> "The own-initiative report "The role of libraries in modern societies", adopted by the European Parliament in October 1998, is the first effort to answer these questions.

The same topics have been dicussed in the United States. They have reached the point where especially the problems of those lacking access to digital resources have been studied. The report Falling Through the Net: Defining the Digital Divide by the U.S. Department of Commerce was released earlier in July 1999.

The report finds that minorities, low-income persons, the less educated, and children of single parent households, particularly when they reside in rural areas or central cities, are risk groups.

The report calls for public policies and private initiatives to expand affordable access to critical information resources. But it also shows,, for the first time as far as I know, that libraries and community centres really can diminish the information gap between haves and not-haves. The 1998 data from the U.S. demonstrates very clearly that community access centers, primarily public libraries, are particularly well used by those groups who lack access at home or at work: *e.g.* unemployed groups used Internet in libraries three times as often as an average citizen.

EARLIER ACTIONS IN EU

In the European Union, there have been some efforts to mobilize "the treasures of the European libraries" since the mid-80'ies. These discussions and resolutions led to two special library programmes under the 3rd and 4th Framework progra-mmes of research and development. The later programme has been known as "Telematics for Libraries".

They have been strongly concentrated in IT, because it has been seen as a good tool to produce better access to the existing, underused library resources. These programmes have had a clear impact in the European library co-operation and development. Benefits of this work come to public libraries indirectly: common standards and working methods help in the end all kind of libraries. But a fact is, that nearly all the libraries active in these EU projects are national libraries or big research and university libraries. Two main exeptions are PubliCA, a network of European public libraries, and ECUP, which was a copyright awareness raising project, and reached public libraries as well. A new beginning was the so called Morgan report in 1997.

In this report libraries were for the first time put clearly onto the place where they belong in the information society. As one result of the Morgan report, the European Commission informed that it will produce a Green Paper about the role of libraries in the information society.

For one or another reason, this was made quite ready but was never published. In this situation the Committee on Culture, Youth, Education and the Media in the European Parliament decided to produce an own-initiative report about libraries. The main reason was that they wanted to influence the big issues under work in the EU, first of all the copyright directive and the 5th framework programme, which will have a direct impact to libraries.

DECISIONS OF THE EP CONCERNING LIBRARY POLICY

In short, when adopting the own-initiative report, the EP (European Parliament) was calling the Commission and/or the member states to following actions:

- Libraries must be taken in account in national and EU information society strategies and in the respec-tive budgets.
- Libraries need more resources for acquiring expen-sive books.
- The Green Paper on libraries by the Commission must be completed.
- The users position must be taken in account in the copyright directive process, the balance must be maintained-this was politically the most important decision in short run.
- Support to libraries was demanded from the 5th Framework programme of research and develop ment, *e.g.* for networking, drafting standards, preser-ving, and transferring information; there is no more named library programme under the 5th framework programme.

- A clearing-house to solve problems of long-term conservation should be founded.
- Studies concerning permanent paper should be done on European level.
- The member states should take care of digitizing their cultural heritage for future.
- There should be studies and concrete support to libraries in licensing matters, which are–will be the next big issue in library work.
- The EU cultural and information budget should be opened to libraries as well, libraries and their co-operation should be taken in account in planning new programmes.
- Problems of legal deposit in international and multinational materials, especially in electronic materials should be solved.
- The member states should provide all types of libraries with modern equipment, particularly with Internet connections.
- Free of charge use of public libraries, in the spirit of the UNESCO Public Library Manifest, was demanded.
- Free and easy access via libraries to material produced with the aid of tax revenues was demanded.
- The members states should organize for their library professionals up-dating education and training.
- A European Union focal point for libraries should be set up.
- The member states should found European infor-mation points at libraries in countries where they do not yet exist.
- Library statistics should be better and more comparable both on national and European level.
- The national Parliament libraries should be opened to the MEP's in countries where this is not yet the practice.

In addition to these, the report strongly stresses that the library financing must be re-thougt in the information society. Without new resources libraries are unable to do everything they are expected to do! After the EP adoption of this report, the European Commission informed that it will next prepare a communication about actions to do. It was stated that the report had already served as a discussion paper, and so the need for the Green Paper had disappeared. The communication is in summer 1999 still under work in the Commission DGXIII/2.

TRADITIONS AND NEW FORMS OF WORK IN THE SAME HOUSE

The European Commission R&D framework programmes have concentrated in IT matters. The three cultural progra-mmes, Caledoskope, Ariane and Raphael, have not been very useful for libraries, because their scope has been quite narrow, *e.g.* the books and reading programme Ariane has concentrated in translations. In the coming framework programme Culture 2000 libraries will have more possibilities to get support also for their cultural actions. What then will be the fate of the traditional tasks of libraries in general? Will the information society wipe out book loaning and poems? These elements will survive, but will get completed by new media forms.

It was stated earlier that culture has a special role in building up the modern society and in mobilizing the capacity of its members The significance of reading is only growing in future. Demands to enlargen and deepen literacy skills get greater and greater. Literacy has a special role in guaranteeing the basic citizen competence to everybody. It is in general interests of the society to offer possibilities to all people for maintaining and developing their literacy. In library work new technologies offer new possibilities to raise service level, too. Good examples can already now be found all over the world, mainly of course in those countries where Internet is used largely.

Some models: Library catalogues are available via Inter-net, the patron can check her/his loaning data from Internet, and even renew the loans a country/areawide information service via Internet and e-mail; there are versions for link libraries or virtual libraries, where libraries collect and describe high-level link-ups discussion lists of librarians, whre they can share their professional skills and knowledge, even take part in developing the library policy of the country/area.

There is one special comment concerning Internet which we have heard both from small libraries with rejected printed collections in Finland and from African libraries: In case you got reach in Internet, the resources your library can offer to the patrons are suddenly multiplied. All of once we have exactly the same resource as British Library or the Library of Congess.

It is amazing, it is revolutionary, and we can use it! In the complicated modern society libraries have many kinds of answers to many demands of the society, as well as those of the citizens.

They have potential means to serve both the information society development and their traditional human-istic tasks. Maybe information technology will even make it easier to combine these elements in future than in the past!

INFORMATION RETRIEVAL IN LIBRARY

In the early and mid-1950s, a critical mass of scientists, engineers, librarians, and entrepreneurs started working enthusiastically on the problem and solution defined by Bush. By 1960s this became a large and relatively well-funded effort and organized activity. Often, there were heated arguments and controversies about the "best" solution, technique, or system.

These arguments brought on the tradition of evaluation, a major staple of IR research and development. What is now TREC started with Cranfield evaluations in the late 1950s and early 1960s. Remarkably, the basic evaluation principles developed then are still the underpinning of TREC today. Calvin Mooers, an active and highly visible pioneer of information science, coined the term *information retrieval* in 1951. The term took hold, and today is a part of the English language.

At that time, Mooers not only coined the term, but also defined the problems to be addressed:

- "Information retrieval embraces the intellectual aspects of the description of information and its specification for search, and also whatever systems, techniques or machines that are employed to carry out the operation.

Today, we would add that IR also and particularly involves interaction in all of these, with all the contextual-cognitive, affective, situational—aspects that interaction embraces. An expanded Mooers' conception is still valid. As it advanced, IR produced a number of theoretical, empirical, and pragmatic concepts and constructs. Numerous IR systems were developed and successfully deployed.

A great many historical examples can be given to illustrate the remarkable evolution of IR systems and techniques, adapting the ever-evolving information technology, from punch cards in the midcentury to the Internet at its close. Based on IR, an online information industry emerged in the 1970s, and grew through its own version of information explosion, as chronicled by Hahn. IR is one of the most widely spread applications of any information system worldwide. It has a proud history. Surely, information science is more than IR, but many of the problems raised by IR or derived from objects and phenomena involved in IR, are at its core.

APPROACHES AND PARADIGM SPLIT

The approach taken by Mooers was to concentrate on the building of systems. This systems emphasis which was formulated early in the 1950s, was the sole approach to IR for some decades. It still predominates in a good part of IR research to this day.

Consequently, most of the IR research and practice concentrated on retrieval systems and processes. However, starting in the late 1970s and gaining steam in the 1980s, a different line of reasoning and research evolved-one that concentrates on the cognitive, interactive, and contextual end of the process. It addressed users, use, situations, context, and interaction with systems, rather than IR systems alone as a primary focus.

The retrieval cluster started splitting into subclusters, as noted by White and McCain, and before by others such as Saracevic and Harter. We now have two distinct communities and approaches to research in the retrieval cluster. They became commonly known as *systems-centred* and *user-centred.* Both address retrieval, but from very different ends and perspectives. The split is not only conceptual, looking very differently at the same process, but also organizational. The systemscentered side is now mostly concentrated in the *Special Interest Group on Information Retrieval* (SIGIR) of the *Association for Computing Machinery* (ACM), while the user-centered cluster congregates around the *American Society for Information Science* (ASIS).

Each has its own communication outlets-journals, proceedings, and conferences. There is less and less overlap of authors and works between the two outlets. We have two camps, two islands, with, unfortunately, relatively little traffic in-between. The systems-centered approach is exemplified by work on algorithms and evaluation based on the traditional IR model, a model that does not consider the users or interaction. The massive research that evaluates a variety of IR algorithms and approaches within TREC is a culmination of this approach.

In contrast, cognitive, situational, and interactive studies and models, involving the use of retrieval systems exemplify the human-centered approach. Following that approach, interactive models, differing significantly from the traditional IR model, started to emerge.

Even in TREC, a group of researchers started an interaction track, but so far have a hard time conceptually and methodologically, thus demonstrating the difficulty in merging the traditional and interactive models and approaches. Let me characterize, in a simplified way, the relationship between the two approaches or subclusters addressing different sides of retrieval.

On the one hand, the human-centred side was often highly critical of the systems side for ignoring users and use, and tried valiantly to establish humans as the proper center of IR work. The mantra of human-centred research is that the results have implications for systems design and practice. Unfortunately, in most human-centred research, beyond suggestions, concrete design solutions were not delivered.

On the other hand, the systems side, by and large, ignores the human side and user studies, and is even often completely ignorant of them. As to design, the stance is "tell us what to do and as suggested, do it." But nobody is really telling, or if telling, nobody is listening.

As a rule, in systems-oriented projects, people and users are absent. Thus, there are not many interactions between the two camps.

Let me provide some examples. A rough analysis of the 1997 SIGIR proceedings found only 3 papers of some 34 that dealt in some way with people and users; in the ACM's Digital Libraries 1997 conference proceedings, of 25 papers only 3 mentioned people and users. If one reads authors such as Dervin and Nilan, and many of their successors, who champion the human centered approach, one gets the impression that there is a real conflict between the two sides and approaches, and that there is an alternative way to the "dreadful" systems approach.

In a way, this stance is a backlash caused by the excesses, failures, and blind spots of systems-centered approaches not only in IR, but also in great many other technological applica-tions. Unfortunately, sometimes the backlash is justified. All of us who work on the humancentered side are not that dismissive of the systems side. But the issue is not whether we should have systems-*or* humancentered approaches. The issue is even less of human*versus* systems-centered. *The issue is how to make human*and *systems-centered approaches work together.* In this sense, a number of works have addressed integrating usercentered and systems-centered approaches in IR, but this has been discussed mostly by researchers from the usercentered side.

Examples are works by:

- Bates,
- Belkin,
- Cool,
- Stein,
- Thiel,
- Fidel
- Efthimidiadis,
- Robertson and
- Beaulieu.

To reiterate, it is not one camp against the other but how can we incorporate the best features of both approaches and make them work jointly. The issue is how to deliver and incorporate the desired design features that will improve systems orientations towards users, integrate them with systems features, and use advantages provided by both, humans and technology. In other words, the issue is *putting the human in the loop* to build better algorithms and to exploit computational advantages. Real progress in information science, and by extension in IR, will come when we achieve this. Lately, the NSF has championed human-centered design involving an interdisciplinary approach to information systems. Hopefully, this will go beyond rhetoric. It is not easy to do. But, that is what research is for—to address difficult, not only easy problems.

PROPRIETARY IR

By the 1980s, the commercial information industry based on IR became successful and profitable. Out of academe, grants, and government, IR became a money-making propo-sition. This, of course, is another and important sign of success. Not surprisingly, a number of former IR researchers, practitioners, and graduates of IR programmes ventured out to become IR entrepreneurs.

Sure enough, throughout information science history there were many entrepreneurs, and they were highly significant in development of the field. But this generation of entrepre-neurs was different. They ventured to develop and market a variety of IR procedures based on algorithms, applicable and scalable to large files, multiple applications, and/or various advanced technologies. It was knowledge industry at its purest. But, as in all commercial knowledge industries, the product was proprietary. While it was not that hard to guess the base of these various proprietary algorithms and how they worked—after all they were derived from publicly available knowledge and experiences, such as those that came from SMART experi-ments—they remain unpublished and "secret."

A new kind of IR evolved, separate from the rest, not communicating as to intellectual advances with the rest. None of these ventures became a high commercial success, as measured by Silicon Valley standards. But the World Wide Web, emerging in the first half of the 1990s, changed all this. The acceleration of the growth of the Web is an information explosion of the like never before seen in history. Not surprisingly then, the Web is a mess. No wonder that everybody is interested in some form of IR as a solution to fix it.

A number of academic-based efforts were initiated to develop mechanisms, search engines, "intelligent" agents, crawlers, and so forth, to help control the Web. Some of these were IR scaled, and adapted to the problem; others were a variety of extensions of IR. Many had few, if any original, developments, besides new packaging or labeling; and a good number were just the usual hype. The wheel was reinvented a number of times. But out of this, and fast, came commercial ventures, such as the pioneering Yahoo!, whose basic objective is to provide search mechanisms for finding something of relevance for users on demand.

And to make a lot of money. These enterprises pride themselves on having proprietary methods by which they are accomplishing the retrieval tasks. The connection to the information science community is tenuous, and almost non-existent. The flow of knowledge, if any, is onesided, from IR research results into proprietary engines. The reverse contribution to public knowledge is zero. A number of evaluations of these search engines have been undertaken simply by comparing some results between them or comparing of their retrieval against some benchmarks.

Some evaluations were done within, others outside of information science. Results were not complimentary. The Web-based proprietary IR is expanding and flourishing outside of the field. It is addressing a vexing problem, the like we have not seen before. But as yet, the success is elusive and questionable.

RELEVANCE

As information science pioneers developed IR processes and systems in the 1950s, they defined as the main objective retrieval of *relevant* information. Effectiveness was expressed in terms of relevance. From then to now, IR is explicitly geared not towards any old kind of information, but towards *relevant information*. Various IR approaches, algorithms, and practices were, and still are, evaluated in relation to relevance. Thus, relevance became a key notion in information science. It is also a complex phenomenon with a long and turbulent history in information science transcending IR, going back to early 1950s. Of course, there was a choice.

Relevance did not have to emerge as the key notion. Uncertainty was one choice suggested by a number of theorists to be the base of IR, and thus to reflect effectiveness. But it did not take. In contrast, uncertainty is the basic notion underlying expert systems. If the pioneers had not embraced relevance, but instead, let's say, uncertainty, as the base for IR, we would have today a very different IR, and probably not that successful. In general, relevance, according to *Webster,* means having significant bearing on matter at hand. As with many other concepts, relevance assumes related but more specific meaning in more specific contexts and applications.

In the context of information science, relevance is the attribute or criterion reflecting the effectiveness of exchange of information between people and IR systems in communi-cation contacts based on valuation by people. With relevance as the criterion, and human judgements of relevance of retrieved objects as the measuring instrument, the measures of precision and recall are widely used in evaluation of IR systems. The strength of these measures is that they involve people—users—as judges of effectiveness of performance. The weakness is the same: it involves judgement by people, with all the perils of subjectivity and variability. Relevance indicates a relation. For relevance, many relations have been investigated.

An consensus has emerged in information science that we can distinguish between several differing relations that account for different manifestations or types of relevance:

- *System or Algorithmic Relevance:* Relation between a query and information objects in the file of a system as retrieved, or as failed to be retrieved, by a given procedure or algorithm. Comparative effectiveness in inferring relevance is the criterion for system relevance.
- *Topical or Subject Relevance:* Relation between the subject or topic expressed in a query and topic or subject covered by retrieved texts, or, more broadly, by texts in the system file, or even in existence. Aboutness is the criterion by which topicality is inferred.
- *Cognitive Relevance or Pertinence:* Relation between the state of knowledge and cognitive information need of a user and texts retrieved, or in the file of a system, or even in existence. Cognitive correspondence, infor-mativeness, novelty, information quality, and the like are criteria by which cognitive relevance is inferred.
- *Situational Relevance or Utility:* Relation between the situation, task or problem at hand and texts retrieved by a system, or in the file of a system, or even in existence. Usefulness in decision making,

appropriateness of information in resolution of a problem, reduction of uncertainty, and the like are criteria by which situational relevance is inferred.

- *Motivational or Affective Relevance:* Relation between the intents, goals, and motivations of a user and texts retrieved by a system, or in the file of a system, or even in existence. Satisfaction, success, accomplish-ment, and the like are the criteria for inferring motivational relevance.

Practically, IR systems assess systems relevance only-that is, they respond to queries-hoping that the objects retrieved may also be of cognitive relevance, and even more so of utility. However, a user may judge an object by any or all types of relevance-for a user they may interact dynamically. Difficulties arise when an object is of system relevance but not of cognitive relevance or utility, or conversely.

If items are of cognitive relevance or utility, but were not reflected in the query, they are not and cannot be retrieved. At the bottom of IR research is a quest to align systems with other types of relevance. People all over have a strong intuitive understanding of relevance, thus, they intuitively understand, without manuals, what IR is all about. This makes IR systems generally understandable and acceptable-a critical attribute in their widespread application.

DISCIPLINARY RELATIONS

Two things introduced interdisciplinarity in information science. First and foremost, the problems addressed cannot be resolved with approaches and constructs from any single discipline-thus, intedisciplinarity is predetermined, as it is in many modern fields. Second, interdisciplinarity in information science was introduced and is being perpetuated to the present by the very differences in backgrounds of people addressing the described problems. Differences in background are many; they make for richness of the field and difficulties in communication and education. Clearly not every discipline in the background of people working on the problem made an equally relevant contri-bution, but the assortment was responsible for sustaining a strong interdisciplinary characteristic of information science. I will concentrate on interdisciplinary relations with two fields: librarianship and computer science. Obviously, other fields, most notably cognitive science and communication, have also interdisciplinary relations, but these are the most significant and developed ones.

LIBRARIANSHIP

Librarianship has a long and proud history devoted to organization, preservation, and use of graphic records and records in other media. This is done through libraries not only as a particular organization or type of information system, but even more so as an indispensable social, cultural, and educational institution whose value has been proven manifold throughout human history, and across all geographic and cultural boundaries.

Researcher defines the library as:

- . . .Contributing to the total communication system in society. . . Though the library is an instrumentality created to maximize the utility of graphic records for the benefits of society, it achieves that goal by working with the individual and through the individual it reaches society.

The common ground between library science and information science, which is a strong one, is in sharing of their social role and in their general concern with effective utilization of graphic and other records, particularly by individuals.

But there are also very significant differences in several critical respects, among them:

- *Selection of Problems Addressed and the Way they were Defined*: A majority of the problems were not and are not addressed in library science;
- *Theoretical Questions Asked and Frameworks Established*: The theories and conceptual frameworks in librarian-ship have no counterpart in information science, and *vice versa*;
- *The Nature and Degree of Experimentation and Empirical Development and the Resulting Practical Knowledge and Competencies Dderived*: There is very little overlap in experimentation and development between the two, and professional requirements differ as well to a significant degree;
- *Tools and Approaches Used:* A most telling example is the very different approach undertaken in relation to utilization of technology in IR and in library automation; and
- *The Nature and Strength of Interdisciplinary Relations Established and the Dependence of Progress on Inter-disciplinary Approaches*: Librarianship is much more selfcontained.

All of these differences warrant a conclusion that librarian-ship and information science are two different fields in strong interdisciplinary relations, rather than one and the same field, or one being a special case of the other. This is not a matter of turf battles, or of one being better or worse than the other. Such arguments, while common between many fields, matter little to progress of either field. But differences in selection and/or definition of problems addressed, agenda, paradigms, theoretical base, and practical solutions *do* matter. Thus the conclusion that librarianship and information science, while related, are different fields. The differences are most pronounced in the research agenda and directions.

Interestingly, research on OPACs, now that they are incorporating more and more IR features, is bringing the two fields in closer relation. Probably, so will the research in digital libraries, but at this time, it is too early to tell. The conclusion is not without heated controversy.

Among other authors, Vakkari contends on information science and librarianship being one and the same field, with the now commonly used name of "library and information science." Does it matter? Administratively yes, very much so, particularly in universities and professional societies. Otherwise, no. The issue is, and always will be, in the problems addressed and solutions undertaken. I contend that they differ significantly.

COMPUTER SCIENCE

The basis of relation between information science and computer science lies in the application of computers and computing in IR, and the associated products, services, and networks. In the last few years, this relation also involves research on the evolving digital libraries, with their strong technological base.

To illustrate the connection, we use a definition by Denning:

- "The discipline of computing is the systematic study of algorithmic processes that describe and transfer information: their theory, analysis, design, efficiency, implementation, and application. The fundamental question underlying all of the computing is: "What can be automated?"

Computer science is about algorithms related to infor-mation interpreted in the first, whereas information science is about the very nature of information and its use by humans, interpreted in the third or broadest sense. Computer science is about symbol manipulation, whereas information science is about content manipulation, where symbol manipulation is the indispensable infrastructure. The two concerns are not in competition, they are complementary—they lead to different basic and applied agendas. Computer science is also many times larger than information science.

A number of computer scientists have been involved in research and development on information and its many spin-offs, to the point of being recognized leaders in information science. Gerard Salton is a prime example. In addition, there are several streams of research and development in computer science that had no connection with the early evolution of information science, but have addressed information problems similar to those in information science. Among others, these include works on expert systems, knowledge bases, hypertext, and human-computer interaction.

More recently, this involves research and development on digital libraries, a "hot", financially heavily supported area by a host of government agencies in the U.S. and many other countries. Bolstered by heavy support, interest in digital library research exploded on the scene in 1990s, attracting the attention of computer scientists from a wide variety of streams, as well as people from many other disciplines. These areas have a significant informational component that is associated with information representation, its intellectual organization, and linkages; meta-information, information seeking, searching, retrieving, and filtering; use, quality, value, and impact of information; evaluation of information systems from user and use perspective; and the like-all traditionally addressed in information science.

Conversely, these streams of computer science research and development provide a different outlook, framework, and approach, and even a different paradigm, not only for information science research and development, but also for its academic and continuing education. Again, as with librarianship, the issue is not about turf. It is about paradigms, theoretical foundations, and pragmatic solutions; and ultimately, it is about their appropriateness to human information problems.

EDUCATION

That education is critical for any field is a truism that hardly needs to be stated. In particular, research lives by education, it cannot be better than the education that researchers receive and then extend and plow back into education. Unfortunately, education in information science has not received the attention that it deserves. This may explain the many difficulties in the field that I have discussed. Educational models that evolved differed to a degree or even substantially from country to country. I am concentrating here on the U.S. models only.

In the United States, two educational models evolved over time. I call them the Shera and Salton models, after those that pioneered them. Both have strengths and weaknesses. Jesse H. Shera was a legendary library school dean from the 1950s until the 1970s at Western Reserve University. Among others, he was instrumental in starting the Center for Documentation and Communication Research in 1955. Shortly thereafter, the library school curriculum started to include courses such as "Machine Literature Searching" and several other more advanced courses and laboratories on the topics of research in the Centre. The basic approach was to append those courses, mostly as electives, to the existing library school curriculum, without modifications of the curriculum as a whole, and particularly not the required core courses. Information science became one of the specialty areas of library science. The base or core courses that students were taking rested in the traditional library curriculum. Information science education was an appendage to library science. A few attempts to spin off information science as an independent degree and curriculum were not followed widely. But Shera's model was. Library schools in the U.S. and in many other countries imitated Shera's model.

They used the same approach and started incorporating information science courses in their existing curriculum as a specialty. Out of this was borne the current designation "library and information science." Shera's model is still the prevalent approach in schools of library and information science. The strength of the Shera model is that it posits education within a service framework, connects the education to professional practice and to a broader and user-oriented frame of a number of other information services, and relates it to a great diversity of information resources.

The weakness is a lack of a broader theoretical frame-work and a total lack of teaching of any formalism related to systems, such as development and understanding of algori-thms. The majority of researchers in the human-centered side, as I described earlier, came from or are associated with this educa-tional environment. Gerard Salton was first and foremost a scientist, a computer scientist, and the father of modern IR.

As such, he pioneered the incorporation into IR research a whole array of formal and experimental methods from science, as modified for algorithmic and other approaches used so successfully in computer science. His primary orientation was research. For education, he took the time-honoured approach of a close involvement with research. Salton's model was a laboratory and research approach to education.

As Shera's model resulted in information science educa-tion being an appendage to library science education, Salton's model of IR education resulted in it being a specialty of and an appendage to computer science education. Computer science students that were already well-grounded in the discipline, got involved in SMART and other projects directed by Salton, worked and did research in the laboratory, completed their theses in areas related to IR, and participated in the legendary IR seminars.

They also published widely with Salton and with each other, and participated with high visibility in national and international conferences. From Harvard and Cornell, his students went to a number of computer science departments where they replicated Salton's model. Many other computer science departments in the U.S. and abroad took the same approach.

The strength of Salton's model is that it:

- "Starts from a base of a firm grounding in formal mathematical and other methods, and in algorithms, and
- Relates directly to research.

The weakness is in that it:

- Ignores the broader aspects of information science, as well as any other disciplines and approaches dealing with the human aspects that have great relevance to both the outcomes of IR research and the research itself, and
- Does not incorporate professional practice where these systems are realised and used. It loses users.

Consequently, this is a successful, but narrowly concen-trated education in IR as a specialty of computer science, rather then in information science.

Not surprisingly, the researchers in the systems-centred approach came out of this tradition. The two educational approaches are completely independent of each other. Neither is connected to the other. Neither reflects fully what is going on in the field. While in each model there is an increase in cognizance of the other, there is no educational integration of the systems-and usercentered approaches.

The evident strengths that are provided by Shera and Salton model are not put together. Their weaknesses are perpetuated. It is high time for communities from each model to try to integrate education for information science. It is an open question whether the human-and systems-centered approaches can fruitfully work together as urged in all those calls for human-centered design until an educational inte-gration occurs.

While library education receives formal attention from the *American Library Association* (ALA), and education for computer science from ACM, no such formal attention is paid by any professional/scientific society to education for information science, or for IR in particular. Neither ASIS nor SIGIR, as primary homes for information science, have been involved to any great extent in educational matters, such as setting of standards or devising model curricula. Clearly, there is a need and an opportunity for more substantive involvement by both organizations in educational issues.

ROLE OF INFORMATION IN PLANNING IN LIBRARY

WHAT IS PLANNING

Planning is a simple process used every day. In the process, one decides where he is, where he wants to be, and how he gets there. Getting to work every day, grocery shopping, preparing for a vacation or trip, and saving for retirement are examples of events that require planning. More formally, planning is an organizational process of envisioning a desired future and developing the necessary infrastructure to achieve it.

WHY PLAN

Overall, the purpose of planning is to achieve excellence in public library service.

Some specific benefits:

- Planning provides information to use in decision-making.
- Planning provides a blueprint for future library development.
- Planning guides decision-makers in setting necessary priorities about who receives what service with what efficiency.
- Planning provides information to use in the allocation of resources, particularly when they are scarce.
- Planning leads to structured positive change resulting in improved library service.

- Planning makes crises less critical.
- Planning encourages staff creativity and cooperation.
- Planning encourages accountability.
- Planning provides a basis for evaluating the library's performance.
- Planning can improve communication and give everyone who works with the library a sense of common purpose.
- Planning pays off—organizations that plan out-perform those that do not.

WHAT ARE THE STEPS IN THE PROCESS

There are many approaches to planning. Significantly, the Public Library Association published a new approach to public library planning; *Planning and Role Setting for Public Libraries: A Manual of Options and Procedures* is designed to meet the special needs of this community. The following is a summary of the eight major steps recommended.

PLANNING TO PLAN

- Organizes the planning process,
- Shapes the planning process to the library's needs and resources,
- Coordinates planning with other management activities,
- Defines the responsibilities of major planning participants, and
- Organizes and trains the Planning Committee.

LOOKING-AROUND

- Identifies information needed for planning,
- Collects information about the library and the comm-unity it serves, and
- Analyses information gathered for planning decisions.

DEVELOPING ROLES AND MISSION

- Describes eight distinct roles, or service profiles, that public libraries may emphasize in providing services to their comm-unities;
- Describes a method of determining which roles are to receive a major commitment in the library and which are to be supported only minimally;
- Guides planners in writing a mission statement as a concise expression of the roles chosen for emphasis;
- Helps the library communicate its service focus to the public, elected officials, and staff.

WRITING GOALS AND OBJECTIVES

- Translates the library's role choices and mission into statements of desired ends or targets,

- Defines goals as long-range and representing a vision of excellence in library service,
- Defines objectives as specific, time limited, and measurable or verifiable, and
- Provides a framework for implementation and evaluation.

TAKING ACTION

- Produces tangible evidence of the library's planning,
- Identifies possible activities to implement the goals and objectives,
- Selects activities best suited to the library's circum-stances and resources, and
- Leads to cycle of annual objective setting and updating of five-year plan.

WRITING THE PLANNING DOCUMENT

- Describes creation of a formal report of the library's planning activities, and
- Provides an opportunity for communication with the public, the library staff, and governing officials.

REVIEWING RESULTS

- Reviews the plan and its implementation activities after a period of time,
- Reviews extent to which objectives were accom-plished, and
- Starts the planning cycle again.

"LEVELS OF EFFORT" AS A PLANNING TOOL

Planning and Role Setting for Public Libraries introduces the concept of "levels of effort," an approach that allows library planners to adapt the process to a particular library's needs, purposes, and resources. There are three levels of effort — basic, moderate, and extensive. Any of these will result in acceptable plans. Each library's level-of-effort choice reflects the interplay of several different factors.

- *Participants:* The more individuals and groups represented, the higher the library's level of effort for planning will be.
- *Resources:* Higher levels of effort call for a propor-tionally greater commitment of the library staff's time and larger expenditures from the library's budget.
- *Library Context:* Libraries serving a community with rapid growth or change, a complex and diverse population, shifting economic conditions, or libraries facing a major change in funding may need to plan at a higher level of effort.

- *Planning Purposes:* What the library expects the planning process to accomplish may affect the level of effort chosen for some planning phases.
- *Planning Structure:* Libraries planning at a basic level of effort may approach many planning activities informally; but as library complexity increases, the planning structure becomes more formal, thus increasing the level of effort.
- *Planning Schedule:* Some libraries may complete their first objectives cycle over a very short time period; higher levels of effort may require twelve to eighteen months to complete.

3

The Role of Libraries in Modern Society

First, the general development of the information society is pushing to re-evaluation of all the institutions which work with information, data, and knowledge-indirectly also with culture. In this connection the roles of education and media have been discussed already quite largely also in the European Union. But libraries-as well as other memory institutions like archives and museums-have not been considered.

Still, there is a clear need in the information society to maintain an institution which is concentrating in collecting and organizing information and offering general access to it. Until now, this work has been underestimated, but I argue the situation will change!

Libraries are especially important now when the whole idea of education is stressing more and more independent learning and acting. All citizens must be able to find and use information. It is the key raw material-but it is a zero resource, if there are no access points to it and if documents are in chaotic order.

Here we can see libraries enter the stage:

- The unique function of libraries is to acquire, organize, offer for use and preserve publicly available material irrespective of the form in which it is packaged in such a way that, when it is needed, it can be found and put to use. No other institution carries out this long-term, systematic work. Culture must be nominated especially: it has an important and unique role in mobilizing resources of human beings. It has been described: To some extent, culture makes its influence felt more indirectly than knowledge, but it is impossible to imagine how people's creative powers could be fully activated without the impact of culture, which extends into the depths of the mind.

The challenge to modern societies is that the basic resource, knowledge, is developing from information in very individual, capricious and unpredictable process.

It cannot be commanded. Still, societies can support this development, *e.g.* by offering access to cultural and knowledge treasures.

This can even be translated into economic language: to get out the best from the human resources in Europe, this resource must be feeded up with rich and various cultural and infor-mation contents! I would like to stress especially the idea of organizing information by libraries.

It is often shadowed by the second important side of library work: offering access. But in the life-long learning and new technology context just all forms of organizing documents are getting more to the focus. This is clear to anybody who has tried to find something from not-so-often-used Internet web sites.

NEW LINES IN THE EU AND IN THE UNITED STATES

In accordance with these phenomenons, there are new political lines in the European Union: The Maastricht Treaty in 1992 launched the cultural aspects. This was only after a long discussion, which made it clear that we have to remember to separate the national view and the European view. The Amsterdam Treaty in 1997 declared citizenship as an important theme.

A significant part of this are a.o. granting information skills and access to information to every European. In addition to this, the European future strategies need to meet the democratic aspects of the information society development. One of the crucial points is again general access to information. Libraries, especially public libraries, are a good tool in all of these new areas. But the European union does not support whichever cultural or citizen concentrated projects in Europe.

In the interests of the European Union there is always to find the European element. So, what can be done in library policy on the European level, taking in account that libraries are primarily a part of national education and cultural policies? The own-initiative report "The role of libraries in modern societies," adopted by the European Parliament in October 1998, is the first effort to answer these questions. The same topics have been discussed in the United States. They have reached the point where especially the problems of those lacking access to digital resources have been studied. The report Falling Through the Net: Defining the Digital Divide by the U.S. Department of Commerce was released earlier in July 1999.

The report finds that minorities, low-income persons, the less educated, and children of single parent households, particularly when they reside in rural areas or central cities, are risk groups. The report calls for public policies and private initiatives to expand affordable access to critical information resources.

But it also shows, for the first time as far as I know, that libraries and community centres really can diminish the information gap between haves and not-haves. The 1998 data from the U.S. demonstrate very clearly that community access centres, primarily public libraries, are particularly well used by those groups who lack access at home or at work: *e.g.* unemployed groups used Internet in libraries three times as often as an average citizen.

EARLIER ACTIONS IN EU

In the European Union, there have been some efforts to mobilize "the treasures of the European libraries" since the mid-80's. These discussions and resolutions led to two special library programmes under the 3rd and 4th Framework programmes of research and development. The later programme has been known as "Telematics for Libraries". They have been strongly concentrated in IT, because it has been seen as a good tool to produce better access to the existing, underused library resources. These programmes have had a clear impact in the European library co-operation and development. Benefits of this work come to public libraries indirectly: common standards and working methods help in the end all kind of libraries. But a fact is, that nearly all the libraries active in these EU projects are national libraries or big research and university libraries. Two main exceptions are Publican, a network of European public libraries, and ECUP, which was a copyright awareness raising project, and reached public libraries as well.

A new beginning was the so called Morgan report in 1997. In this report libraries were for the first time put clearly onto the place where they belong in the information society. As one result of the Morgan report, the European Commission informed that it will produce a Green Paper about the role of libraries in the information society. For one or another reason, this was made quite ready but was never published. In this situation the Committee on Culture, Youth, Education and the Media in the European Parliament decided to produce an own-initiative report about libraries.

The main reason was that they wanted to influence the big issues under work in the EU, first of all the copyright directive and the 5th framework programme, which will have a direct impact to libraries. I was nominated the rapporteur of the own-initiative report. The report was adopted almost unanimously and with a very encouraging discussion in the Plenary session of the Parliament in October 1998.

DECISIONS OF THE EP CONCERNING LIBRARY POLICY

In short, when adopting the own-initiative report, the EP was calling the Commission and/or the member states to following actions:

- Libraries must be taken in account in national and EU information society strategies and in the respective budgets.
- Libraries need more resources for acquiring expensive books.
- The Green Paper on libraries by the Commission must be completed.
- The users position must be taken in account in the copyright directive process, the balance must be maintained-this was politically the most important decision in short run.
- Support to libraries was demanded from the 5th Framework programme of research and development, *e.g.* for networking,

drafting standards, preserving, and transferring information; there is no more named library programme under the 5th framework programme

- A clearing-house to solve problems of long-term conservation should be founded.
- Studies concerning permanent paper should be done on European level.
- The member–states should take care of digitizing their cultural heritage for future.
- There should be studies and concrete support to libraries in licensing matters, which are–will be the next big issue in library work.
- The EU cultural and information budget should be opened to libraries as well, libraries and their co-operation should be taken in account in planning new programmes.
- Problems of legal deposit in international and multinational materials, especially in electronic materials should be solved.
- The member states should provide all types of libraries with modern equipment, particularly with Internet connections.
- Free of charge use of public libraries, in the spirit of the UNESCO Public Library Manifest, was demanded.
- Free and easy access via libraries to material produced with the aid of tax revenues was demanded.
- The members states should organize for their library professionals up-dating education and training.
- A European Union focal point for libraries should be set up
- The member states should found European information points at libraries in countries where they do not yet exist.
- Library statistics should be better and more comparable both on national and European level.
- The national Parliament libraries should be opened to the MEP's in countries where this is not yet the practice.

In addition to these, the report strongly stresses that the library financing must be re-thought in the information society. Without new resources libraries are unable to do everything they are expected to do! After the EP adoption of this report, the European Commission informed that it will next prepare a communication about actions to do. It was stated that the report had already served as a discussion paper, and so the need for the Green Paper had disappeared. The communication is in summer 1999 still under work in the Commission DGXIII/2.

TRADITIONS AND NEW FORMS OF WORK IN THE SAME HOUSE

The European Commission R&D framework programmes have concentrated in IT matters. The three cultural programmes, Caledoskope,

Ariane and Raphael, have not been very useful for libraries, because their scope has been quite narrow. *E.g.* the books and reading programme Ariane has concentrated in translations. In the coming framework programme Culture 2000 libraries will have more possibilities to get support also for their cultural actions. What then will be the fate of the traditional tasks of libraries in general? Will the information society wipe out book loaning and poems?

PROBLEMS AND OPPORTUNITIES FACING LIBRARIES IN INDIA

Library and information services are fundamental to the goals of creating, disseminating, optimally utilising and preserving knowledge. They are instrumental in transforming an unequal society into an egalitarian, progressive knowledge-based society. It is well known that in India most of the libraries function in the government sector.

These are in academic and research institutions and under the public library system, which is again under the state and central governments. At present, education being a state subject and coming under the purview of different apex agencies, there is no common direction or coordination among them. It is imperative that all libraries (public, academic, research and special) change gear and develop at an accelerated pace. Developments in information communication technology (ICT) have enabled libraries to provide access to all, and also bridge the gap between the local, the national and the global. Yet the Library and Information Services (LIS) sector in India has not kept pace with the paradigmatic changes taking place in society.

There are a few libraries which are using state of art technologies to disseminate knowledge to their respective user community. There is lack of cooperation among the libraries of different organisations and which cause the lack of union catalogues at national level. The national library failed even to do this immense task. One of the major problems faced by LIS sector in India is lack of bibliographic control at national level which causes duplication in research. A considerable number of libraries had not been developed bibliographic databases of their documents for putting them on network.

To summarise, the major constraints faced by the libraries which militate against effective dissemination and use of information are:

- A considerable percentage of the population is illiterate or functionally literate making libraries of minimal use to them.
- Poor resource allocation for infrastructure improvement and collection development for public libraries.
- Lack of sufficient sanctioned posts, forcing most services to be operated by voluntary Non-professional staff, which damages information organisation and services.
- Lack of national policies promoting ICT as a tool for development of library systems and services.

- Lack of adequate trained manpower in the use of IT.
- Lack of funds for acquiring necessary hardware and software facilities.
- Resistance on the part of library staff to change from their traditional practices to the use of IT.

Despite the problems, Library and Information Services (LIS) sector in India has got remarkable achievements. Efforts had been made to set up networks at local, regional and national level to deploy information and communication technologies and to build electronic information sources. Besides INFLIBNET at the national level to support university and college libraries, a number of other national networks and various library networks have also been developed including NICNET (National Informatics Centers Network), ERNET (Education and Research Network), CALIBNET (Calcutta Library Network), DELNET (Developing Library Network), etc.

A number of educational institutions are members of such networks. These networks, especially INFLIBNET and DELNET, are engaged in compiling union catalogs, creating various databases of experts, providing training to library staff, ILL, online facilities, reference service, assistance in retrospective conversion,,etc. To overcome the problem of financial crunch and the rising costs of journals, librarians have formed consortia to subscribe all the required journals and databases. Some special libraries and research organisations have established consortia known as FORSA (Forum for Resource Sharing in Astronomy) to share electronic access to journal literature.

NISCAIR (National Institutes of Science Communication and Information Resources), one of CSIR labs, has formed a consortium for CSIR labs for accessing e-journals and databases. In order to solve the problem of universities and college libraries, UGC launched a major initiative called UGC-INFONET that provides high speed Internet connections so as to have electronic access to professional literature including research journals, abstracts, review publications, and databases from all areas in science and technology, as well as in social sciences and humanities.

The Ministry of Human Resource Development (MHRD) has set up the "Indian National Digital Library in Science and Technology (INDEST) Consortium" for the subscription to electronic resources for 38 academic institutions, including the Indian Institute of Sciences, Indian Institute of Technology, Regional Engineering Colleges, Indian Institute of Managements, and about 60 centrally-funded/aided government institutions through the consortium. For the improvement of quality of library and information services through the systematic acquisition, organisation and dissemination of knowledge, various library associations have been set up at national and state level.

They annually organised conferences, seminars and training Programmes to trained and update library professionals with latest development in LIS.

Recently libraries and research organisations realise the importance of digital libraries and they started the work of digitisation of important documents. NISCAIR and the Department of Indian Systems of Medicine and Homoeopathy (ISMandH) have entered into an agreement for establishing a Traditional Knowledge Digital Library (TKDL) on Ayurveda. TKDL will be available in English, German, French, Spanish and Japanese Since, these languages account for more than 98 per cent of the international patent applications.

TKDL in the first phase targets Ayurveda. But as a whole it would encompass, in addition to Ayurveda, Siddha, Unani, Yoga, Naturopathy and Folklore medicine. The Indian Institute of Science (IISc), Carnegie Mellon University (CMU), the International Institute of Information Technology, Hyderabad (IIITH) and many other academic, religious and government organisations, totaling about 21 'Content Creation Centers', have become partners in the Digital Library of India (DLI) initiative for the digitisation and preservation of Indian heritage present in the form of books, manuscripts, art and music.

Each centre brings its own unique collection of literature into the digital library. DLI has a vision to build a universal digital library of world knowledge. One million books have already been available through this project. India perhaps has one of the oldest and largest collections of Manuscripts in the world. These manuscripts are in different languages and scripts; written on different materials such as birch bark, palm leaf, cloth, paper,etc. They are in the custody of libraries, museums, monasteries, mutts and individuals.

A significant proportion is not preserved scientifically. Experts estimate that almost all palm leaf manuscripts may perish due to wear and tear over next 50 to 100 years. In this regard the National Mission for Manuscripts has taken a step to save the most valuable, intellectual property of our cultural inheritance. The missions has started a pilot project for digitising the manuscripts in five states across India covering five caches of manuscripts and for the same four digitising agencies have been selected.

Importance of open access archives, institutional repositories and open access journals has been realised by the library and information professionals in India. This movement has been accelerated by the availability of open source software namely DSpace, EPrints, Greenstone,,etc., Indian Institute of Science, Bangalore, INFLIBNET Centre, Ahmedabad and Documentation Research and Training Centre (DRTC), Bangalore are the leading institutions who made this movement a great success. Among the top 25 publishing countries, India ranks 12th for the overall number of journals, but drops to 18th for journals with online content. At present there are more than 150 open access journals in India.

The open access journals in India are mainly initiated by six journal publishers, namely, Indian Academy of Sciences, Indian National Science Academy, Indian Medlars Centre of National Informatics Centre, Medknow Publications, indianjournals. com and Kamla-Raj Enterprises.

The Indian Institute of Science was the first in the country to set up and interoperable institutional archive ePrints@IIScr. The archive now has more than 7000 records, with over 90 per cent having full text. Presently there are 25 institutional archives in India which are registered in the Registry of Open Access Repositories (ROAR). An open access statement is likely to be ready by this year.

The CSIR also has a plan to setup a national digital repository of research literature. NISCAIR has already started to work on the project known as National Science Digital Library. National knowledge Commission is also formulating similar open access policies and guidelines for the higher education and R and D sectors to improve access to research literature and disseminate research literature to the global communities.

The National Knowledge Commission has submitted its report to the government on how to redefine the information services sector. The report of Knowledge Commission on library sector suggests that "Every state should establish a registry and archives of knowledge based digital resources which should be made accessible to all".

LIBRARIES – AN INVESTMENT IN OUR FUTURE

Libraries provide the physical and virtual spaces that are an integral part of an overarching system that provides continuous opportunities for learning from birth to senior age. By offering all New Yorkers the opportunity to acquire the knowledge they need to be informed and engaged participants in an open democracy, libraries empower individuals. Library "profit" is demonstrated through both the promotion of economic enterprise and the social return on investment. Libraries continue to undergo tremendous transition as they move to virtual services in response to changes in technology and the expectations of their patrons, and as they facilitate not only the use of existing information, but also production of new information through online communities and efforts to preserve local history.

One significant change is the increasing convergence among traditionally different types of libraries in the services they offer. Such convergence includes online access to digital resources, the re-tasking of library space, the need for staff skilled in virtual librarianship and collaborative learning, as well as more customary types of service. Because of the continuing centrality, complexity and diversity of today's knowledge creation and information distribution environments, it is important that our students and residents be equipped with both print and digital literacy skills — how to find, evaluate, and effectively use information from a variety of sources and formats.

Literacy – and in particular digital literacy — lies at the heart of the mission of all libraries. Regardless of the many levels of technological change, libraries remain the embodiment of Americans' "right to educate themselves", a critical necessity in a knowledge economy where everyone must relentlessly improve their skills throughout their lifetime.

The library is what makes lifelong learning for *all* residents both possible and practical, including, and perhaps especially, for those with special challenges such as the disabled, homeless and economically disadvantaged. People unable to respond to new challenges and invest in their own abilities are likely to become an economic liability, unable to participate fully in society.

Libraries continue to represent a community investment in a vision of a better tomorrow through sharing information, knowledge and, hopefully, wisdom. They are the repositories for the collective memory of our communities, our state, and our nation, and offer us an institution that reflects the American dream of self-help and equity. Today's libraries are busier and more vibrant than ever because of, not in spite of, the dramatic impact of digital technology. But even though they have a well established and well respected brand, libraries suffer from outdated public attitudes based on misperceptions that are limited to their traditional roles, stereotypes and the constant assault of competing commercial information providers.

UNIVERSAL RECOMMENDATIONS –FOR ALL LIBRARIES

The themes of Access, Information Literacy and Sustainability are woven through all libraries in our state and nation. Though each serves its unique community, all share these values.

MODELS FOR SUCCESS

Over six decades ago the State of New York outlined its vision for universal access to information for all residents through its creation of library systems. This remarkably successful model has evolved to embrace nearly all the libraries within our state, creating a framework and foundation for the fulfillment of this dream.

The notion that any and every child or adult may follow their curiosity to its fullest extent, accessing resources from around the world, is today a reality for most, but not all, of our state's residents.

Vibrant libraries of all types, enjoying the robust support of their community or constituency and working in partnership with their library system and its collaborative systems are able to bring these resources into their communities. We have the potential to fulfill this vision for all.

RECOMMENDATIONS

To assure that tomorrow's libraries continue to be a vibrant and vital part of all New Yorkers' lifelong learning experience, all libraries must:

- Improve the marketing of library services to all clientele and communities by rebranding libraries while addressing the erroneous perceptions about the need for libraries in a digital world.

- Develop better tools for advocacy, and identify library champions at all levels of governance: university and school boards, town and city management, State Education Department, Board of Regents, New York State Legislature and Executive branch.
- Collaborate to integrate services and collections of all types of libraries while developing a transparent and seamless world of library services that are ubiquitous and instantaneous, yet personalised and flexible, serving all ages and needs.
- Seek operational and cost efficiencies in light of technological opportunities, energy efficient facilities, and online service delivery methods.
- Develop economic justifications for the investments that governments, communities, individuals and philanthropic organisations are asked to make in libraries, and enhance the role of libraries as economic drivers for their communities.
- Recruit technologically savvy staff and train current staff in virtual librarianship while influencing higher education to appropriately educate tomorrow's service providers.
- Function at the front lines of e-resources (including e-books) purchasing, licensing, digital rights management, digital curation, resource-sharing, and preservation; and advocate for the delivery of open content as embodied in initiatives such as the Digital Public Library of America or the Berlin Declaration on Open Access to Knowledge in the Sciences and Humanities.
- Actively address issues concerning the privatisation of information and its impact on traditional models of library services, defending residents' rights to free access, free lending and the intersharing of materials among libraries.
- Create collaborative partnerships with all cultural and educational organisations in the state to offer our residents the most comprehensive educational opportunities available anywhere in the world.

SCHOOL LIBRARIES (P-12)

School libraries are deeply engaged in the implementation of the New York State P-12 Common Core Learning Standards. There is a well documented connection between student achievement and effective school libraries. The role of school librarians is evolving as they teach students information literacy to be savvy information consumers, producers and judges of appropriate content in all formats.

School librarians increasingly collaborate with teachers in designing curricula, developing learning experiences, and providing technical infrastructure that are ideally placed to support differentiated instruction and facilitate special programmes for the gifted as well as students with special needs. The school librarian is unique in that he/she addresses the depth and breadth of the entire curriculum, and leads in teaching a 21st Century curriculum of enquiry, problem solving and content creation.

MODELS FOR SUCCESS

The best school libraries are fully integrated into the P-12 learning experience and are at the hub of each campus, reaching into every classroom as well as into students' homes. Based on the research findings of the recent Information Brief: The Impact of School Libraries on Student Achievement published by the NY Comprehensive Center, it is clear that with the shift to the Common Core Standards and a commitment to five key elements of the Regents reform agenda, school libraries with certified school librarians play an important role in student achievement, curriculum development and instruction. Information and digital literacy is recognised as a critical aspect of each student's education.

The school librarian is a true educational partner with every teacher and administrator in providing the best possible learning experience for each child.

RECOMMENDATIONS

The Board of Regents and State Education Department should formulate policy and regulation that will:

- Adopt and implement a statewide information fluency curriculum framework, aligned with the New York State P-12 Common Core Learning Standards, which, through certified school librarians and a strong library programme, will provide equitable access to information and digital literacy instruction and tools. Such a framework will further the schools' ultimate goal of preparing students, beginning at the elementary level, with the literacy and digital skills and knowledge needed for career or college.
- Expand the existing Commissioner's Regulations to require a certified elementary school librarian in every school to strengthen instructional leadership in meeting the P-12 Common Core Learning Standards, and enforce library staffing regulations in all public schools.
- Create incentives to encourage school districts to actively expand and promote access to the school library collection of online resources, e-books, and Web 2.0 tools, available 24/7, to create learning and enrichment opportunities that reach beyond the school day and encourage yearround learning.
- Create incentives to encourage school districts to adopt flexible scheduling to support full academic day access to school librarians, school library resources and information and digital literacy instruction.

- Create incentives for school libraries to collaborate with other libraries and communities to result in full-time, full-year access to information that will further opportunities for all students.

THE PUBLIC LIBRARIES IN THE KNOWLEDGE SOCIETY

THE LIBRARIES IN A STATE OF FLUX

The municipal reform in 2007 had major consequences for the library service. The number of libraries decreased and the remaining libraries grew in size. The reform thus underlined and intensified various tendencies in library development over the past many years.

The public library is in a state of flux. *Library service to children* from 2008 that chose as its point of reference the changes in children's use of the library. Thus this report had a strong focus on one target group and on how the library can develop new services to that group.

The present report also focuses on the target group, but slightly more on the institution–the public library. Based on a number of societal needs and new opportunities the report also considers how the library can be developed as an institution. The library offer is changing rapidly, but it continues to be much sought after.

Two out of three Danes use the public library, and 29 per cent of the adult population visit the library at least once a month. In 2008 the public libraries registered more than 34 mil. visits. This makes the library one of our most popular, public cultural offers, and this has been the case for many years. But the way we use the library is undergoing a change. On the one hand the loan of physical materials – books, CDs etc. – is falling.

In the period 2000-2008 the public libraries' loan of physical materials has thus fallen by 22 per cent, from ca. 62 mil. to app. 48 mil. materials. On the other hand the use of digital offers is growing, an offer that spans from downloads of music and e-books to renewals of loans via the library's homepage. Bibliotekernes Netmusik, where as a library user you can via your municipality download music for free, experienced over 2,5 mil. downloads in 2008 – an increase of 48 per cent compared with 2007.

One explanation of the change in borrowing patterns could be that the technology and media development has resulted in new media habits on behalf of the library users. At the same time the libraries' consistently high visiting figures show that they have succeeded in reorganizing and revitalizing themselves and continue to be attractive.

This happens by developing new library services, particularly digital services, but also by turning the library into something more than just a collection of materials, so that the physical library maintains its desirability.

Today the library is also a place for being and meeting, where one for example gets instruction, uses the Internet or gets help in the local citizen service centre. However, borrowing books remains the main reason why Danes visit the library. The latest cultural habits survey from 2004 shows that 85 per cent of adult library users visit the library to borrow books and journals. The same tendency becomes apparent in more recent studies.

In a Gallup poll conducted on behalf of the Danish Library Association, the Union of Danish Librarians and HK Kommunal (white collar workers' union (municipal) in 2009, "borrowing books" is the most frequent reason for visiting the library, followed by "borrowing electronic media", "taking the children to the library" and "watching events".

There is in fact also a growing interest in the library's non-users, as can be seen from the large number of new initiatives, which the libraries participate in at municipal level. In many cases these have a social aspect, and the library is here used as a partner in a targeted initiative towards certain target groups.

This effort is particularly relevant in the light of the challenges that globalization presents to less resourceful citizens. The focusing on non-users also has another angle, which is i.a. clearly expressed in former minister for culture, Carina Christensen's strategy Culture for everybody from 2009. Here the emphasis is on the value of participating in a cultural community and the individual citizen's benefit from cultural offers. The strategy suggests that all citizens should be able to take advantage of the cultural offers and consequently–that the cultural institutions focus more purposefully on non-users.

THE POLITICAL BASIS FOR THE COMMITTEE'S WORK

The appointment of the Committee on the Public Libraries in the Knowledge Society was decided by the minister for culture in connection with several consultations in Folketingets Kulturudvalg (parliamentary cultural committee), which took place in the wake of a large number of public library branches being closed down during the first year of the municipal reform. The discussion fuelled by this naturally included the media and technology development.

A suggestion for a more extensive, interdepartmental committee work was rejected by the minister, who referred to the work that had already been done by the Globalisation Council. The committee's work builds on the report *Future library service to children* from 2008. The report contains a number of recommendations as to how to make sure that a strong library offer continues to be available to all Danish children.

In 2008 the Danish Agency for Libraries and Media also published the report *The public libraries after the municipal reform*, which analysed the development within the public library area with particular focus on any consequences due to the municipal reform. The report concluded that the closure of the branches in 2006-2007 was a natural adaptation of the library service, and that at the same time it demonstrated a prioritisation in order to deliver a more up to date and value-enhancing library offer.

With the report from the Committee on the Public Libraries in the Knowledge Society we now have a number of recommendations as to how this prioritisation can be made so that the public libraries also in future will be able to meet the public's need for enlightenment, education and cultural activity. The committee presents its recommendations within an expenditure-neutral framework with the perspective that it may be both necessary and correct with local changes of priorities within the library field in order to support and strengthen the public library in the knowledge society.

THE COMMISSION'S ASSIGNMENT: MANDATE FOR THE COMMITTEE ON THE PUBLIC LIBRARIES IN THE KNOWLEDGE SOCIETY

The committee must focus on continuous development of the public libraries in Denmark. This includes the public libraries' interaction with other libraries and relevant institutions. Focus must be on the libraries as an easily accessible offer to everybody. The committee must build on the report *Future library service to children* and pay particular attention to service to youngsters and adults. The committee must assess the public libraries' role in relation to the challenges facing the knowledge society, the globalisation strategy's focus on education, lifelong learning and societal cohesive force. The committee must assess to which extent there is basis for establishing new concepts for a library service that meets the public's needs in terms of enlightenment, education and cultural activity, and close to the citizens.

Likewise the committee must asses the possibilities for continuous development of traditional core services such as literature dissemination. In particular, the committee must asses the need for further development of the libraries' digital infrastructure and the interaction between digital and traditional services.

The committee must furthermore describe models for the mediation of digital cultural heritage and licensed digital media and models for various forms of learning and inspiration activities (*e.g.* in relation to citizens with poor reading and IT skills). The committee must likewise give examples of new partnerships, including inter-institutional cooperations and binding networking commitments.

Finally the committee must assess the need for competence development of library staff. On the basis of its analyses the committee must put forward recommendations and suggestions as to how the strategy's objectives can be realised within the present legislation and existing division of labour between state and municipalities. The committee's suggestions must be expenditure-neutral. The committee is composed upon appointment, so that the minister for culture appoints three members, while Local Government (KL), Danish Library Association, Association of Library Directors, Danish Research Library Association, the Regional Libraries, Union of Danish Librarians and Børne-og Kulturchefforeningen each appoints a member. The Danish Agency for Library and Media's director general is chairman of the committee, and the Agency is the committee's secretariat. The committee must have completed its work primo 2010.

MODERN DIGITAL LIBRARY SYSTEM

Invenio is an integrated digital library system originally developed at CERN to run the CERN Document Server, currently one of the largest institutional repositories worldwide. It was started over 15 years ago and has been matured through many release cycles. Invenio is a GPL2 Open Source project based on Apache/WSGI + Python + MySQL architecture. Its modular design enables it to serve a wide variety of usages, from a multimedia digital object repository, to a web journal, to a fully functional digital library.

The development strategy used to implement Invenio ensures it is flexible in any layer. Being based on open standards such as MARCXML and OAI-PMH 2.0 its interoperability with other digital libraries is guaranteed. Being originally designed to cope with the CERN requirements for digital object management, Invenio is suitable for middle-to-large scale digital repositories. Records can be of any nature. This presentation will introduce the different features of Invenio, their usage in the CERN context and how other institutions and projects are also driving some of its development.

USAGE

Besides being used to run the CERN Document Server, Invenio has also been chosen by several other big institutions or projects. Among them it is about to be used to serve the SPIRES High Energy Physics information through the recently launched INSPIRE service, that will become the repository of reference for high energy physics. It is used by the EPFL. ADS has expressed interest to move to an Invenio-based platform, while starting a collaboration at the data level between astrophysics and high energy physics worlds.

For example in Spain Invenio is already used by the *Dipòsit Digital de Documents* (DDD) and by the "Repositorio Digital de la Universidad de Zaragoza". Recently the European Commission has chosen Invenio to become part of two important projects D4ScienceII, and OpenAIRE, with the latter having the goal to set up a portal where all the EC funded research project documents will be available.

FEATURES

Let us demonstrate the key Invenio features by following the lifetime of a record in the system, from ingestion to dissemination.

As an integrated digital library, Invenio is built to allow the management of digital objects and the meta-data associated with them. Meta-data are stored in the MARCXML format, which has the flexibility to store any kind of information and which can be easily converted, thanks to XML style-sheets to any other meta-data format.

INGESTING RECORDS

Data and Meta-data can enter into Invenio powered repositories through different ways. They can be manually deposited by an author, through custom and fully configurable web interfaces, backed by an equally configurable workflow architecture, that lets the submission administrator set up any kind of procedure triggered by a deposition. Meta-data and data can as well be harvested regularly from OAI-PMH compatible repositories.

Data can also be input into the system from any non-standard format by writing ad-hoc conversion scripts either in XSLT or in the proprietary BibConvert's language. Users also have the possibility to upload records by sending e-mails that will be parsed automatically. The system can be configured to accept submission by robots thanks to the availability of a simple web API.

DIGITAL OBJECT MANIPULATION

Fully fledged tools to integrate and manipulate digital objects are available. In particular Invenio can manage multiple formats for the same document, multiple revisions, automatic conversions between formats, automatic stamping of PDF documents with watermarks, creating icons, automatic text extraction to allow for full-text searching, automatic meta-data extraction and many more. Data consistency is also ensured by MD5 checksum being continuously verified.

INDEXING AND RANKING

All the new records ingested into the system and their modifications are indexed by a very fast indexing engine that has been developed in-house. All the indexing stages are configurable; which metadata fields to index, how to extract tokens, which language is expected in order to apply stemming and removing stop words, and so on. A plug-in based ranking engine takes care of creating special indexes to be used at search time for sorting results based on word similarity, citations, download statistics, and to present citation networks.

CURATING RECORDS

Curators have powerful web-based tools to manipulate records, whilst maintaining change histories, auto-completion of fields based on fully configurable knowledge bases, multi-record modification, assisted duplicate record finding and an efficient AJAX-based record merging tool, and so on. Curators can also exploit flexible tools to perform meta-data compliance checks against configurable rules.

Automatic tools are also available to extract citations and references from scientific papers and to extract keywords based on a given ontology, to enrich the available meta-data. Distributed curation activities can be instantiated through integration of Invenio with RT, one of the most famous open source ticketing systems.

DISPLAYING RECORDS

Bibliographic records can be displayed in any format, thanks to an easy and fully-configurable formatting layer, which allows creation of record-based rules to choose which representation of a record to use, while each representation can be fine tuned to fit any particular need. Thus any kind of content can be hosted and properly displayed, such as multimedia documents, books, address book contacts, and so on.

Records can be organized in a flexible hierarchical structure using real and virtual collections. Each collection can in turn be customised to choose the look and feel and the kind of features enabled.

The whole web appearance of Invenio can be fully customised thanks to an integrated templating system, thus facilitating integration of Invenio into an existing institutional portal. Since Invenio is being developed in an international environment it supports internationalization and comes translated already in 25 different languages.

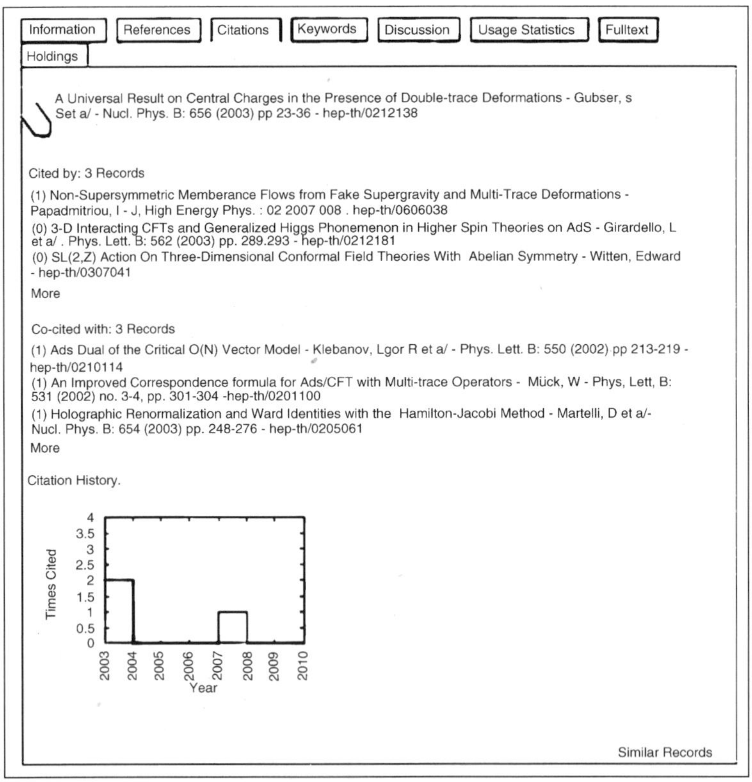

SEARCHING AND BROWSING RECORDS

A powerful search engine resides at the core of Invenio figure. Supporting a Google-like syntax, it can be used to dig into the repositories in a very easy way, while allowing the more experienced users to take advantage of many advanced features such as regular expressions, range queries, selection of meta-data, and many more. Results can be clustered by collections and ranked with respect to word similarity, number of citations, downloads based rankings, and any other pluggable algorithm. Any search query can automatically turned into an RSS feed to add to a personal news aggregator. Thanks to integrated support for MODS and UnAPI standards, search results can be stored in Zotero, a powerful Firefox plug-in useful to organize a personal digital library. The system offers users powerful citation and author analyses.

COLLABORATIVE TOOLS

Invenio integrates several collaborative and typical web 2.0 tools such as baskets, to store and share records or external resources with other users, personal e-mail notification alerts, record commenting and reviewing, internal web-based messaging tools, approval/reviewing work-flows.

EXPORTING RECORDS

Data and meta-data can be exported in several ways, the most important being through OAI-PHM protocol and by means of a pluggable exporting module.

AUTHENTICATION AND AUTHORIZATION

While offering for free local accounts management, Invenio can be integrated with institutional user databases to delegate the authentication phase and to exploit externally available user details. Using the *role based access control* (RBAC) model of Invenio one can define a list of roles, attach users to particular roles, and grant rights to perform actions such as view-restricted-collections based on user group membership, user IP address, and more.

CIRCULATION

Invenio supports the operation of a physical library by integrating a circulation module, as well as by supporting inter library loans. Users can submit loan requests, and follow the request status, the librarians have a web interface to accept/reject loan requests, to send overdue letters, to set up sub-libraries, etc.

CREATING JOURNALS

As an example of an application that has been built on top of the core Invenio, the web journal module lets repository administrators create online web journals with regular issues built from articles stored in the repository itself. A specific appearance can be set up in order to have a layout providing journal-like reading experience. This is currently used today for producing the official CERN Bulletin, which is issued every two weeks.

4

Organisational Change in Library Automation

IDENTIFICATION OF THE ISSUE

The example is only one instance of the large-scale changes that affect people's work lives. These types of changes raise many important issues for managers, from the level of director to unit supervisor. Some issues are primarily technological. What equipment will be needed? Is the technological infrastructure in place? Will the system crash when the date changes to January 1, 2000? Other issues are more social. How will the employees react? Will they accept the change or resist it? Can the change process be made easier? Unfortunately, this second group of issues can be easily overlooked. Managers often do not address human issues adequately, even though they are aware of them, and even though they consider their employees, clients, and other people to be important.

CHANGE ISSUES IN THE PUBLIC AND PRIVATE SECTORS

While the specific issue of library automation is located principally in the public sector, the processes and challenges of change are common to both areas.

HUMAN FACTORS IN LIBRARY AUTOMATION

Librarians, staff and patrons must make a number of adjustments as a result of any library automation project, whether it is an original implementation or a migration. One key area is the relationship between people and technology. People have to change the way they behave and think to work effectively in an automated environment. They skim through cards to find a catalogue record in a manual system. To find a catalogue record in an automated system they use computer commands.

In a migration scenario, this might be a change from typing keyboard commands to choosing buttons or menu items on a graphical interface. For long-term employees, this requires yet a third 'mental map.' These demands for change easily lead to stress reactions of fear or anger, especially when they are large-scale or frequent. Smith mentions several sources for these emotions, such as loss of control, worries about identity and security in the workplace, and breakdowns in interpersonal relationships. It is no wonder that people often resist change. However, Smith cautions against regarding human responses solely as a barrier to change. For leaders who pay attention to social issues, these responses provide valuable feedback and help to implement a more successful system.

HISTORICAL PERSPECTIVE

The early history of library automation can be divided into three phases, the Developmental Phase, the Operational Phase, and the Integrative Phase. The development phase was the period of early experimentation up to the early seventies. During this period a small number of institutions engaged in automation projects. While management hoped that systems could be transferred from one institution to another, this was not the case with these early efforts. Libraries did not have similar computer operating systems, they did not have standardised procedures, and they could not agree on outputs.

However, the development of the MARC record was a significant development that allowed libraries to communicate bibliographic records in a standard format. The operational phase, in the mid-to-late seventies, saw the expansion of automation in a wider variety of libraries. Vendor-supplied systems, shared computer resources, and networking made this possible. Since, libraries were no longer forced to develop their own systems from scratch, it was an easier and less expensive task. During this phase most library automation projects still focussed on discrete tasks, such as check-in or circulation. Operational areas were not integrated, and the overall workflow stayed basically the same, "it has been utterly possible to use the automated system as inefficiently and ineffectively and with as little knowledge of what is going on as with the manual system". Montague proposed that the next phase would be an integrative phase, in which the automation systems would cut across operational lines, actually change the way libraries do business, and improve service.

There were a number of obstacles during these stages of library automation:

- Lack of direction and oversight from library managers to systems staff;
- Lack of technical training for library managers;
- Failure to develop long-range plans;
- Lack of up and down communication between managers and staff;
- Lack of staff input;
- Lack of staff training;
- Lack of feedback mechanisms.

Overall, it appears that the several problems, training, oversight, input, feedback, all involved a general lack of communication.

MIGRATION—SECOND GENERATION SYSTEMS

Since, many libraries, including Notre Dame, have or plan to migrate to second generation library systems, it is important to consider whether the obstacles are the same. One view is that they are not the same. Migrations are said to be easier than initial implementations. Although there may be some staff apprehensions, staff morale is reported to improve. A significant advantage is that second-time buyers have a better understanding of what they want in a system, and focus more on quality and customer support, instead of low bids. There is one potential source of resistance, which is never present in an initial automation project, that is a hostile 'soon-to-be former vendor.' Another important distinction is whether the library is migrating after successful implementation of a system which simply no longer meets their needs, or whether the library is desperately seeking a new system after a failed effort.

The reaction of librarians to this viewpoint is to be mixed. Some libraries have reported a very similar degree of 'techno stress' during migration projects, with similar emotional responses. Staff are required to change procedures, and in many cases the new procedures are not clear-cut—of course, the procedures in the 'old' system were not clear-cut in the beginning either. On the other hand, the majority of directors in a survey of 33 libraries that had undergone system migrations felt that 'promoting' the system change to the staff was unnecessary. This seems to be primarily due to staff frustration with the old systems, providing a clear motivation for change.

The worse the original system, the less staff resistance there was to migration. However, there were still some symptoms of technostress. Many found the vendors training programmes to be inadequate, consisting of 'canned' presentations were did not apply to local needs. Due to 'rush jobs,' the staff at many libraries did not have adequate time to become familiar with the new system before it was made available to the public. In one particularly egregious case, the staff and patrons were given access to the system at the same time. The staff 'hated this.' A two-month lead-time between staff and public access gave optimum results.

PRIVATE SECTOR EXPERIENCES

While library automation, *per se*, is not a major issue in the for-profit world, automation in general definitely is. As such, experiences in the private sector provide helpful comparisons. One very familiar theme from corporate settings in the need to consult with users prior to any sort of migration or automation project. This is true even with systems that are not central to the users' jobs. Gaudin relates several stories of companies that tried to implement new systems without consulting users. One case involved replacing a mainframe e-mail system with a desktop system. After the company spent $3 million, the employees rejected it because it was not fast or stable enough.

In another case, FedEx introduced a scheduling system without consulting their own employees. This became one of the issues in a potential strike against the company. One manager pointed out the importance of remembering that 'users might like their old systems'. This is an important lesson for library managers to remember in a migration, especially when the original system was basically successful. Even a failed system may have features the employees liked. Another illustration is provided by Norman's study of a failed automation effort. An attempt to introduce the CASE system in a management information firm provides valuable lessons for both sectors.

The goal of the CASE project was to establish a 2-1 ratio of CASE workstation usage among the MIS staff and achieve a 10 to 15 per cent increase in productivity. The project is considered to be a failure, because people are not using it. The company has lost business to competitors who do use the system. Norman identifies a number of factors in the CASE implementation, which contributed to its failure. From the beginning, the decision to implement CASE was made by a small high-level committee, without involving staff. There was a successful pilot project, following which the company attempted to expand the system. Their main methodology was a staff-training programme. Management assumed that if they provided training, the programmers would use the system. While the training was described as 'adequate,' it was informational only, and there was no effort made to change attitudes. The most critical barrier identified in the study was the high learning curve for using CASE. Management did not make any effort to reduce this learning curve. Instead, each work group that attempted to use the system had to learn it on their own. There was no sharing of tricks or shortcuts, or any help given by those who had already started using the product to new users. Interdepartmental friction and a rigid chain-of-command that stifled communication between units prevented this type of cooperation.

A related factor was the lack of any visible benefits or rewards for using CASE. Instead rewards were based on completing projects under-time and under-budget. Since, CASE is intended to increase productivity, it might seem that this would reward its use. But "this means that the rewards are indirect and totally dependent upon the successful use of the tool". In conjunction with the high learning curve, this becomes a negative incentive – the system is likely to slow production in the short-term, until the learning curve is past. If the programmer fails to learn it quickly, rewards are lost rather than gained.

THEORIES AND STRATEGIES FOR CHANGE

In discussing theories of organisational change, many theorists divide changes into different types. Before delving too deeply into specific strategies for change, I would like to examine the relationship between library automation projects and descriptive theories.

CONTINUITY

In the Age of Unreason, Handy tells us that "Change is not what it used to be". He distinguishes continuous and discontinuous change. Continuous change is gradual and predictable, with one situation leading into the next. This is relatively comfortable for most people. But he asserts that the changes in the workplace now are discontinuous. That is, changes are abrupt and unpredictable, and hence, far less comfortable. Handy frequently links discontinuous change to technology. As such, it is easy to reach the conclusion that a library automation project is a discontinuous change. People who worked with paper switch to online systems, and their jobs are altered or even eliminated. But we should not be too quick to classify it this way. Particularly in the early automation projects, automated tasks were substituted for manual tasks on a one-to-one basis. Because of this, there was no drastic change in the overall workflow; even when specific tasks were drastically altered. It could be argued that automation has had a more significant impact since, that time, as library systems have become integrated.

CALM AND TURBULENT WATERS

Robbins focuses on the frequency of change. He uses two metaphors, 'calm waters' and 'whitewater rapids.' In the calm-waters scenario, change is the exception. Most of the time is spent in a state of equilibrium, until some crisis forces a change. After the change is past, the organisation regains a new state of equilibrium. In the white-water scenario, change is continuous, though in a different sense than Handy uses the word.

There is no state of equilibrium; instead one period of change is followed directly by another. It is very tempting to identify library automation projects with the 'calm water' metaphor. In fact, Saunders uses a very similar model in her article on library system migration. First various forces bring about a need for change, which requires unfreesing process. This is followed by a period of instability. When this is over, the library establishes a new state of equilibrium, as new patterns and procedures are frozen into place. Because automation efforts are not made frequently, this model appears to be a good match.

In an original automation project, the library has been using a manual system as long as it has been in existence. Once the project has been completed, the library will continue to use the new system indefinitely. Even in a migration project, the library may have been using its old system for many years, and certainly would hope the new system would be long-lived. One potential problem with this model is that it ignores the wider picture of overall changes. At the same time as a library is contemplating an integrated library system, the staff may be dealing with new online indexes, electronic journals, e-mail systems, computer operating systems, and even a building renovation. Taken in this larger context, the white water metaphor seems more appropriate to the library environment. It is often not just the project at hand that causes problems for staff and users, but the 'unrelenting demand' of changes in many areas. Another issue is the continuing change following the implementation of an automated system due to new releases and upgrades to the system.

Even after a new system is fully implemented, it may not be as 'calm' as the old manual system. One significant problem with the white-water model as a model for change is that it suggests a reactive style of management with unplanned changes. But most library automation and migration projects are planned, as are many of the other changes affecting the library staff. This model seems most apt for dealing with the external changes impacting an organisation.

THE FOUR MOTORS OF CHANGE

Van de Ven and Poole give a more fully fleshed taxonomy of change. They identify two crosscutting distinctions, the level and the mode of change. The level of change is whether the change involves single or multiple entities. The mode of change is either prescribed or emergent. A priori changes are planned, predictable or follow set rules or patterns. Emergent change is discontinuous and unpredictable.

This combination yields four 'motors of change:'

- Life-cycle (single entity, prescribed);
- Teleological (single entity, emergent);
- Dialectical (multiple entities, emergent); and
- Evolutionary (multiple entities, prescribed).

While these motors can be separated in theory, most real-life changes involve interaction between them. The four motors model provides a more complete description of organisational change, and avoids over simplification problems. If we examine library automation projects in this e-context of the four motors of change that Van de Ven describes, as suggested, find rather complex interactions. The teleological theory, which is characterised by planning and goal setting, provides the closest description of the first stage in an automation project. Libraries may have a variety of motivations for undertaking an automation or migration project.

In the case of migration, this might include negative factors, like dissatisfaction with the current vendor, as well as positive ones, like a desire to expand capabilities. These motivations provide the Aristotelian final cause for the project. Most libraries engage in goal setting activities, such as compiling lists of desired features. This stage may be described as teleological in Van de Ven's scheme because it primarily involves one entity and the process is emergent. At the beginning of this stage, it is not clear where it will finish. Although the process is planned the goals are identified during the process, and may provide a dramatic break with the existing manual or automated system. The dialectical motor may be present to a lessor extant, as different stakeholders interact with each other, and occasionally present conflicting goals. This teleological description fits most, but not all migration projects. For 79 per cent of cases in a migration survey, the projects were planned. But in some cases, the libraries did not have time to develop plans due to legal or financial problems. In those cases, the teleological motor would only apply in a trivial sense, if at all. Those cases are obviously not ideal scenarios. Towards the end of the selection process, the library must compare its goals and desires to the actual systems available. At this point, the process could be described as dialectical, involving the library and the vendors who would like to supply the system. Vendors and librarians both regard this process as different for migration projects compared to first-time automation efforts.

In a first-time automation, libraries tend to rely on numerical evaluation of vendors' proposals and claims. In migration projects, libraries find site visits to be the most effective way to evaluate quality and hands-on work issues. At some point either during the final selection process or shortly after a vendor is chosen, the process shifts to a life-cycle model. The life-cycle motor is also primarily concerned with the library as a single entity. At this point, the plan, which was developed in earlier stages, becomes the guide for the process.

The library engages is a series of steps that were laid out in the plan, possibly on a strict timeschedule. This includes all of the steps technically necessary to implement the system as well as steps to prepare the users. This process is imminent in, or prescribed by the plan, and is much more predictable than the earlier stages. The library may have even planned for contingencies. Once the actual conversion in done, and the new system is live, the process become somewhat less predictable. Procedures that worked on paper or in test may fail under the pressure of real-life use.

While none of the motors seem to be completely dominant at this point, the evolutionary theory is closest. Procedures that work 'survive' while others are discarded. The changes may still be described as imminent, however, because they are constrained by the system. The others motors continue to play some role, as plans are made and carried out, and different stakeholders disagree on various issues. The dialectical motor may become dominant from time-to-time as the vendor announces new releases, or the library recommends enhancements for the system. At these times the possibilities for change are less constrained, and the results become more emergent.

STRATEGIES

The authors who describe actual automation projects also list key lessons and make recommendations. There are a number of general, and some very specific, suggestions along with a couple of common threads. One of the common threads is communication. Whether it is between management and employees, between systems and users, or between the employees at large, it seems that more communication is always better. A related thread is the need to involve the users in the process as early as possible. Several of the authors suggested that users should be involved at the very beginning, during the selection process. Montage, Norman, Gaudin, Hallmark and Smith all cite lack of user involvement in the selection or planning stage as an obstacle to successful implementation. Since, these two threads stand out, we may conclude that if any overall strategy is too be effective, it must include a high level of communication and user participation.

STRATEGIES FROM THE CASE IMPLEMENTATION

Norman described three change strategies in his evaluation of the CASE implementation. These strategies could be used independently or in conjunction with each other.

Rational-empirical

This strategy focuses on training and information. It is presumed that teaching people to use the system and providing a rational explanation of why it is better will lead them to use it. This strategy could easily be applied to a library automation or migration project, as many of the authors indicated the importance of training programmes.

Normative-educational

This strategy focuses on group strategies for promoting acceptance of the new systems and providing motivation to use it. First, identify the attitudes that create resistance, and then develop programmes to change them. This is similar to developing training sessions in the rational-empirical strategy. The difference is that the sessions are intended to develop positive attitudes instead imparting information.

Power-coercive

In this strategy individuals are induced to use the new system by the threat of loosing their job or other benefits. This can be a fairly direct approach to implement change, but it also runs a high risk creating bad feelings, job dissatisfaction, and tension between management and employees. Threats, whether explicit or implicit, will also add to the fear and anxiety already identified as an obstacle to change. A variation of this strategy can be applied in a positive way by offering employees incentives for change. While this is can be regarded as a power-exercise it is less confrontational. In the CASE implementation, the main strategy that was applied was the rational-empirical strategy.

The normative-educational strategy was largely ignored, and the power-coercive strategy was inconsistently applied. Management made statements that employees were required to use the system, but did not follow-up when it was not used. Management also did not provide any direct positive incentives. This strategy may also be applied to library systems in the sense that when the old system is shut-off, employees will not be able to perform their duties without using the new system.

PHASED IMPLEMENTATION

Saunders recommends a strategy of phased implementation. The idea of this strategy is to minimize the impact of the new system has on staff by introducing modules in a gradual fashion. For example, a library might implement cataloguing or acquisitions functions first, and circulation latter. This strategy has some advantages. Successful implementation of one module should increase staff willingness to use another. Also, management can deal with the staff in smaller groups, concentrating on the area currently being automated, instead of dealing with all areas at once. The chief drawback of this strategy is found when the current system is already well integrated.

In this case, phased implementation may mean that user's are initially presented with a system that has fewer features than their previous system. There may also be technical difficulties that preclude phased implementation, as the two systems are not likely to communicate with each other well, if at all. Where it is usable, this strategy should also be combined with other strategies. Saunders specifically emphasises the importance of training and communication issues.

PARTICIPANT-ORIENTED CHANGE

Zeffane advocates the strategy of participant-oriented change, which is based on the premise that change works best when comes from the bottom up rather than from the top down. One reason for this premise is that if the employees introduce change, then they will not have an authority figure to rebel against. It is also based on the idea that collegial affiliation is a positive motivation for change. That is, employees will be more motivated to help with a changes initiated by someone at, or close to, their level. To use participant oriented change, management needs to shift the responsibility for change away from themselves and towards the employees.

This strategy goes beyond considering the users' needs, or soliciting input, to actually delegating authority to the participants. This strategy takes advantage of the fact that the employees who are closest to the hands-on work have the most detailed knowledge about it. This also frees the upper management from concentrating on this level of detail, and to concentrate on overall strategic planning. This strategy may not be effective in all types of organisations.

There are some essential elements for participative strategies to work. First, the employees given responsibilities for change must be well informed. Second, the employees must understand and agree with the mission of the organisation. Unless these requirements are met, management cannot expect that the decisions will be beneficial to the organisation. The third requirement is that this style of change must be supported by the organisation culture. The management must be comfortable with this type of delegation.

MANAGEMENT FUNCTIONS

The traditional roles of management are planning, organisation, coordination and control. These can be applied to these change strategies.

RATIONAL-EMPIRICAL

The rational-empirical strategy is primarily concerned with dispensing information, presuming that the plans for change have already been made. It involves the organising function of management, in the sense that the managers determine what information needs to be given to which employees in order to implement the changes. It also involves the control function, in that the management is seeking to influence behaviour through the information it dispenses.

NORMATIVE-EDUCATIONAL

The normative-education strategy is concerned with influencing attitudes and behaviour. As such, it involves the control function of management, but in an indirect manner. That is, rather than controlling behaviour directly, the management attempts to instill attitudes which are likely to result in the desired behaviour. Like the rational-empirical strategy, it also involves the coordinating function, as managers decide who should be involved in which programmes.

POWER-COERCIVE

The power-coercive strategy concerns the management role of control in a straight- forward fashion. It is mainly concerned with seeing to it that the change decisions are carried out as directed. To ensure this, it dispenses rewards or penalties to individuals or groups depending or whether they have implemented the changes. In the extreme, employees who fail to change are fired.

PHASED IMPLEMENTATION

Phased implementation involves both the planning and coordinating functions to a large degree. Planning includes determining the order in which to implement the modules and setting timetables for each phase. Coordination includes meshing together the efforts of different groups associated with each phase, and ensuring that each module is integrated with the previous ones when it is brought into production. As more modules are brought into the 'live' mode, coordination becomes essential in order to see that the different areas function smoothly.

PARTICIPANT-ORIENTED CHANGE

Participant oriented change involves the coordinating function of management. Since, much of the planning and decision making is delegated downward to the staff, management must integrate these plans and decisions. This is particularly important when implementing an integrated library system, as the activities of staff in one area will have more impact on other areas than they are accustomed to. The actual delegation of these responsibilities to employees involves the organising function. Determining how and to whom these responsibilities are delegated is in important part of the change process.

This may involve organising employees into self-managed teams, work groups, or interdepartmental task forces. How these groups are organised, the amount of authority they have, and how they will interact with each other are crucial decisions.

COMMON CHARACTERISTICS OF KNOWLEDGE ORGANIZATION SYSTEMS

It is often said that humans are inherent organizers. From an early age, children play sorting and matching games. We cope with our ever-changing world by comparing new objects or experiences with those with which we are familiar, identifying patterns and categorizing what is new into our existing frame of reference. The emphasis on developing comprehensive KOS's can be seen in the writings of our earliest philosophers, many of whom continue to influence our view of the world. For example, Aristotle's effort to categorize knowledge into groups is reflected in our language, our education, and our science.

The original classification scheme of the Library of Congress, used between 1800 and 1814, was based on the philosophical works of Sir Francis Bacon and inherited from the English tradition. Beginning in 1814, the influence of Thomas Jefferson can be seen on the Library of Congress collection. Jefferson, who reclassified the library, reflected a more humanist philosophy. There is no single knowledge classification scheme on which everyone agrees.

Michael Lesk speculates that while a single KOS would be advantageous, it is unlikely that such a system will ever be developed. Culture may constrain the knowledge classification scheme so that what is meaningful to one culture is not necessarily meaningful to another. Therefore, we live in a world of multiple, variant ways to organize knowledge.

Despite their diversity, KOSs have the following common characteristics that are critical to their use in organizing digital libraries:

- The KOS imposes a particular view of the world on a collection and the items in it.
- The same entity can be characterized in different ways, depending on the KOS that is used.
- There must be sufficient commonality between the concept expressed in a KOS and the real-world object to which that concept refers that a knowledgeable person could apply the system with reasonable reliability. Likewise, a person seeking relevant material by using a KOS must be able to connect his or her concept with its representation in the system.

TYPES OF KNOWLEDGE ORGANIZATION SYSTEMS

A review of some typical knowledge organization systems shows their scope and applicability to a variety of digital library settings. While there are specific definitions for many of these KOSs in the computer science and information science literature, and even in standards documents, there is debate over these definitions. Terms are often used, particularly in the popular press and in the book trade, in non-standard ways. Reflecting the scope of this practice, a recent *National Information Standards Organization* (NISO) work shop on electronic thesauri emphasized the need to improve the definitions of "terminology relating to terminology".

The descriptions given here provide an overview of possible systems for organizing digital libraries. The descriptions are based on characteristics such as structure and complexity, relationships among terms, and historical function. The list is not comprehensive; nor are the definitions of these terms contained in specific standards documents. They are grouped into three general categories: term lists, which emphasize lists of terms often with definitions; classifications and categories, which emphasize the creation of subject sets; and relationship lists, which emphasize the connections between terms and concepts.

Term Lists

Authority Files

Authority files are lists of terms that are used to control the variant names for an entity or the domain value for a particular field. Examples include names for countries, individuals, and organizations. Non-preferred terms may be linked to the preferred versions. This type of KOS generally does not include a deep organization or complex structure. The presentation may be alphabetical or organized by a shallow classification scheme. A limited hierarchy may be applied to allow for simple navigation, particularly when the authority file is being accessed manually or is extremely large. Examples of authority files include the Library of Congress Name Authority File and the Getty Geographic Authority File.

Glossaries

A glossary is a list of terms, usually with definitions. The terms may be from a specific subject field or from a particular work. The terms are defined within a specific environment and rarely include variant meanings. Examples include the *Environmental Protection Agency* (EPA) Terms of the Environment.

Dictionaries

Dictionaries are alphabetical lists of words and their definitions. Variant senses are provided where applicable. Dictionaries are more general in scope than are glossaries. They may also provide information about the origin of a word, variants and multiple meanings across disciplines. While a dictionary may also provide synonyms and through the definitions, related words, there is no explicit hierarchical structure or attempt to group them by concept.

Gazetteers

A gazetteer is a list of place names. Traditional gazetteers have been published as books or have appeared as indexes to atlases. Each entry may also be identified by feature type, such as river, city, or school. An example is the U.S. Code of Geo-graphic Names. Geospatially referenced gazetteers provide coordinates for locating the place on the earth's surface. The term *gazetteer* has several other meanings, including an announcement publication such as a patent or legal gazetteer. These gazetteers are often organized using classification schemes or subject categories.

Classifications and Categories

Subject Headings

This scheme type provides a set of controlled terms to represent the subjects of items in a collection. Subject heading lists can be extensive and cover a broad range of subjects; however, the subject heading list's structure is generally very shallow, with a limited hierarchical structure. In use, subject headings tend to be coordinated, with rules for how they can be joined to provide concepts that are more specific.

Examples include:

- The Medical Subject Headings (MeSH); and
- The Library of Congress Subject Headings (LCSH).

Classification Schemes, Taxonomies, and Categorization Schemes

These terms are often used interchangeably. Although there may be subtle differences from example to example, these types of KOSs all provide ways to separate entities into "buckets" or broad topic levels. Some examples provide a hierarchical arrangement of numeric or alphabetic notation to represent broad topics. These types of KOSs may not follow the rules for hierarchy required in the ANSI NISO Thesaurus Standard and they lack the explicit relationships presented in a thesaurus.

Examples of classification schemes include:

- The Library of Congress Classification Schedules,
- The Dewey Decimal Classification, and
- The Universal Decimal Classification.

Subject categories are often used to group thesaurus terms in broad topic sets that lie outside the hierarchical scheme of the thesaurus. Taxonomies are increasingly being used in object-oriented design and knowledge management systems to indicate any grouping of objects based on a particular characteristic.

Relationship Lists

Thesauri

Thesauri are based on concepts and they show relation-ships among terms. Relationships commonly expressed in a thesaurus include hierarchy, equivalence and association or relatedness.

These relationships are generally represented by the notation:

- BT (broader term),
- NT (narrower term),
- SY (synonym), and
- RT (associative or related term).

Associative relationships may be more detailed in some schemes. For example, the *Unified Medical Language System* (UMLS) from the National Library of Medicine has defined more than 40 relationships, many of which are associative. Preferred terms for indexing and retrieval are identified. Entry terms point to the preferred terms to be used for each concept. There are standards for the development of monolingual thesauri and multilingual thesauri. In these standards, the definition of a thesaurus is fairly narrow.

Standard relationships are assumed, as is the identification of preferred terms, and there are rules for creating relation-ships among terms. The definition of a thesaurus in these standards is often at variance with schemes that are tradi-tionally called thesauri. Many thesauri do not follow all the rules of the standard but are still generally thought of as thesauri. Another type of thesaurus, such as the *Roget's Thesaurus*, represents only equivalence. Many thesauri are large; they may include more than 50,000 terms. Most were developed for a specific discipline or a specific product or family of products. Examples include the Food and Agricultural Organization's *Aquatic Sciences and Fisheries Thesaurus* and the *National Aeronautic and Space Administration (NASA) Thesaurus* for aeronautics and aerospace-related topics.

Semantic Networks

With the advent of natural language processing, there have been significant developments in semantic networks. These KOSs structure concepts and terms not as hierarchies but as a network or a web. Concepts are thought of as nodes, and relationships branch out from them. The relationships generally go beyond the standard BT, NT, and RT. They may include specific whole-part, cause-effect, or parent-child relationships. The most noted semantic network is Princeton University's WordNet, which is now used in a variety of search engines.

Ontologies

Ontology is the newest label to be attached to some knowledge organization systems. The knowledge-management community is developing ontologies as specific concept models. They can represent complex relationships among objects, and include the rules and axioms missing from semantic networks. Ontologies that describe knowledge in a specific area are often connected with systems for data mining and knowledge management. All of these examples of knowledge organization systems, which vary in complexity, structure, and function, can provide organization and increased access to digital libraries.

THE ORIGIN AND USE OF KNOWLEDGE ORGANIZATION SYSTEMS

In the physical library, classification schemes such as *Library of Congress* (LC), Dewey Decimal System, and the Universal Decimal Classification reflect, among other things, the need to store a single item at a single location on a shelf. To provide multiple access points beyond the limits of a single physical location, subject headings are applied. Libraries use subject heading schemes such as LCSH, Sears, or other specialized schemes developed for specific content or specific collections. At the level of specific content, libraries have used authority files to control variant forms of personal, organizational, and geographic names. However, KOSs can be found in settings other than libraries. An awareness of the KOSs available from alternative sources is valuable when considering the development of digital libraries for a specific audience.

Abstracting and Indexing Services

Abstracting and indexing (A&I) services developed as an outgrowth of traditional bibliographies and the explosion of journal literature. In the sciences, the development of A&I services was spurred by the post-World War I concerns about inadequate access to scientific information. In the 1950s, investment in A&I services was fueled by the Cold War and Sputnik. Abstracting and indexing services in the humanities, such as the Bibliography of the History of Art or the *Modern Languages Association* (MLA) Bibliography, generally took a different growth path than did their scientific and technical counterparts, but they also quickly became important resources for scholarship in the online environment.

The scope of A&I services varies from broad discipline-oriented services to narrowly defined aspects of the literature and subdisciplines. Special KOSs, such as thesauri and subject categories, were developed to support A&I services and their specific products and audiences. These organizations applied increasingly complex schemes to provide subject access to the literature in a variety of subjects.

By the 1960s, A&I services were moving from the provision of printonly products to print and online services through large online vendors such as Dialog. Later, the products were distributed on CDROM and now, increasingly, on the Web. In many cases, the KOSs migrated from print to electronic media following the products they supported. While increased computing power, more sophisticated search engines, and more independent end-user searching have led to changes in some KOSs, most have retained their importance, even in the Web environment.

For many years, the KOSs related to A&I services were applied only by catalogers and indexers trained in using the KOS indexing for a particular product or products. The primary users of KOSs were librarians and other professional searchers. However, the proliferation of electronic data, the explosion of electronic publishing, and increasing concerns about the difficulty of locating information have led to a renewed interest in these KOSs for use not only by professionals but also by end users.

Publishers

As publishers have migrated to electronic composition systems, they have become increasingly involved in the production of A&I products. Large journal publishers such as Academic Press and Elsevier have developed their own systems to provide bibliographic records linked to the full text of documents. As the content of online journals has grown, it has become necessary to move from systems that provide browsing by table of contents and journal issue to systems that support searching by both free text and by KOS. Electronic journals have resulted in additional KOSs, particularly classification and categorization schemes. For example, Elsevier's Web site has a subject categorization scheme to provide access to individual Web sites of its more than 2000 titles.

Trade, Professional, and Governmental Organizations

A variety of authority files and classification schemes are used to support business and commerce. They range from the *Standard Industrial Classification* (SIC) code and the *North American Industrial Classification System* (NAICS), used in procurement and government statistics, to disease codes used to communicate patient illnesses and treatments among physicians, hospitals, and insurance companies. As more organizations develop Web sites, additional KOSs are being developed to support them.

Internal Projects

Organizations are among the most prolific creators and users of KOSs. Developers of corporate intranets and knowledge management systems have discovered hundreds of specific classification schemes, glossaries, categorization schemes, and other vocabularies in use within organizations. Many of these are geared towards specific tasks and are, therefore, very narrow both in subject scope and target audience. However, for these audiences, they can also be rich sources of information. For example, the *Department of Energy* (DOE), *Environmental Management Science Programme* (EMSP) and the Office of Scientific and Technical Information are developing a digital library to support EMSP programme managers.

Programme managers and researchers have developed "needs categories" and "science categories" to organize the *Environmental Science Network* (ESN). The categories are used primarily to support the process of grant submission and award; however, the ESN also uses them to provide access to related material from within DOE and from other distributed databases from the EPA, the Department of Defence, and NASA. Vocabulary is currently being organized around these categories for use with a Web mining tool that will provide highly relevant Web resources for project managers in specific areas.

LIBRARY AUTOMATION IN DEVELOPING COUNTRIES

When Information Development was launched in 1984, library automation was, looked at from today's perspective, very much in its infancy. The largest libraries in the world such as the Library of Congress and the British Library had sizeable databases of catalogue records. University library catalogues were available on-line within their institutional four walls and library circulation was also automated, but data was generally confined to the institution that held it since, there was no network resembling the internet. In 1983 the JANET network had begun to connect the universities in the United Kingdom, and some catalogues were beginning to be available online from other institutions. The most common way of accessing remote data if there was a possibility at all was by dial-up modem using ordinary phone lines and a modem or an acoustic coupler in which the phone handset was pushed into a rubber holder to ensure no extraneous noise seeped into the phone line when it was transferring electronic signals between computers. Businesses including libraries were also connected by dedicated phone lines to locations where their computers were located when they were remote. But most automation was firmly confined to the institution where it was based. Twenty five years ago was also the beginning of the period when computers were being introduced as desk top computers, with IBM PCs and subsequently IBM PC lookalikes. Personal computers were about to make a huge impact on automation in libraries as no longer was it necessary to have a dedicated air-conditioned room to house computers.

In the early days cataloguers had to have terminals on their desks to enable access to the catalogue but eventually all staff had PCs for general administration so no longer was it was the responsibility of the library budget to purchase desk-top computers. Modems were in fact used to access remotely catalogues for bibliographical purposes, to search databases like Medline. It was already possible to dial up databascs such as the British Library's BLAISE database or the US National Library of Medicine's Medline. But these facilities required good phone lines and were not available outside Western Europe and the United States.

There was no such thing as 'full text' then. Computers did not have the capacity to store so much data and data stored was often coded to ensure that it did not take up more space than was necessary. 25 years ago, while most libraries in industrialised countries had not only computerised their catalogues but also computerised their circulation, in developing countries there was very little library automation outside that organised by the United Nations agencies such as FAO's AGRIS and IAEA's INIS and these were very much in their infancy or in their planning stages.

To return to the situation in industrialised countries. In the early 1990's catalogues began to be accessible on the internet but were not web-based and required the catalogue software to be run interactively across the Internet using various different protocols. By the end of the decade, true web-based catalogues using the power of hypertext were available. Libraries began to include in their catalogues digital resources internally held and externally held (predominantly external). MARC formats thenceforward incorporated a field 856 used to link to an external resource by means of a URL (the internet address).

Users of the catalogue could click on a link and go straight to a digital resource that could be anywhere in the world. Subscriptions were possible to electronic journals but they were often not available in developing countries or if they were available the bandwidth of tehinternet in those countries was not enough to enable the materials to be read. Digital library software became available and UNESCO encouraged its implementation in developing countries by making Greenstone available free-of-charge, a digital library software package developed at Waikatu in New Zealand. Links could be made from a library catalogue to material in such a digital library. Material available on the internet which might not be easily accessible in institutions in developing countries with low bandwidth could be downloaded or sent on CD-ROM to the digital libraries and hosted locally.

The Soros Foundation set up eIFL (Electronic Information for Libraries) with the aim of creating national purchasing consortia. They have since, become involved in supporting other activities such as promoting library automation systems, mindful of the fact that without a catalogue of print and digital materials the library user cannot easily find out what is accessible. eIFL supported the

European Union funded project to implement NewGenLib, a system under development in India, in Aleppo and Al Baath university libraries in Syria alongside providing them with licences at a reasonable price to access electronic resources.

INASP, the International Network for the Availability of Scientific Publications, was set up by the International Council of Scientific Unions (ICSU) in 1992. Aware of the need to establish good catalogues in order to access scientific litreature, they have also participated in some library automation projects. The Andrew W. Mellon Foundation, well known for philanthropic projects in developing countries, is also supporting the development of a new library automation system at Duke University, the Open Library Environment (OLE). Although there is no participation from developing countries at this stage it is likely that any open source package developed would be supported with necessary tailoring in line with the needs of developing countries wherever they might be different.

The main feature in the last 25 years then has been in the expansion of computers into every aspect of libraries. Possibly the biggest change has been the development of digital libraries, acquiring, transforming or accessing data in digital format. In developing countries this methods of digitisation has taken place to a certain extent.

TRENDS IN THE INDUSTRIALISED WORLD

Library systems in developing countries have obviously developed alongside systems in the industrialised world. First we should look at systems for large institutions. The majority of library systems have been developed in the United States. Many commercially available integrated library systems were developed by universities for their own use and later made available to a wider audience. Dynix was one such, developed for a university library and later sold around the world to universities, public libraries and special libraries. Other systems were based from the outset on cooperatives, such as TALIS which originated as BLS, the system of BLCMP (Birmingham Libraries Cooperative Management Project) which was a cooperative set up with government funding in the 1960s.

This project was one of two established from the beginning by OSTI, the UK Office of Scientific and Technological Information, to support cooperative cataloguing. They had less incentive to expand outside their country of origin as it was their aim to serve a cooperative all of whose members were equal. In 1967, the Ohio Colleges Library Centre was established to bring library automation to Ohio academic institutions by sharing costs. OCLC as it is now has developed from being a cooperative between libraries in Ohio to being an international cooperative, and at one time promoted a library management system.

Then they ceased to support it returning eventually to the market by acquiring OLIB, an Oracle based library system. Its vision is to connect libraries of the world. Originally, as with BLCMP, it was a shared cataloguing system receiving records from participating libraries and adding them to a database which in turn could be used by member libraries to populate their own catalogues. Records were transferred between computers initially by sending large magnetic tapes, a thing of the past, from the Centre to the remote libraries. Later they were transferred by telephone lines and subsequently the transfer was done by a client computer, a PC in a remote institution, accessing the Centre's servers by the Internet. Jumping to the present, OCLC have established Worldcat which could act as a large union catalogue for the world if every library in the world added its holdings.

This concept is called Cloud Computing, on the basis that the computer is somewhere remote and no one knows or cares where exactly it is! To return to library systems established in individual institutions, VTLS (Virginia Tech Library System), another large library automation system, always had an interest in working with developing countries and have a large number of installations in the Third World after having expanded into Eastern Europe as well. Another popular system, Aleph, is based in Jerusalem surrounded by a number of developing countries some of which have considered installation though by far the largest share of the market is in Europe.

As for cooperatives like OCLC, there has existed for many years in former Yugoslavia a miniature version of OCLC, COBISS (Co-operative Online Bibliographic System and Service), which since, the break-up of Yugoslavia has expanded to include Albania and Bulgaria on the same basis as other ex-Yugoslav states. They act as a cooperative cataloguing agency but they also keep data on research projects. This institution would be a good model for other regions to adopt. Now and again a commercial library system has been licenced to a developing country institution which has subsequently found it difficult to pay the maintenance fees. Maintenance in any case is often more expensive in a developing country because of economies of scale and distance from the supplier. Additionally there may be problems caused by shortages of foreign exchange.

Now the internet reaches much of the world, distance is not so important. But there have been many instances of institutions retaining a package but not paying maintenance fees and therefore not updating it. Marshall Breeding keeps records of as many library automation packages and the sites where they are used as he can find the information. He publishes the results each year in Library Journal. The latest was published on the web in January 2009. He reviews the market as well as providing statistics about library automation suppliers.

This is a useful guide to make comparisons with developing countries. Unfortunately in his tables he makes only the distinction between the US and the rest of the world. However he also includes a general review and this year he reported that the use of Open Source packages is increasing mainly bring provided by third parties. For example, a company called Equinox provides support for the Open Source package Evergreen.

PACKAGES WHICH HAVE HAD AN IMPACT IN DEVELOPING COUNTRIES

Large libraries in developing countries had always had a certain amount of access to library automation systems. For example, the National Library of Venezuela had a system found in many US academic libraries called NOTIS. However this library's catalogue is still not available on the web. A number of countries in the former Soviet Union use IRBIS, the CDS/ISIS clone developed by the Russian National Library for Science and Technology. But ordinary libraries, public and academic, in developing countries have always lacked a wealth of possibilities for library automation. Hardware used to be expensive, and relatively speaking is still expensive for developing countries. Other problems raised by writers on the subject range from the power supply to the problems of training staff. Another issue not often raised is the need for collaboration both within and between institutions to get library automation project off the ground and then maintain it. This is a much more complex activity than a pre-automation situation where there is a library card catalogue maintained by cataloguers and used manually by staff and library patrons. Smaller systems than the ones developed for universities or networks have been developed which could be regarded as being similar sized to CDS/ISIS, for instance Inmagic and Tinlib. Some of these were not very easy to use and were not well maintained. Others were adopted by consortia or organisations in the industrialised world with branches in developing countries such as the British Council.

The main problem in developing countries has been support because of their remoteness and so those packages offering less support would be more attractive as they would be less expensive overall. This may well change in the future with the increase in the power of the internet and the next 25 years will surely see a difference in the availability of and the charges for support.

CDS/ISIS

CDS/ISIS has undoubtedly had a huge influence on library automation in developing countries. This author reviewed the package onits twentieth anniversary. Time and again, libraries have begun automation. There is even a reference to a library which began with Tinlib and has migrated to CDS/ISIS. Since, CDS/ISIS is well mentioned in the litreature, concerning library automation in developing countries, it will not be covered here.

However the most interesting feature which has become available over the last five years in CDS/ISIS is a Z39.50 import facility which is available as part of IsisMARC, and which enables MARC records from external sources to be downloaded into a CDS/ISIS database compatible with the version of MARC of the records. CDS/ISIS is not essentially a library management system, rather a database management system aimed at bibliographic records which by their very nature are variable length (with for example book titles being of indeterminate length) rather than fixed length which is the case for most data processing systems. Because it is attractive to small institutions with little funding and because of its parentage (UNESCO), it has attracted a certain kind of institution, for example those in the development community. UNESCO developed a DOS version in 1985 and a Windows version which was available for many years as a beta test version but was eventually released around 1998.

However libraries were already requiring to place their catalogues on the web and a number of organisations began to develop compatible web-based systems which could be used by institutions which were developing databases for in-house use on Windows or DOS versions of CDS/ISIS. The main developer of the official version was BIREME with WWWISIS but already others were available such as Webisis. CDS/ISIS is no longer being developed by UNESCO but BIREME in cooperation with UNESCO is leading the development of ABCD on an Open Source basis.

Tinlib

Tinlib was a package which was used extensively in British Council libraries. In Ilorin Nigeria it was used from 1996 as reported by Adewoye. The library had by 2001 almost replaced its card catalogue by the OPAC. The chapter was optimistic about the future and reporting on the use of other electronic resources. However e-mail and the internet were not then available. However, TINLIB had its problems. It was not an easy system to use and contracts for it dwindled outside developing countries and it ceased to be supported. Adeyoyin describes in 2004 how the Development Policy Centre Library in Ibadan migrated their catalogue from Tinlib to CDS/ISIS.

DEVELOPING COUNTRY SCENARIOS

It is of course a fallacy to make assumptions that all developing countries will have approached and will approach library automation in the same way. The wealth of the country the distribution of that wealth and the culture of the residents will make a difference.

Nigeria and other African Countries

Nigeria has oil money and had automation early, being one of the first users of CDS/ISIS for mainframe computers. Already in1989 Eyitayo could write a paper on the attitude of automated library system vendors to investing in Nigeria. Many respondents hoped to open an office and increase their marketing. Enakrire describes a few instances in Africa where automation has been implemented, indicating that, except for branches of international organisations, it depends on the generosity of donors. In Makerere University in Uganda, the library has benefited from donor funding through the African Virtual University Library Initiative of the World Bank to equip the library with computers and installed Internet connectivity. Other university libraries are developing their information service as they are also benefiting from the Programme for the Enhancement of Research of (PERI) under the sponsorship of the International Network for the Availability of Scientific Publications (INASP).

Through PERI, donors have paid subscriptions on behalf of libraries in Africa to access web-based journals. The University of Ibadan had a long history of automation, having begun in 1979. Georgina D. Ekpenyong wrote in 1997 about the history so far. The University of Ibadan Library was already seen as a leader in Nigeria. At that time they used CD-Rom extensively to provide bibliographic data. They took training seriously but did not yet have an OPAC. In 2008, the John D. and Catherine T. MacArthur Foundation in Chicago awarded grants totalling US $7.1 million to expand academic and research programme and strengthen staff development at two Nigerian universities as part of the Foundation's efforts to improve higher education in Africa. The result is that they signed up to VTLS, Virginia Tech Library System, a commercially available package developed originally as Virginia Tech's own system.

Thailand

In Thailand there were efforts in the 1990s to computerise the libraries with foreign-based systems being purchased. Thammasat University library had Dynix, supported from Ameritech's Australia office, and planned to move to Ameritech's new system Horizon. In 1997 the university library sent three cataloguers to Middlesex University to learn to use Horizon. Since, then they have implemented Horizon and exchange of experience took place between Middlesex University and Thammasat University until the Systems librarian at Thammasat moved to a different post around 2006. Many universities in Thailand are able to purchase these systems often through local distributors of international or American packages. Early on though, CDS/ISIS was used and at Thammasat University they used it for databases of journal articles.

OPTIONS FOR DEVELOPING COUNTRIES

Developing countries depend on developments in the industrialised world but they do not necessarily benefit from the same options as the industrialised world can use. Moreover, some of the options may be much more attractive in developing countries or at least may seem to be so.

Developing a Library System

One solution for organisations in developing countries which might have problems with paying organisations in foreign currency but which have good local technical staff is to develop their own software system. One interesting example of this is the University of Colombo in Sri Lanka. They had begun to automate in 1991 by using CDS/ISIS and then later adopted CDS/ISIS for Windows when it became available. In 2002, Seneviratne and Amaraweera reported in Information Development that in Sri Lanka there was discussion on developing a library automation system to bridge the gap between CDS/ ISIS and what commercial software was able to provide, such as Alice for Windows (UK commercial) and LibSys (Indian).

In 1997 the National Agency for Research Energy, Science and Agriculture (NARESA) now the National Science Foundation, used the CDS/ISIS DOS version to handler acquisitions, cataloguing, serials management, Current Awareness Services as well as cataloguing and indexing; this package called PURNA was then used in 34 special and academic libraries. AGRIS using CDS/ ISIS was widely influencing libraries in the agricultural sector and the Windows version was then used in the National Library of Sri Lanka for its union catalogue.

Now they are using Genisis, a package to make it easy to implement BIREME's WWWISIS on the web, development of which was undertaken in France by Pierre Chabet but for which a manual was written in Sri Lanka (partially a translation from the documentation in French) by Ms. Deepali Talagala Director/Information of the Sri Lanka Scientific and Technical Information Centre based at the National Science Foundation in Colombo Seneviratne and Amaraweera discussed in their paper the features a system would need and the platforms, hardware and operating system, most used and as a result decided to make a prototype using MS Access on Windows. Development took two phases.

Firstly a web-based interface to physically dispersed databases with a user-friendly front-end reported by Kumara et al in 1998, and a library automation system described in a BSc dissertation by DMS Dilrukshi, 1999 NetLib—a library management system through the Internet. In 2002 a prototype had been developed and the system was due to be maintained by the Computing Service Centre of the University of Colombo. Unfortunately there is a high overhead in developing and maintaining systems especially for a small client base.

In the UK all university libraries have commercial systems. Newcastle, used to have their own system in the 1980s but only Lancaster remained, eventually contracting with Ex Libris to take Aleph in 2001. By 2008 both the University of Colombo and the National Library of Sri Lanka had signed up to Softlink Europe's Alice system, a system used by the British Council worldwide (for example in Oman, Jordan and Sudan: the catalogue of the British Council in Sudan is available on the internet) and so has proven maintenance in developing countries. So developing one's own system is not to be recommended: Eyitayo noted that despite the availability of numerous off-the-shelf systems, most libraries in Nigeria that have attempted automation have chosen to commission expensive and time-consuming in-house projects, most of which have suffered severe set-backs and in most cases are not adequate for library work and often lack the capability for sharing information and interconnection with other systems.

Open Source

In the context of moving towards commercially supported systems, it is interesting to see that CDS/ISIS was attractive to libraries in developing countries. It was available without charge and so there was no danger of not being able to pay for it. Of course it was supported by an organisation with as much prestige though not so much turnover as many industrial companies. It also operated on a legal footing. Institutions had to sign a licence agreement to use the software. No doubt many institutions obtained the software illegally but the software was protected in law by the licence agreement. UNESCO were more concerned with illegal copies being made and sold for illegal profit than with institutions using the software without being officially licenced since, the spirit of the software following the ethos of the developer Giampaolo Delbigio was that it should enable institutions to participate in worldwide record sharing at many different levels. Nevertheless there was established a network of distributors which is still in place. Some acted merely as local distributors sending out the software on diskettes by post and thereby easing the burden of the hard-pressed office in UNESCO dealing with this. Other distributors were able to provide support usually of a limited nature though sometimes of a more extensive nature akin to the commercial support that is found in the large-scale library automation systems. The shareware movement was in place when CDS/ISIS was released in 1985.

In 1984, Andrew Fluegleman programmed a communications software package, PC-Talk and Jim Knopf a file management application called PC-File a year before the IBM PC was released and called it Freeware. The developers wanted to avoid commercial distribution networks and distribute the software over the now seemingly primitive and slow dial up systems whereby PC users could transfer programmes by dialling up a central computer using a modem and phone lines. The idea was that users would download the software, test it and if they liked it make a small contribution to the developer to support further development. Knopf established the term freeware as his own and no one else could use it.

There were other microcomputers around at the time, most notably the Apple Macintosh and others which are only part of history such as the BBC Microcomputer, though none ever reached the level of popularity that the IBM PC with the Microsoft Windows operating system has now reached. Incidentally Fluegleman distributed his software with the source code which led to many other developers producing their own versions and PC-Talk was improved and sold on by other developers such that Fluegleman lost control of it. Knopf however established a multi-million dollar company on the basis of PC-File. In 1983 Bob Wallace created PC-Write which became a well used word processor and was used extensively in developing countries. Because the word freeware was reserved he called it shareware. The concept was pretty much the same. Over the years, freeware and shareware became less used as concepts probably because the most used programmes for business purposes were monopolised by Microsoft with the operating system and Microsoft Office applications. Shareware was in a sense reborn with the open source movement. It is difficult to see any difference between Open Source and shareware but the Open Source Movement has been supported from the outset by large foundations such as the Soros Foundation which founded the Open Society Initiative. In English 'Open Source' means freely available source software which developers can use to advance the software in question. In all these cases, software developed is free though usually developers ask for a voluntary contribution. They cannot be sold on. Open Source does not necessarily mean free-of-charge but there is an implication that the availability of the source code will enable organisations to acquire and develop it for free. CDS/ISIS was no shareware or open source but many of the features of open source and shareware were responsible for the popularity of CDS/ISIS.

For example, Open Source has the possibility for users with access to programming skills to make their own developments. CDS/ISIS has a feature of being able to write programme exits which enable further development. Unlike open source the source code was not made widely available but UNESCO did make it available to BIREME in Brazil where further developments have taken place. Moreover, in the Soviet Union the Russian National Library for Science and Technology developed with permission from UNESCO IRBIS, a functionally equivalent package copied from the DOS version of ISIS.

The Open Source movement gained much greater political credibility than the earlier movements did and UNESCO came under pressure to support the movement. They now have on their web site a Free and Open Source software portal. Because of UNESCO's lead in this concept, CDS/ISIS came under pressure to be declared open source in the early 2000s. But the source code is still not available. This author believes it would lead to many different versions of the software that could generate records in databases that were no longer compatible with each other. Moreover, Open Source is seen by some as the solution to some of the problems facing the library softwarc industry. Is Open Source all it promises to be? Over the last few years there has been a spate of mergers in the library systems industry led by the equity market resulting in a trend to discontinue the development if not the support of library systems when a company has acquired more than one such package. This severely inconveniences the using institutions which have to migrate from one system to another. Would open source be a protection against this? Open Source has become so much a fashionable option for library software that the International Federation of Library Associations and Institutions held a meeting in Senegal prior to the annual conference's meeting in Durban South Africa.

The proceedings are illustrative of the views on Open Source. The argument in Savard's introduction goes that Open Source may help to smooth out the inequalities between industrialised and developing countries. The connection with commerce is weaker than with commercial software but it is not non-existent. In industrialised countries libraries often use third-party services to support Open Source. This means the connection with the commercial world strengthens. There is no way put from paying for support. The question is who pays and there is not much difference between paying a developer or a third party.

In the conclusion of these proceedings, Diop feels there are clearly economic advantages to adopting an open source software solution but agrees that mastering open source software can take a lot of time and effort because library and information professionals are often isolated. User communities need to be built up to provide mutual help. However it remains to be seen what will be the impact of open source on library automation, particularly integrated library systems in the industrialised world. A pessimistic outcome might be that the institutions using such software feel no differently being supported by the commercial open source support companies than by the current range of commercial companies who promote systems they themselves own.

THE CURRENT SITUATION AND FUTURE PROSPECTS

Making predictions is a very hazardous occupation in anything to do with computers since, the future only tends to bring surprises. Developments in many developing countries are not as advanced as might be expected and in some places there is still a problem with electric supply: Adebibo reporting on usage of catalogues by students at the University of Ilorin in Nigeria stated: "Most respondents claimed to know how to use the card catalogues and OPAC but only a few use them. The possible reason for this low level use of the OPAC is power outages, which have become the rule in Nigeria rather than an exception. Overall, as the power of the internet increases, particularly its bandwidth and its reliability, library automation in developing countries will have the same capabilities as the industrialised world, but not the finance to support it.

In developed countries it is felt by some that the future of library automation lies in open source (outside the control of commercial suppliers) or 'Cloud Computing' (very much controlled by commercial suppliers who provide software on their own hardware and the clients access the data via the Internet). However if solutions to library automation are hosted services in the industrialised world, the suppliers of the service would be able to charge developing countries as little as they wish on the basis that every amount, however little, is profit. This has happened with hosted electronic journals where deals have been made by publishers to cover entire countries which are less than the licence fee required for a university in the west. As suggested, see if this happens. As with e-journals, it needs a champion like eIFL to promote to the suppliers the benefits of their working with developing institutions in what may be perceived as an altruistic way.

CONCLUSION

The participant oriented change strategy provides the best overall approach to managing library automation and migration projects. Of the strategies which have been outlined, it offers the highest degree of employee communication and participation. These are the same areas that caused the most problems if they were inadequate. One of the chief advantages of this strategy is that it involves the users of the system at the earliest possible stage of the project. That is during the teleological process of identifying reasons for the project and setting goals or criteria for a new system. Involving the employees at this stage reduces the need for normative attitude-adjusting sessions latter in the process. This is not to say that managers who adopt this strategy can just ignore employee attitudes later on. Change will still be stressful, and people may still resist it at various points. But, management will not have to invest as much effort in convincing staff that the new system is better if the staff were involved in selecting it. The rational-empirical strategies of employee training programmes will still have a role to play, as the process moves on. As was demonstrated in the failed attempt at implementing the CASE system, this strategy is not sufficient by itself. But users must learn how a new system works if they are to use it at all. Within the overall context of participant oriented strategy, other employees provide much of that training. With their hands-on experience, employee led training can be more effective than vendor supplied 'canned presentations'.

This also promotes an atmosphere in which employees will be comfortable sharing their learning experiences, tricks and shortcuts following implementation. The other two strategies, phased implementation and power-coercive can not be recommended across the board. The power-coercive strategy is divisive, and is likely make the change harder instead of easier. This strategy aggravates fears about job security, which is one of the sources of change anxiety. While a degree of control needs to be maintained, a threatening approach is not desirable as a general strategy.

The strategy of phased implementation will be helpful for some situations, but not for all. For libraries currently using manual systems or automated systems that are not integrated, this method may help to ease the transition. For libraries that already have a well-integrated system, it could create even more chaos. Within the context of participant-oriented change, the choice of whether to include it rests with the employees who actually work with the system.

5

Serials and Book Selection in Library

SERIALS SELECTION

From the eighteenth century, the journal has been an important mechanism for communicating scientific findings, advances in techniques, and changes in accepted practice in medicine and other health professions. Journals continue to constitute the core of health sciences library collections. But biomedical journals now face price increases, dwindling number of personal and institutional subscribers and the threat that print publications will be overshadowed by electronic forms of scientific communication. They also face various changes in the title, the publishers, emerging or splitting, editorship, supercession, ceasing, format or size, numbering, or frequency.

RESPONSIBILITY FOR SELECTION

Because a decision to subscribe to a journal is often a long-term one, with a financial commitment over several years, selection is rarely left to a single person, although the final decision is often so.

Selection Committee

This is the practice in academic medical libraries and in large hospital libraries, as suggestions or requests are brought to the committee for review. Criteria for evaluation are agreed upon and an evaluation form is used to collect data for decision-making and to document decisions. The information should be recorded in a consistent manner on a standard form to allow comparisons.

The information may include the following: Title, publisher, frequency, starting date, cost, coverage of contents by standard indexing and abstracting services and online databases, published rankings or reviews, interlibrary loan data, information about purchase requests, information about other titles in the subject field, evidence of peer review of articles, assessment by faculty or hospital staff, availability in other affiliated library, relevance to the parent organisation's programmes. The frequency to committee meeting may vary from monthly to semiannually.

External Reviewers

These may be faculty or other health professional staff without forming any group. A form similar to the one used for selection committee may be used, preferrably with a sample issue of the journal. The library may use departmental representatives for this purpose. The librarian has to set a plan for follow-up.

Selection Criteria

Although selection criteria previously dealt with apply to all types of library materials, there are some unique characteristics of the journal format that need to be considered:

- *Quality*: Although no single measure will be sufficient to judge quality, there are several factors to be taken into account:
  - — *Publisher*: Who is he? How reputable is he as a scientific publisher? Is the publisher a professional society or association? Is the membership of such society or association international? National? Regional?
  - — *Editors*: Are they recognized? What is their institutional affiliation? are they themselves writers as well? Does the editorial board include prominent names?
  - — Editorial review.
  - — *Authors*: Are they members of the editorial board? What is therc affiliation?
  - — Content.
    - *a. Research Journals*: Research journals should publish articles that follow the accepted format for describing scientific research.
    - *b. Clinical Journals*: These may be evaluated by practitioners for selection.
    - *c. Review Journals*: These require more selectivity than the previous types because they do not report new information, and reviews on similar topics may cover much of the same ground.
- Writing and Style:
  - — *Writing Style*: Articles should be readable. The writing should be grammatically correct, well organised and clear.
  - — *Abstracts*: These should be informative.
  - — *References*: These should be pertinent, thorough and up-to-date. Citations should be complete and accurate.
- *Accessibility of Content*: The inclusion of the journal in indexing services may be a criterion for selection. Inclusion in a selective database may also be used for this purpose.
- *Bibliometric Indicators*: Bibliometrics, or statistical bibliography,

analyses literature by numerically examining the publications of a discipline. Data can be used to identify journals with the greatest number of articles on a subject or that cover greatest percentage of the literature. But bibliomteric data must be used cautiously as a selection tool, as articles may be cited for multiple reasons and not necessarily to indicate useful research or clinical content.

- *Physical Quality*: It is to be noted here that not all countries have equal access to high-quality paper and printing.
  - — *Illustrations*: Clarity and definition in reproduction of radiographs, photographs and other images. Use of colour may be important in some fields.
  - — *Paper and Binding*: This may not be a factor to be considered as a factor for selection, although using acid-free paper is relevant for material preservation.
- *User Needs*: Patient care and current research needs are driving forces for selection. One indicator of need is the number of requests made to obtain copies of articles through interlibrary loan or document delivery services. The departmental representatives for selection may be a source for identifying department needs.
- Local Availability.
  - — Whether the title is available in another library of the parent organisation.
  - — Duplication is becoming less likely except for heavily used items.
  - — Availability through a network to which the library subscribes.
  - — Reliance on remote collections or document delivery services.
- *Cost:* The judgement on the benefit for cost may be difficult, and subject experts should be called upon for advice.

Electronic Journals

Electronic journals may be categorized either by availability of electronic and print parallels or by mode of access.

The first will result in:

- Electronic journals that have an electronic version only, such as Online journal of current clinical trials.
- Electronic journals that are versions of print journals, such as New England journal of medicine.

The second will result in:

- Electronic journals that are available through a commercial vendor.
- Electronic journals that are locally accessible through CD-ROM, floppy disk or other electronic format loaded on a library workstation or parent organisation's network.

The issues that electronic journals pose for libraries are not substantially different than those posed by print journals. Information on availability of electronic journals may be obtained from the Association of Research Libraries (ARL) in both print and electronic format.

SERIAL ITEM AND CONTRIBUTION IDENTIFIER (SICI)

The SICI standard defines a coding structure to assign unique identifiers to serials. The code builds on the *International Standard Serial Number* (ISSN) for the serial item portion of the identifier. The SICI code is derived algorithmically from bibliographic information about the serial and/or article and may be generated by the creator/publisher of the items and contributions, by a third party vendor such as a document delivery supplier or abstracting and indexing service, or by the library which acquires and holds the materials.

Use of the SICI code in a computer system allows the items and contributions to be uniquely identified in many library automated transactions including ordering, claiming, bibliographic database linking, ILL and document delivery, check-in, reserve room, and rights management and royalty collection. The code was designed to be compact enough to be easily converted to a barcode. SICI has also been assigned a use value in the Z39.50 bib-1 attribute set. This assignment allows the SICI to be used as a qualifier in a Z39.50 information retrieval search. SICI also could be used as the identifier in conjunction with an ILL Protocol request, EDI order, or a GEDI electronic document transmission.

SAMPLE RFP LANGUAGE

The following are examples of language that could be included in an RFP to address SICI compliance:

- The system must support the use of the Serial Item and Contribution Identifier as specified in ANSI/NISO Z39.56. Describe how your system implements SICI for both serials and contributions. Discuss how the SICI is stored, indexed, and searchable.
- Discuss how your system does SICI code matching and validation.

Assessing compliance

It is more likely, currently, to find support of SICI at the Serials Item level than the Contribution level in a library system. However, the use of the Contribution Identifier through the entire ILL or document delivery cycle is becoming more crucial. Even libraries that do no currently identify items at the contribution level should look for a system that allows the code's use. Since the standard allows that some data elements can be omitted when creating a SICI, the algorithms a system uses to match or validate SICI codes can be complex. Demonstrations and tests of this functionality should be requested from the vendor.

The 1996 version of the standard changed the rules for Title Code, clarified the distinction between serial items and contribution identifiers, added a method for indicating the medium of the material, and better delineated the segments of the identifier. Libraries should confirm that the system supports the changes in this version.

DATA ELEMENTS FOR BINDING LIBRARY MATERIALS

Z39.76 identifies and defines common data elements used to process and track library materials for binding when information about the material is exchanged between a library management software system and a binding preparation software system. Use of the specified data elements in an automated library system can reduce duplicate data entry when preparing binding orders, improve accuracy and consistency of binding labels, and allow for more automation of binding processes. The standard incorporates other identifying codes and standard numbering systems such as ISBN, ISSN, and SICI.

Holdings information fields are based on the MARC 21 Format for Holdings Data. The standard does not define any of the communications protocols required for the information exchange, but the expectation is that EDI is utilized for the transfer of data.

Sample RFP language

The following are examples of language that could be included in an RFP to address Z39.76 binding data elements compliance:

- The system must support ANSI/NISO Z39.76 Data Elements for Binding Library Materials. Define which binding element fields are included by default in the system and discuss how optional elements are handled.
- Describe how binding element information is input and how it is linked to the bibliographic and holdings record information to ensure consistency.
- Describe the process for generating binding information from the system to send electronically to a vendor. Describe the methods and formats for exporting binding information to a file.
- Identify which communications protocols can be used to transmit binding information.

Assessing compliance

A small subset of the data elements defined in the standard is considered mandatory; these elements should be supported in the selected system. Many of the optional fields are defined as such only because they would not be utilized with every binding order thus it is likely that many of the optional fields would be desirable to have. Additionally, some libraries may be using a binding preparation software package that might require some of the standard's optional data fields. The evaluation team should review all the optional elements and identify the additional fields that would be "mandatory" to their library's binding process. Determine how the desired optional data elements are supported and how easily additional data elements can be added at a later time. Ask if there are any limitations on the number of binding related fields which the system can support. Determine that the system supports both serial and non-serial materials in the binding processes and that the binding module can access needed data from the serials and acquisition modules. Have the vendor create a test file of binding data from the system as it would look when transmitted and verify that the information is compiled and reported correctly. If the library's binding vendor accepts electronic transmissions, a test transmission to that vendor and the vendor's verification of how the data was received would be useful.

Clarify with the vendor which communication protocols are supported for binding information. If the system supports EDI transmission for acquisition and claiming activities, can it also be used for the binding transmission? If the binding data is exported to a file, determine what file formats are available and if these are compatible with what the library and the binding vendor use.

SELECTION SOURCES

There are several sources or information about journals:

- *Advertising and Announcements*: Advertisements may be sent directly by publishers, or are published in library or medical journals. Vendors also alert libraries in various ways: through lists, order forms, and online information systems. Publishers' catalogues may also be used.
- *Sample Issues*: These are sent by the publisher as sample or trial issues, which often may be requested and sometimes purchased.
- *Core Lists:* Lists of key journals, sometimes together with some other library materials are compiled. The following are examples:
- *User Recommendations:* The library can encourage users to suggest new titles using request form available in the library, whether manually or electronically.
- *Interlibrary Loan Requests*: Repeated requests from users to obtain articles from a journal should prompt the library to consider a subscription.
- *Reviews:* There are scientific journals that publish reviews of new titles. Among these journals are Nature and Serials review.
- *Indexes*: Lists of journals indexed for major indexing services are used to make a judgement on titles already identified. Announcement of titles added can alert selectors to them. Examples of these lists are:
  - — List of journals indexed in Index Medicus. New titles are announced in *NLM technical bulletin*.

— Serial sources for the BIOSIS Previews Database.
— Chemical Abstracts Service Source Index.

- *Other Sources*: There are general sources that cover a wide range of subjects. Among these are the following:
  — Ulrich's international periodicals directory. Bowker.
  — Standard periodical directory. Oxbridge.
  — New serial titles. OCLC.
  — Faxon's librarians' guide to serials.
  — EBSCO's librarians' handbook.
  — Computer databases such as OCLC, RLIN, SERLINE (an NLM database)
  — Serials review. Ann Arbor: Pierian. Quarterly

It has to be noted here that all such sources are also available in machine-readable form.

BOOK SELECTION

Books assist in the dissemination of information by providing a convenient means of access to recorded knowledge. It is true that a medical book is out-of-date when it is published, but this does not invalidate its use as a digest of available knowledge in a physically handy form.

The main categories of books are:

- *Quick Reference Books:* Dictionaries, directories, pharmacopoeias, data book. These are essential items in every collection. Now many of these books are also available in CD-ROM format.
- *Standard Works of Reference*: These provide access to knowledge in depth in subject at an advanced level. They are usually too detailed to serve as textbook guides to their subjects.
- *Postgraduate Textbooks:* The need to specialize is paramount and the number of courses leading to future qualifications is numerous in medicine. This ensures a good market of textbooks at the postgraduate level. They are among the most heavily used materials in the medical library.
- *Texts for Basic Study:* There is virtually no topic in the undergraduate level which is not suitably covered by this type of material.
- *Monographs*: A monograph consists of a treatise on a single subject, and it is always an advanced level work. They may also appear in series.
- *Theses and Dissertations:* Most of the smaller medical libraries do not hold this type of material and larger one will onlyhold those originating in their own parent organisations. If required, it is usual to have them collected by a central body such as national or depository libraries.
- *Pamphlets and other Ephemera:* Pamphlets are short topical and written

with a particular object in view. They may quickly lose their currency. They may be ordered and treatedas books. Many useful pamphlets are available free particularly from pharmaceutical companies.

- *Reports:* A report is a work written by a task force or particular group specially commissioned to study a particular issue or problem. They may be difficult to trace. Reports may also emanate from important bodies in the profession. Research reports in, for example, the pharmaceutical industry may be confidential. Another example of reports is the annual report of a research or teaching institution. Government departments generate a great deal of report literature, of which many are on social and medical subjects.
- *Conference Proceedings:* The quality of this type varies from carefully edited account of important meetings to mere photolithography of the authors' typescripts with little editing and no index.

Responsibilities

- Responsibilities for book selection should be formally agreed upon, and the flow of information and decisions clearly delineated. If most of the selection is distributed among several persons, a manual describing both the responsibilities and the process is useful. This manual promotes consistency and thoroughness in carrying out the functions
- In small libraries, there is little confusion regarding who has what responsibility. But in large libraries the situation is different as procedures need to document how selection tools are handled:
  - — Who sees advertising materials, how they are divided, for instance by subject, how they are marked for follow up
  - — If books reviews are used, the routing process should be established
  - — Method of transmitting ordering information from the selector to the acquisitions unit
  - — If interlibrary loan requests are to be reviewed, there must be a mechanism for receiving the information.
- The link between selection activity and the budget allocations must be established, whether the individual selectors have any fund management responsibilities or not.

SOURCES FOR BOOK SELECTION

Selection tools for book selection should be both alerting and evaluative to be convenient for selection. They may be in the form of bibliographies, review or advertising materials, and may be in print and/or electronic formats. Other sources are relevant for selection.

The various sources may be summarized as follows:

- *Publishers' Flyers and Catalogues*: Libraries usually receive a lot of announcements from the publishers about the availability of new books. Moreover, many publishers produce various types of catalogues for their publications, sometimes including previously published editions which are still in print. It is necessary for the library to be on the mailing list of the publishers in the disciplines that concern the library. Visiting their web sites is now enabled as well.
- *Vendors' Flyers and Catalogues*: Many vendors do the same thing as publishers. Make sure that you are regularly informed of their offerings. Some provide altering service, in print or electronically, of new titles.
- *Recommendations from Users*: This should be encouraged. Request forms must be readily accessible. Remember that they themselves receive flyers and catalogues from publishers and sometimes complimentary copies of new titles.
- *Interlibrary Loan Requests:* Although particularly appropriate for journal selection, they may be also relevant for selecting books that are not brand new.
- *Bibliographies and Library Catalogues:* Bibliographies are of several categories as there are national biblio-graphies, subject bibliographies both total and selective, author bibliographies, bibliographies of bibliographies, etc. Some of these bibliographies include health sciences while there is one devoted to medicine which is Medical books in print of Bowker.

Another tool that is considered here is what is usually called core lists:

- *British Council*: Core list of library materials: medicine.
- *EMRO*: List of basic sources in English for a medical faculty library. 8th ed. 1999.
- *Royal College of General Practitioners*: Books for general practice and primary health care. London, 1992. Regularly revised.
- *Royal College of Psychiatrists:* Lists of books suitable for a psychiatric library 1988-1993. London, 1993. Re-gularly revised and updated.
- *Royal College of Psychiatrists:* Key books for a psychiatric library. London. Regularly revised and updated.

Moreover, the most comprehensive catalogue of health sciences books is CATLINE. This is NLM's online catalogue. NLM Locator, which includes CATLINE, AVLINE for audiovisuals, and SERLINE for information on journal titles, is now available on the Internet.

- *Book Reviews*: There are two types of book reviews:
  - — Those published in professional and scientific journals. Examples of such journals are:

a. *JAMA:* Journal of American Medical Association
b. Lancet
c. British medical journal
d. British journal of hospital medicine
e. Nursing times
f. Journal of advanced nursing
g. New England journal of medicine
h. Bulletin of the Medical Library Association

There are journals not limited to health sciences such as Nature, and Science, and Library journal:

— Those that are fully devoted as journal to reviews. Some of these reviews cover medicine among the disciplines that they serve. Among them, are the following:
a. *New Technical Books*: New York Public Library (10/year).
b. *Technical Book Review Index:* JAAD Publications (monthly).
c. *Science Books and Films*: American Association for the Advancement of science (5/year).
d. *The Bookseller:* Whitaker (weekly).
e. *Contemporary Psychology*: A journal of reviews. American Psychological Association (monthly).
f. *Directory of Published Proceedings*: Series SEMT-Science, Engineering, Medicine and Technology. InterDok (10/year)
g. *Choice:* Association of College and Research Libraries (11/year).
h. *British Book News*: The British Council (monthly).
i. *American Book Publishing Record*: Bowker (monthly).
j. *Cumulative Book Index*: H.W. Wilson (11/year).

The outstanding example of book reviews is the new publication of Doody Publishing set up in 1993. This publication is entitled Doody's journal: health sciences book reviewing, issued bimonthly and evaluates about 250 titles in each issue. It can be accessed on Internet.

A British version is under discussion:

- *Approval Plan*: Although approval plans are concerned with acquisition. The selection function of the approval plan is summarized as follows:
  — The library supplies the vendor with a detailed profile of its requirements in specific fields, together with any budgetary limits, and the publishers to be considered;
  — The supplier selects and regularly supplies the materials as specified in the profile;
  — The library monitors the materials supplied and have the right to return any item received;

- If the percentage of returns is high then the library should review the plan and take required action, which may include changing the supplier.
- The approval plan does not fit with small medical libraries.

SELECTION IN SPECIAL SETTINGS

Electronic Resources

Selection decisions of electronic resources parallel those of print materials in many ways, but they are treated separately, because their unique characteristics introduce additional factors to collection decision-making and because these formats can affect information delivery, budgeting, equipment, and staffing. Electronic resources play an essential role in every health sciences library. But they are usually expensive, and thus may consume a great portion of a library's budget. So a greater degree of care should be taken in making decisions regarding what the library will provide to its users.

As knowledge-based computer programmes in clinical medicine and other health care disciplines are improved and gain wider acceptance, they appear more commonly as library resources, especially if they can be accessed remotely from offices and clinical care sites. Selection of computer software by students, hospital staff, faculty, clinicians, or researchers should be guided by the library's collection development policy. The policy should address the criteria by which these resources are selected. Scope, depth and audience will define the boundaries.

There are several types of software that may be acquired by health sciences libraries:

- Bibliographic
- *Full Text*: Books and journals
- Numeric or factual databases
- Clinical assist programmes for diagnosis or treatment decisions
- Educational software
- Applications software, such as word processing, analytical or statistical packages, file management, telecommunications, authoring software, graphics software (note here that such software is general pur-pose not resources)
- Administrative functions or staff support
- Criteria of Resources for Selection
  - *Scope*: The resource must fit the subject scope of the library.
  - *Depth*: The intensity of collecting in a discipline will dictate how many resources the library will acquire, or the degree of specialization needed.
  - *Audience*: The selection should answer the question whose needs should the library intend to serve with the software? Different

clientele will require different resources. Computer-based resources for student use should usually be selected with advice and recommendation from faculty or potential users.

- Selection Principles:
  - — The resource should fit the mission of the library, and the scope and depth defined in the collection development policy, it should meet users' needs;
  - — Specific criteria should address the content, the user interface retrieval software, the format, and the hardware and software required by the resource;
  - — Careful investigation and evaluation of the cost-effective-ness of different formats should precede any decisions. An information policy both for the library and for the parent organisation will help guide these decisions.
- Selection Criteria:
  - — Content:
    - *a.* Quality of the material presented.
      - i. Authoritiveness of content
      - ii. Expertise of the authors
      - iii. Reputation of the producer
      - iv. Comprehensiveness of the information
      - v. Quality of the images, if important
    - *b.* *Currency*: Regular updates should be provided.
    - *c.* *Content Usefulness*: Such as:
      - i. Interactive capabilities of testing
      - ii. Simultaneously hear and see as required
      - iii. Combine text and images, sound and movement
      - iv. Highly accurate and up-to-date knowledge
      - v. Able to show relationships and probabilities, and suggest possibilities
    - *d.* Relationship to Print Publications.
      - i. Whether additional material is added
      - ii. Convenience of access, amount of demand, need for permanent presentation
      - iii. Are updates offered electronically through networks?
  - — User Interface:
    - *a.* Ease of use.
    - *b.* Software functions.
      - i. The search engine or other control functions should be powerful enough to support the resource;
      - ii. Response time should be snappy;
      - iii. Use of Boolean operators, adjacency feature, saving searches or search strategies are enabled.

c. Printing and Downloading Capabilities.

d. Duplication of Print Publications. When the software duplicates to a large extent a print publication, the library must determine whether the electronic version offers additional features, such as easier search, use hypertext, reformat information, manipulation or animation of illustrative material, extraction and manipulation.

e. Compatibility with Other Resources.

f. Documentation and Guides.

— *Format*: The library has several formats to choose from:

a. In print

b. On stand-alone CD-ROM

c. On CD-ROM on a LAN

d. By tapes mounted on local institutional network

e. By various routes to a remote utility through a gateway

The following factors should be considered in making this choice:

a. *Users*: Consider the likely users; if they are very few, the cost and support may not be justified.

b. *Expected Use*: The number and frequency of use.

c. *Accessibility*: Convenient access.

d. *Content*: Whether formats differ in comprehen-siveness or specialized contents. Compare the interface and performance characteristics. Updating.

e. Costs.

f. *Equipment*: Compatibility with local systems.

g. Legal Issues:

i. Licensing

ii. Restrictions to making backup copies, downloading, and printing

iii. Possibility of sharing

— Hardware, Software, and Space Requirements.

a. Space:

i. The facilities should be conducive to the types of use that will be made of them.

ii. Whether the workstation has to be an open area.

iii. Whether the resources can be used effectively in the available setting.

b. Workstation Configuration.

i. Networking is to be provided.

ii. Adequate number of workstations to ensure effective use of the resources.

iii. Avoid workstations dedicated to single resource, except for those that will be heavily used, such as MEDLINE, or the library's catalogue.

c. Compatibility.
   i. Is the resource compatible with existing equipment?
   ii. Is the memory sufficient and the machine fast enough for the type of content, such as images?
   iii. Does the new software conflict with any other resources on the same equipment?

d. Additional Software.
   i. Does the resource require specific software such as operating system or database loader?
   ii. Audio and video require additional component.
   iii. Is the existing hardware adequate to accommodate the required software?

Reference Collections

The policy for reference collection should relate to the general collection development policy, whether it forms part of it or written separately. All selection criteria applied to books in general apply here as well. It remains to cover here the types of materials that form the reference collection and the selection sources of reference items.

Types of Materials

Reference collections are used to locate the following:

- *Directory Information*: Brief factual information about people, institutions, organisations, programmes.
- *Data:* Compilations of such information as statistical data, biological facts, chemical compositions, drug descriptions.
- *Definitions:* Collections of medical terminology, foreign language, specialized nomenclature.
- *Descriptions:* Short or encylcopaedic summaries of diseases, procedures, biological processes, historical events.
- *Bibliographic Information:* References or abstracts by subject, author, citation, historical period, or source.

To enable this, the following types of materials have to be provided:

- *Bibliographies:* Examples include the various core lists and other sources for selection of books, journals and electronic resources mentioned previously.
- *Business or Corporate Information about Health Care Industry:* Examples: The medical and health information directory; the Patersons guides series; Research centres directory; World of learning; Encyclopedia of associations; the Medical and health care marketplace guide; the Foundations directory; Directory of medical and health care libraries in the United Kingdom and Republic of Ireland.

- *Dictionaries: Examples*: Dorlands illustrated medical dictionary; Stedman's medical dictionary; the International dictionary of medicine and biology; Taber encyclopedic dictionary; Segen's dictionary of modern medicine; the encyclopedia and dictionary of medicine, nursing and allied health; Jablonski's dictionary of syndromes and eponymic diseases; Mangalini's directory of syndromes; Encyclopedia of human biology; Sloane's medical abbreviations and eponyms; the Acronyms, initialisms and abbreviations dictionary; Mosby's medical, nursing and allied health dictionary.
- *Directories and Biographical Sources:* Examples are the various medical directories published in many countries of the world, such as the UK Medical directory.
- *Drug and Chemical Information:* Examples are the various pharmacopoeias published in many countries.
- *Funding Sources:* Some are listed under the second type mentioned.
- *Handbooks and Manuals:* This also includes style manuals. Examples: Merck index; CRC handbook of chemistry and physics.
- *Health Legislation, Regulations and Standards:* These are published and documented in various countries.
- *Indexes and Abstracts*: Many are available in both print and electronic formats. Examples include:
  - — Index Medicus (Medline);
  - — Science citation index (SCISEARCH);
  - — Current contents;
  - — Excerpta medica (EMBASE);
  - — Cumulative index to nursing and allied health (CINAHL);
    Hospital literature index (Health Planning and Administration);
  - — Biological abstracts (BIOSIS Previews);
  - — Chemical abstracts (CA Search);
  - — Psychological abstracts (Psych-INFO);
  - — CANCERLIT;
  - — PDQ;
  - — TOXLIT.
- *Statistical Compilations:* Many countries and health associations publish statistics on different aspects of health. WHO publishes World health statistics annual.
- *Tests*: Examples include: Mental measurements yearbook; stromborg's Instruments for clinical nursing research.
- Yearbooks and annual reviews.
- *General Works:* Most reference collections include a small number of general reference works such as an encyclopaedia, dictionary, almanac, directories of local organisations, an atlas.

- *Textbook Collections:* If the library does not maintain a reserve collection. A representative collection of textbooks in the reference collection may provide convenient access to students who need information for assignments or patient care questions.
- *Electronic Resources:* There is an increasing number of electronic reference sources covering the range of print sources, including bibliographic and fulltext databases, handbooks, encyclopaedias, directories, and textbooks. The data is stored on CD-ROM, floppy disks, hard drives and mainframe or minicomputers. Some are duplicates or enhancements of printed sources or mainframe sources, such as CD-ROM versions of MEDLINE, others incorporate several publications or resources. Another electronic resource is the OPAC (Online Public Access Catalogue) were one or more workstations are dedicated for them.
- *Ephemeral Materials*: Collection of pamphlets, information sheets, brochures, and even reprints or bibliographies are maintained as adjuncts to reference collections. This collection may also include press clippings. A policy for selection criteria and guidelines for weeding and retention should be developed and followed.

BOOKSTACK DIMENSIONS

Manufacturers of wood library shelving follow a standard format of overall section heights and depths. Thc same is true for manufacturers of steel cantilever-style shelving; however, it is a different dimensional format from that adopted by wood shelving manufacturers. A critical difference between wood and steel shelving manufacturers occurs when dimensions are published.

- Wood Shelving: Industry-standard width for wood shelving section is: 36" wide. All other widths are generally considered custom widths, and are factory-manufactured to actual field dimensions and carry a price increase.
- Cantilever-style Steel Shelving: Industry-standard width for a steel shelving section is: 36" wide, with 30" and 24" wide widths available. It is very rare for a steel shelving manufacturer to factory-build shelving to custom widths.

CANTILEVER-STYLE STEEL SHELVING DIMENSIONS

Cantilever-style steel shelving manufacturers dimensions are considered to be nominal. A double-faced, Cantilever-style steel shelving that is described as " a section is 84" high x 24" deep" is, in fact, 84" in overall height, but actually somewhere close to 24-." in depth. A singlefaced, cantilever-style steel shelving that is described as " a section is 84" high x 12" deep" is, in fact, 84" in overall height, but actually somewhere close to 13-." in depth. When developing shelving space plans utilizing Cantilever-style steel shelving, this is a critical concept to master, especially where space is tight and one must struggle to maintain adequate legal and accessible aisles. Growth is a dimension concept used in applying actual stack unit dimensions to actual plan layout and physical building spaces. Conceptually, growth is the factoring in of actual stack unit depths that are greater than published nominal dimensions, plus the growth in length of assembled ranges due to the insertion of reinforcing gussets between frames, as their thickness increases the length. Often, architectural floor plans are drawn using nominal dimensions, therefore, it is important to realize that the aisle will be diminished in width by the amount of growth which results from factoring in the oversize actual shelving dimensions. One should also add from ö." to 2" to the shelving width dimension when including decorative end panels at range ends, as aisle width will be determined by clearance between end panel edges at the entrance end of the aisle.

WOOD SHELVING DIMENSIONS

Wood library shelving dimensions are considered to be actual dimensions. Wood shelving that is described as "a section is 82" high × 24" deep" are exactly, and actually, those overall height and depth dimensions.

AUDIOVISUAL COLLECTIONS

Audiovisual materials comprise an important segment of many health sciences libraries. But they usually have requirements (such as space, equipment and funding) that make them different from collections of other materials.

Collection development for audiovisuals is different from those for other materials in the following aspects:

- Selection of audiovisuals is more user-driven than that for other formats;
- Previewing is required in the selection process, whether this takes place in the library or at the supplier's place.

Audiovisuals supports all aspects of educational programmes in both academic settings and hospitals (whether for staff or patients).

SELECTION CRITERIA

In addition to the general criteria of selection previously discussed, the following additional criteria may be considered:

- *Audience:* The library's interest in the audience which may be professional, academics, or general public including patients and patient families, should be documented in the collection development policy and taken into account in the selection process.
- *Equipment Availability*: The following questions have to be answered: Does the library already own the proper equipment so that users can view or listen to the programme? Are users likely to have access to

compatible equipment at home or in their departments? Can the item be used on patient to other broadcast networks?

- *Appropriateness of Format*: Is the format in which the material is presented the most useful one to convey the information? Slides *vs.* videotapes, audiovisual *vs.* print, motion *vs.* still images, audiotape *vs.* printed description.
- *Origin of Format:* does the audiovisual conform to national standards: slides may differ in size.
- *Rental or Permanent Acquisition*: Can the need be satisfied through rental? Is there sufficient recurring demand to justify a purchase? Is it possible to borrow particular items from other library or institution?
- *Restriction on Use:* Are there special guidelines which must be followed regarding the use of the title, such as prohibition on group showings? If it is difficult to monitor and enforce such restrictions, it may not be advisable to procure the item.
- *Cost*: Is the item worth the investment?

Grey Literature

Grey literature is defined as the " literature which is not readily available through normal bookselling channels, and therefore difficult to identify and obtain". Examples of grey literature include reports, technical notes and specifications, conference proceedings and preprints, translations, official publications, supplementary publications and data, trade literature. It has to be noted that not all materials in all these categories are grey.

Grey materials are characterized by the following:

- Poor availability
- Poor bibliographic information and control
- Non-professional layout and format
- Low print run

Types of Grey Literature in Health Sciences

- Government Information.
  - — The grey titles issued by government departments. These may outnumber the other normal publications in some countries.
  - — The health agency documents, including circulars.
  - — Documents produced by national statutory and non-statutory bodies, academic units and voluntary sector.
  - — *Health Authority Literature*: This includes:
    - *a.* Minutes and agenda papers
    - *b.* Annual reports
    - *c.* Public health reports
    - *d.* Strategic plans

e. Working party plans
f. Statistical series and bulletins
g. Medical audit plans
h. Policy documents
i. Research and surveys
j. Health needs assessment surveys
k. Public opinion surveys
l. Financial statements

— Documents of other relevant authorities, such as the ministries of interior, housing, transport, labour, sports and even police service.
— Grey literature of health service providers in both public and private sectors. This literature also includes research activities and statistics.

Sources for Selection

There are services concerning grey literature in various fields. They are normally with national covering although some may be international.

The following are examples:

- *Government Reports Announcements and Index. Virginia*: NTIS. This publication has three major headings related to health sciences in its subject categories:
  — Biomedical technology and human factor engineering
  — Health planning and health services research
  — Medicine and biology
- Scientific and Technical Aerospace Report (STAR). NASA. This has the following parts concerning health sciences:
  — Life sciences
  — Aerospace medicine
  — Behavioural sciences
  — Man/system technology and life support
  — Space biology
- Energy research abstract (ERA). US Department of Energy. It has:
  — Biomedical sciences, basic studies
  — Biomedical sciences, applied studies
  — Health and safety
- British reports, translations and theses. Boston. Spa: The British Library Document Supply Centre. It has: 06 biological and medical sciences.
- System for information on grey literature in Europe (SIGLE). The European Association of Grey Literature Exploitation (EAGLE). It is a bibliographic database holding contributions from 9 European countries.

- For librarians seeking German language grey literature in medical and health care, there are two publications:
  - — FTN (Forschungsberichte aus Technik und Nat-urwissencha ften). Weinheim: VCH Verlag. This is a bibliography of projects sponsored by the German Federal Ministry for Research and Technology.
  - — Bibliography of medicine. Munich: K.G. Saur. This is a bibliography of German-language publications outside the book trade, and includes literature from Switzerland and Austria.
- PASCAL Bibliographies internationales. Paris INIST. This is an international bibliography with French emphasis covering science and medicine.
- Ethnic minorities health. Bradford: Bradford Community Quarterly bulletin covering conference proceeding, theses and much useful grey literature.
- The Cumulative index to nursing and allied health literature (CINAHL). It is useful for dissertations, standards and conference proceedings.
- *Health Service Abstracts. Oldham:* Department of Health Leaflets Unit. Monthly. It includes books, book chapters, NHS executive publications, reports and periodical references.
- *The European Union Biomedical and Health Research. Brussels:* European Commission. 3/year. It concentrates on national research into medical and health problems in Europe.
- Health Care Literature Information Network (HECLINET). Berlin: Institut für Krankenhausbau, Dokumentation Krankenhauswesen. Bimonthly. It covers the entire range of European literature, both grey and white, on hospitals and health care. It includes conference reports, theses and company publications.
- Conference papers index. Louisville, NY: Data Courier. Monthly. It covers published and unpublished papers.
- WHODOC. Geneva: WHO. Bimonthly. It lists all WHO publications, including periodicals, technical and policy documents, as well as documents emanating from WHO funded programmes.

Other disciplines, such as food and environment, are covered in international databases.

They include:

- *AGRIS. Rome*: Food and Agriculture Organisation (FAO). It has a print version, AGRINDEX.
- CAB abstracts. London: Commonwealth Agricultural Bureau.
- AGRICOLA. US National Agricultural Library. It has a printed version: bibliography of agriculture.

- International register of potentially toxic chemicals (IRPTC). Nairobi: United Nations Environment Programme (UNEP).
- Environmental Chemical Data and Information Network (ECDIN). European Communities at Ispra (Italy) Establishment. This is a factual database.

Consumer Health Collections

During the 1980s and 1990s, increasing attention has been given to the provision of information on health care issues to patients, relatives, carers and wider public. The information provided is called "Consumer Health Information (CHI)'. Deve-lopment of consumer health information is now a necessity dictated by law in some countries.

It has significant benefits:

- It leads to more truly informed consent
- It leads to increased patient's understanding and satisfaction
- It leads to increased compliance with treatment
- It leads to quicker and less stressful recovery from illness and surgery.

The increased availability of health information for lay people has also been influenced by the WHO declaration of " Health for All by the year 2000 " which says:

- "Health for all will be achieved by people themselves. A well informed, well motivated and actively participating community is a key element for attainment of the common goal".

Consumer health collections exist to serve library users seeking authoritative information, in clearly understood language, about normal anatomy and physiology, diseases, conditions, treatments and other health care topics. Besides the general public users of these collections include medical school students seeking materials to help explain health and disease concepts to patients and their relatives. Others include primary care physicians, nurses and faculty members. It may be part of the reference collection, or on its own. But it is not always the responsibility of the medical library to contain consumer health collections. In some cases it is the responsibility of the parent organisation's public relations unit, while in other cases the responsibility rests with a variety of statutory and voluntary agencies, as it is rather common for the ministries of health and other health authorities to provide this information. Yet in other cases, the responsibility rests with public libraries.

Selection Criteria

The general selection criteria previously mentioned apply here.

But further criteria may be given:

- *Presentation of Information*: This includes the writing style, easiness of use, presence of index and table of contents, illustration, presentation of alternatives and presence of citations and sources.

- *Audience*: The collection development policy should document the audience to be served, to be taken into account in the selection process.
- *Pathway to Additional Information:* The item should have bibliographies, reading list, referral sources and resource organisations.
- Qualifications of the Author and Publisher.
- Currency.

Rare Book, History of Medicine and Archives Collections

Rare book, history of medicine and archives collections, are not found in all health sciences libraries. The difference between collection development in general, and that of rare books derives from the nature of the books themselves. Thus policies governing it are frequently singled out for special consideration in overall collection development policy statements. A distinction is often made between rare book collections and history of medicine collections, under the assumption that the latter are generally comprised of secondary works, the materials are collected in the same manner as other books for the medical library collections, and they are kept in open stacks with the rest of the library's collection.

Rare books are primary research materials, require more proper storage and security controls than the general stack collection, and may also be used as showplace for the parent organisation. The archives collection of the parent organisation is different and is not common in medical libraries as it may be under the responsibility of another department of the parent organisation.

If it exists, it may include: official correspondence, minutes, books of account, publications of the parent organisation, books by and about staff and students including alumni publications, theses from the parent organisation or its staff, records of parent organisation's clubs, associations, and societies catalogue, newsletters, personal papers of the more eminent members of the staff, and photographs. It may also contain records from other local health-related organisations, such as affiliated hospitals.

Selection Criteria

Additional to generic criteria, there are further ones that need to be considered:

- *Presence of other Editions of the Same Work*: In addition to availability of other editions or printings, there may be need for specific edition with special features. Some large libraries may require that all editions of a work be acquired for comparison.
- *Availability of a Facsimile Edition*: Facsimile editions may be useful as reading copies.

- *Physical Condition*: The physical condition may be the reason for selection as the item may be different from modern works. Items that need restoration are not usually acquired.
- *Cost:* This must be appropriate.
- *Research Value of the Artifact over Content:* This concerns signed or annotated copies, special bindings and illustrations. Works of particular publishers may be of interest.
- *Provenance*: Previous owners of the copy. Whether the copy is a stolen copy.
- *The Subject in Context*: This means that the copy may show whether the discipline changed over time.
- *Format:* Formats other than books may figure prominently in rare book and history of medicine collections.
- For archives there must be a policy for retention and disposal of the materials rather than a selection policy.

PLANNING FOR COLLECTIONS

One of the keys to the success of any library project is to provide enough shelving to meet the requirements for planned collections. There are various ways of calculating the shelving requirements for a project, ranging from using a simple mathematical calculation based on an average number of volumes per shelving unit to using sophisticated software applications, such as Libris Design, which will calculate the shelving requirements on a collection-by-collection basis. To plan the shelving for a project, a number of decisions must be made once the size of the planned collections has been determined.

These decisions should be made during the programming phase in order to allocate enough space in the building for collections. The criteria which determine the number of bookstack units and the space required include: shelf capacity or number of volumes per shelf, shelf depth, stack height and/or number of shelves per unit, selection of single or double-faced shelving units, and aisle width. The width, depth and aisle requirement for the stack unit will determine the footprint or amount of space required for each stack unit. The net square footage allocated for each shelving unit is the amount of space that is necessary to house the shelving unit plus space in front of the unit for a person to stand.

The net square footage typically includes regular (side) aisle space, which is shared with the adjacent shelving unit and an allotment of space for main and end aisles. Space allocation for single-faced units ranges from 10 to 14 square feet per unit and for double-faced units, from 18 to 22 square feet. The number of stack units required will be determined by the size of the collections divided by the capacity per unit.

For example: if the capacity for fiction volumes is 336 volumes per full height double-faced unit and the on-shelf collection size is projected at 3,360 volumes, then the number of stack units required will be ten. The total collection space required will be the sum of the space requirement for each individual collection. This equation is the number of units required x net square footage per unit = stack area required. The space requirement for fiction collection of 3,360 volumes is:

- 10 (units) x 18 (square feet per unit) = 180 (assignable square feet)

CAPACITY

Capacity is defined as the number of volumes capable of being shelved on a linear foot of shelf. The horizontal running length of a shelf is its linear length or width. A typical standard 3' wide section of shelving has shelves that provide three linear feet of storage per shelf. Typically, the published capacity for a collection will use volume numbers that will produce 25 per cent of excess space per shelf. The shelves will not be full using these calculations. Optimum capacity for a working collection requires shelves that are only 70 to 75 per cent full.

This extra space is not considered future growth space, but is the space required for collection management, efficient reshelving, interfiling of new acquisitions and multi-volume sets. The capacity per shelving unit will vary based on the collection being housed. The factors involved in determining the capacity are volumes per linear foot (by collection type) and number of shelves per shelving unit. Capacity of a shelving section is then an arithmetic calculation of volumes per foot x shelf length (width) x number of shelves. A 90" high x 36" wide, single-faced shelving section, consisting of one base and six adjustable shelves would have a total of seven shelves. The equation illustrating the capacity for fiction books at eight volumes per linear foot housed on a single-faced shelving unit is:

- 8 (volumes per linear foot) x 3 (linear feet) x 7 (shelves) = 168 (volumes)

SHELVING HEIGHT

One of the most critical decisions to be made in planning for shelving is the height of the stack unit. The height of the unit will determine the number of shelves per unit, which, in turn, will determine the capacity for each unit and the number of units required to house the planned collections. Manufacturers offer shelving units in various heights. The most common standard heights are 42", 66", 78", 84" or 90" high. This height refers to the height of the vertical (upright) component of the shelving unit. Units hold from two to seven shelves per side for storing collections.

Other *non-standard* heights including 36", 45" and 60" are also available. Frequently 60" high units are substituted for 66" high units to exempt the units from the seismic requirements in the State of California which refer specifically to units *over* 60". The height of the shelving selected will depend on the type of material housed. Younger children's materials are typically shelved on 42" and

66" high units and adult and young adult materials are typically housed on higher units. The shelving height selected will vary from library to library and often depending on the requirements for supervision of a particular area with shelving over 66" high blocking sight lines. In specific cases accessibility requirements will affect the height of the shelving selected.

Accessibility

Shelving height in most collection areas is unrestricted unless an attendant will not be available, and then it is limited to 54" above the finished floor. The exception is current periodicals, which must be accessible with a maximum side reach of 54" above the finished floor (48" preferred), and a front reach of no more than 48" above the finished floor. To accommodate this reach, shelving units can be no higher than 66" inches, or three sloped display shelves high. Additionally, collections such as the large print collection should reflect the physical challenges of the elderly and the visually impaired, with shelving that is not too high or too low. Heavier materials such as automotive repair manuals, oversized books, or telephone books might also be shelved on lower units.

SHELVING DEPTH

Along with the width and aisle requirements, the shelving depth will determine the footprint or amount of space required for each stack unit. Since stack units are available in various depths, library planners must select the proper size shelf for the materials being stored.

- Flat bookshelves 8" deep are still available as standard, but are virtually never used.
- Most collections can be accommodated on a flat 10" deep bookshelf.
- The use of a 12" deep shelf is common for reference, technical or scientific collections and pre-school collections, where some substitution of a 12" divider-type shelf is desirable.
- Periodical display shelving is always designed as being a minimum of 12" deep due to the use of a 12" deep flat shelf for back issue storage.
- Most manufacturers will have available a 16" deep shelf section, which has application for oversize book storage, but may be used for flat newspaper storage, or may be outfitted with hinged periodical display shelves on a 16" deep flat storage shelf for extra deep back issue storage facilities.

STACK AISLE REQUIREMENTS

In addition to the width and depth of the shelving, the aisle allowance is the third determining factor in the amount of space allocated for each stack unit. Stack aisles are pedestrian paths located in stack areas. Stack aisles include Main Aisles, Side Aisles, Range Aisles, and End Aisles. Aisle requirements for libraries in California are found in Section 1106B.6 of Part II of Title 24 of the California Code of Regulations.

- Cross aisles that run parallel to the stack aisles, which are intended to break up the side aisles into increments, are also known as range aisles. These are required to be 36" wide to meet accessibility requirements.
- End aisles run perpendicular to side aisles and may have books on one side. These must also be a minimum of 36" wide; 44" is required in some cases.
- Main aisles are those aisles, which are the principle accessible routes, and must be a minimum of 44" wide in California.

Stack Aisles and the Americans with Disabilities Act

Aisles in stack areas must comply with accessibility requirements. Side aisles, which run parallel to stack sections, can be no longer than 20 to 21 feet (6 to 7 stack sections) without a cross aisle (range aisle) provided to break up the side aisles. Both side and range aisles are required to be 36" wide. Main aisles are principle access routes which run perpendicular to side aisles and must be a minimum of 44" wide. End aisles run perpendicular to side aisles and must be a minimum of 36" wide. They can serve a single-faced section of stacks and in certain instances 44" may be required. Range and side aisles in magazine and other display area must be a minimum of 44" wide.

Stack Aisles and Column Spacing

In addition to planning the space required to house collections, determining the aisle requirements early in the project can provide valuable information to the architect and structural engineer. The stack aisle requirement and the column spacing should be coordinated to create a satisfactory stack layout. Without this advance coordination valuable space can be lost when aisles are blocked or valuable stack units lost to unexpected columns. In planning the structural requirements, a bay or module is the space between four columns and with good planning this dimension should equal some multiple of the stack unit width and the shelving aisle requirement.

A 2' base shelf with a 3' aisle requirement would indicate an ideal column bay of some multiple of 5' in at least one direction. This would typically be a distance of 25' from one column to another. Including the column dimensions for a 6" square column, the measurement is taken from mid-column to mid-column to produce an ideal module of 25'6". If 4' aisles are requested, then the column bay would be based on a 6' module and 24'6" or 30'6" might be the ideal module. The dimension in the other direction might be based on multiples of 3' with a 6" column at the end of every 5th or 6th range depending on the structural requirements of the facility.

6

Computer-Based Library Information Systems

COMPUTER TECHNOLOGY

But things changed fast. By the 1990's a university student would typically own his own computer and have exclusive use of it in his dorm room. This transformation was a result of the invention of the microprocessor.

A microprocessor (uP) is a computer that is fabricated on an integrated circuit (IC). Computers had been around for 20 years before the first microprocessor was developed at Intel in 1971. The micro in the name microprocessor refers to the physical size. Intel didn't invent the electronic computer. But they were the first to succeed in cramming an entire computer on a single chip (IC). Intel was started in 1968 and initially produced only semiconductor memory.

In 1969 they were approached by Busicom, a Japanese manufacturer of high performance calculators. Busicom wanted Intel to produce custom calculator chips: one chip dedicated to the keyboard, another chip dedicated to the display, another for the printer, etc. But integrated circuits were expensive to design and this approach would have required Busicom to bear the full expense of developing new chips since, these chips would only be of use to them. But a new Intel employee convinced Busicom to instead accept a general purpose computer chip which, like all computers, could be reprogrammed for many different tasks. Intel argued that since, the chip could be reprogrammed for alternative purposes, the cost of developing it could be spread out over more users and hence, would be less expensive to each user. The general purpose computer is adapted to each new purpose by writing a programme which is a sequence of instructions stored in memory.

TYPES OF COMPUTERS

A computer is a machine that can be programmed to manipulate symbols. *Its principal characteristics are:*

- It responds to a specific set of instructions in a well-defined manner;
- It can execute a prerecorded list of instructions (a programme);
- It can quickly store and retrieve large amounts of data.

Therefore computers can perform complex and repetitive procedures quickly, precisely and reliably. Modern computers are electronic and digital. The actual machinery (wires, transistors, and circuits) is called hardware; the instructions and data are called software.

All general-purpose computers require the following hardware components:

- *Central Processing Unit (CPU)*: The heart of the computer, this is the component that actually executes instructions organised in programmes ('software') which tell the computer what to do.
- *Memory (fast, expensive, short-term memory)*: Enables a computer to store, at least temporarily, data, programmes, and intermediate results.
- *Mass storage device (slower, cheaper, long-term memory)*: Allows a computer to permanently retain large amounts of data and programmes between jobs. Common mass storage devices include disk drives and tape drives.
- *Input device:* Usually a keyboard and mouse, the input device is the conduit through which data and instructions enter a computer.
- *Output device*: A display screen, printer, or other device that lets you see what the computer has accomplished.

In addition to these components, many others make it possible for the basic components to work together efficiently. For example, every computer requires a bus that transmits data from one part of the computer to another.

COMPUTER SIZES AND POWER

- Computers can be generally classified by size and power as follows, though there is considerable overlap:
- *Personal computer*: A small, single-user computer based on a microprocessor.
- *Workstation*: A powerful, single-user computer. A workstation is like a personal computer, but it has a more powerful microprocessor and, in general, a higher-quality monitor.
- *Minicomputer*: A multi-user computer capable of supporting up to hundreds of users simultaneously.
- *Mainframe*: A powerful multi-user computer capable of supporting many hundreds or thousands of users simultaneously.
- *Supercomputer*: An extremely fast computer that can perform hundreds of millions of instructions per second.

SUPERCOMPUTER AND MAINFRAME

Supercomputer is a broad term for one of the fastest computers currently available. Supercomputers are very expensive and are employed for specialised applications that require immense amounts of mathematical calculations. For example, weather forecasting requires a supercomputer.

Other uses of supercomputers scientific simulations, (animated) graphics, fluid dynamic calculations, nuclear energy research, electronic design, and analysis of geological data (*e.g.,* in petrochemical prospecting). Mainframe was a term originally referring to the cabinet containing the central processor unit or 'main frame' of a room-filling Stone Age batch machine.

After the emergence of smaller 'minicomputer' designs in the early 1970s, the traditional big iron machines were described as 'mainframe computers' and eventually just as mainframes. Nowadays a Mainframe is a very large and expensive computer capable of supporting hundreds, or even thousands, of users simultaneously.The chief difference between a supercomputer and a mainframe is that a supercomputer channels all its power into executing a few programmes as fast as possible, whereas a mainframe uses its power to execute many programmes concurrently.

In some ways, mainframes are more powerful than supercomputers because they support more simultaneous programmes. But supercomputers can execute a single programme faster than a mainframe. The distinction between small mainframes and minicomputers is vague, depending really on how the manufacturer wants to market its machines.

MINICOMPUTER

It is a midsize computer. In the past decade, the distinction between large minicomputers and small mainframes has blurred, however, as has the distinction between small minicomputers and workstations. But in general, a minicomputer is a multiprocessing system capable of supporting from up to 200 users simultaneously.

WORKSTATION

It is a type of computer used for engineering applications (CAD/CAM), desktop publishing, software development, and other types of applications that require a moderate amount of computing power and relatively high quality graphics capabilities. Workstations generally come with a large, high-resolution graphics screen, at large amount of RAM, built-in network support, and a graphical user interface.

Most workstations also have a mass storage device such as a disk drive, but a special type of workstation, called a diskless workstation, comes without a disk drive. The most common operating systems for workstations are UNIX and Windows NT. Like personal computers, most workstations are single-user computers. However, workstations are typically linked together to form a local-area network, although they can also be used as stand-alone systems.

PERSONAL COMPUTER

It can be defined as a small, relatively inexpensive computer designed for an individual user. In price, personal computers range anywhere from a few hundred pounds to over five thousand pounds.

All are based on the microprocessor technology that enables manufacturers to put an entire CPU on one chip. Businesses use personal computers for word processing, accounting, desktop publishing, and for running spreadsheet and database management applications.

At home, the most popular use for personal computers is for playing games and recently for surfing the Internet. Personal computers first appeared in the late 1970s. One of the first and most popular personal computers was the Apple II, introduced in 1977 by Apple Computer. During the late 1970s and early 1980s, new models and competing operating systems seemed to appear daily.

Then, in 1981, IBM entered the fray with its first personal computer, known as the IBM PC. The IBM PC quickly became the personal computer of choice, and most other personal computer manufacturers fell by the wayside. P.C. is short for personal computer or IBM PC.

One of the few companies to survive IBM's onslaught was Apple Computer, which remains a major player in the personal computer marketplace. Other companies adjusted to IBM's dominance by building IBM clones, computers that were internally almost the same as the IBM PC, but that cost less. Because IBM clones used the same microprocessors as IBM PCs, they were capable of running the same software.

Over the years, IBM has lost much of its influence in directing the evolution of PCs. Therefore after the release of the first PC by IBM the term PC increasingly came to mean IBM or IBM-compatible personal computers, to the exclusion of other types of personal computers, such as Macintoshes. In recent years, the term PC has become more and more difficult to pin down.

In general, though, it applies to any personal computer based on an Intel microprocessor, or on an Intel-compatible microprocessor. For nearly every other component, including the operating system, there are several options, all of which fall under the rubric of PC Today, the world of personal computers is basically divided between Apple Macintoshes and PCs.

The principal characteristics of personal computers are that they are single-user systems and are based on microprocessors. However, although personal computers are designed as single-user systems, it is common to link them together to form a network.

In terms of power, there is great variety. At the high end, the distinction between personal computers and workstations has faded. High-end models of the Macintosh and PC offer the same computing power and graphics capability as low-end workstations by Sun Microsystems, Hewlett-Packard, and DEC.

INTERNET SEARCHING IN LIBRARY

In 300 B.C., the Library of Alexandria held some half million scrolls and served as a cultural centre for the world, uniting the thoughts of Greek, Egyptian, Macedonian and Babylonian culture. The Letter of Aristeas, the library had "a large budget in order to collect, if possible, all the books in the world." Whole fields of study such as geometry and grammar grew from the scholars who had the fortune to travel to and study at Alexandria.

In 2003 A.D., the Internet forms a distributed library of billions of pages, one that is accessible to anyone, anywhere in the world, at the click of a mouse. Every day hundreds of millions of 'trips' to the library start with a query to an Internet search engine. If I want to research a topic such as 'Library of Alexandria,' I can type those words to a search engine and in less than a second have access to a list of 14,000 pages, sorted by their usefulness to the query. This unprecedented ease of access to information has revolutionised the way research is done by students, scientists, journalists, shoppers, and others. It opens up an online marketplace of products, services, and ideas that benefits both information providers and seekers; sellers and buyers; consumers and advertisers.

How is it that an Internet Search engine can find the answers to a query so quickly? It is a four-step process:

- Crawling the Web, following links to find pages;
- Indexing the pages to create an index from every word to every place it occurs;
- Ranking the pages so the best ones show up first; and
- Displaying the results in a way that is easy for the user to understand.

Crawling is conceptually quite simple: starting at some well-known sites on the web, recursively follow every hypertext link, recording the pages encountered along the way. In computer science this is called the transitive closure of the link relation. However, the conceptual simplicity hides a large number of practical complications: sites may be busy or down at one point, and come back to life later; pages may be duplicated at multiple sites and must be dealt with accordingly; many pages have text that does not conform to the standards for HTML, HTTP redirection, robot exclusion, or other protocols; some information is hard to access because it is hidden behind a form, Flash animation or Javascript programme.

Finally, the necessity of crawling 100 million pages a day means that building a crawler is an exercise in distributed computing, requiring many computers that must work together and schedule their actions so as to get to all the pages without overwhelming any one site with too many requests at once. A search engine's index is similar to the index in the back of a book: it is used to find the pages on which a word occurs. There are two main differences: the search engine's index lists every occurrence of every word, not just the important concepts, and the number of pages is in the billions, not hundreds. Various techniques of compression and clever representation are used to keep the index 'small,' but it is still measured in terabytes, which again means that distributed computing is required. Most modern search engines index link data as well as word data.

It is useful to know how many pages link to a given page, and what are the quality of those pages. This kind of analysis is similar to citation analysis in bibliographic work, and helps establish which pages are authoritative. Algorithms such as PageRank and HITS are used to assign a numeric measure of authority to each page.

For example, the PageRank algorithm says that the rank of a page is a function of the sum of the ranks of the pages that link to the page. If we let PR(p) be the PageRank of page p, Out(p) be the number of outgoing links from page p, Links(p) be the set of pages that link to page p and N be the total number of pages in the index, then we can define PageRank by,

$$PR(p) = r/N + (1 -_{,}) \sum_{i} \subset Links(p)^{PR(i)/Out(i)}$$

where r is a parameter that indicates the probability that a user will choose not to follow a link, but will instead restart at some other page. The r/N term means that each of the N pages is equally likely to be the restart point, although it is also possible to use a smaller subset of well-known pages as the restart candidates. Note that the formula for PageRank is recursive— PR appears on both the right-and left-hand sides of the equation.

The equation can be solved by iterating several times, or by standard linear algebra techniques for computing the Eigen values of a matrix. The two steps are query independent—they do not depend on the user's query, and thus can be done before a query is issued with the cost shared among all users. This is why a search takes a second or less, rather than the days it would take if a search engine had to crawl the web anew for each query. We now consider what happens when a user types a query. Consider the query, where the square brackets denote the beginning and end of the query, and the quotation marks indicate that the enclosed words must be found as an exact phrase match.

The first step in responding to this query is to look in the index for the hit lists corresponding to each of the four words 'National,' 'Academies,' 'computer' and 'science.' These four lists are then intersected to yield the set of pages that mention all four words. Because 'National Academies' was entered as a phrase, only hits where these two words appear adjacent and in that order are counted. The result is a list of 19,000 or so pages. The next step is ranking these 19,000 pages to decide which ones are most relevant. In traditional information retrieval this is done by counting the number of occurrences of each word, weighing rare words more heavily than frequent words, and normalising for the length of the page.

A number of refinements on this scheme have been developed, so it is common to give more credit for pages where the words occur near each other, where the words are in bold or large font, or in a title, or where the words occur in the anchor text of a link that points to the page. In addition the query-independent authority of each page is factored in. The result is a numeric score for each page that can be used to sort them best-first. Traditionally this is done by listing a short description of each result in rank-sorted order. The description will include the title of the page and may include additional information such as a short abstract or excerpt from the page.

Some search engines generate query-independent abstracts while others customise each excerpt to show at least some of the words from the query. Displaying this kind of query-dependent excerpt means that the search engine must keep a copy of the full text of the pages at a cost of several more terabytes.

Some search engines attempt to cluster the result pages into coherent categories or folders, although this technology is not yet mature. Studies have shown that the most popular uses of computers are e-mail, word processing and Internet searching.

Of the three, Internet searching is by far the most sophisticated example of computer science technology. Building a high-quality search engine requires extensive knowledge and experience in information retrieval, data structure design, user interfaces, and distributed systems implementation.

Future advances in searching will increasingly depend on statistical natural language processing and machine learning techniques. With so much data—billions of pages, tens of billions of links, and hundreds of millions of queries per day—it makes sense to use data mining approaches to automatically improve the system. For example, several search engines now do spelling correction of user queries. It turns out that the vast amount of correctly and incorrectly spelled text available to a search engine makes it easier to create a good spelling corrector than traditional techniques based on dictionaries. It is likely that there will be other examples of text understanding that can be done better with a data-oriented approach; this is an area that search engines are just beginning to explore.

OPEN DATA, INTERNET RESOURCES WEB SITES AND LITERACY

The public, graphic Internet is a young technology. It is so young that it has only endured one significant change.

It has morphed from being a passive information tool where large companies and organisations posted documents and has become, as well, a place where anyone can and does contribute opinions about events and thoughts or their personal lives.

We are beginning to see a third major change in the web. This change is characterised by people being sent information that their profile suggests they might like to receive. Singles Around Me (SAM) is a dating app for smartphones. It links to social media profiles and lets users know when single people who match their interests are physically close, in any city. This is a huge shift from a web that provided passive web pages waiting to be viewed.

FOUR PRIORITIES FOR THE 21ST CENTURY PUBLIC LIBRARY SERVICE

- Place the library as the hub of a community.
- Make the most of digital technology and creative media.
- Ensure that libraries are resilient and sustainable.
- Deliver the right skills for those who work for libraries.

The key issues emerging in this research are similar to those we handle with the wider arts and cultural sector. It is because there is such a close fit with the Arts Council's five long term goals that we will be able to develop solutions to these challenges from which both libraries and arts organisations can benefit.

PLACE THE LIBRARY AS THE HUB OF A COMMUNITY

We know that, in future, many people are likely to lead more isolated lives. More will work from home and more will live alone. Opportunities to meet in free public spaces for a wide variety of purposes will be increasingly important. Our findings show that libraries will continue to be valued as trusted, safe, democratic places that offer valuable resources and expertise to support the activities of the people who use them.

Libraries' physical space will be more flexible and integrated with a virtual presence that includes web-based reading groups, social networking and links to other online resources. People will engage in creative and cultural activities as well as reading and learning, exchanging ideas, conversation and knowledge.

Space shared with community based services (such as council, health, business support, and learning organisations) will be better for local people, and will bring benefits such as skills exchanges, reaching more people and cutting costs.

The challenge: the use of a library's space:

- Re-think the way library spaces are used to encourage shared and creative activity while continuing to welcome those who want to explore on their own
- Integrate the library's physical and virtual spaces
- Sustain enough spaces offered by libraries to meet the needs of their communities

MAKE THE MOST OF DIGITAL TECHNOLOGY AND CREATIVE MEDIA

Digital technology is developing rapidly and will continue to have a major impact on the way we obtain and consume information, culture and the written word. Beyond the library building, people will expect a more interactive experience and to be able to gain access to library services all day, every day, particularly while on the move.

Libraries should be at the heart of digital innovation. They should develop their role in actively connecting communities and helping people to experience, experiment with and master new technologies. Digital technology will be the key to future library service delivery but our research points out that its true potential will not be achieved unless the principle of an open, enabling ICT infrastructure is agreed by local authorities and library services.

This would allow libraries to innovate, and to share or jointly adopt services more efficiently. By making it easier to develop national services and enable local innovation, people will get access to more resources, information and support. Many assume that digital information sources and online services are accessible to everyone.

But a digital divide still exists because a significant number of people lack the confidence, the necessary skills or the desire to make effective use of technology. Some who do, are held back by poor digital connections or can't afford them. Public libraries will ensure that no-one needs to be left behind or excluded.

The challenge: using technology:

- Improve the quality and consistency of the virtual library experience
- Develop an open ICT infrastructure that encourages innovation and better service
- Enable libraries to lend the full range of e-books, including remotely

DELIVER THE RIGHT SKILLS FOR THOSE WHO WORK FOR LIBRARIES

Our research indicates that one of the major challenges facing public libraries in the future is ensuring that library staff have effective leadership and delivery skills for a rapidly evolving service. Librarians will need to be active in their communities, encouraging people to get involved with their library. That involvement will include local people identifying what their priorities are as well as volunteering and community managed services.

Supporting people in using digital resources competently and confidently will become increasingly important. Those who work in libraries will need to improve their skills in organising and helping users to find their way through complicated information sources. They will become more pro-active in inspiring new services in partnership with others, and their leaders will need to be more entrepreneurial and adept in communicating and marketing their services.

Our research indicates that not enough people working in libraries are equipped to tackle these changes and take on these roles, and that current training is not always relevant for the current and future needs of those working in public libraries.

The challenge: developing the skills of those who work in libraries:

- Ensure those responsible for libraries have the right range of skills and experience to lead their services successfully
- Encourage those working in libraries to offer creative and innovative ways to use library spaces, books and other resources
- Ensure that library staff have the skills to develop and respond to digital developments and to support digital users.

IMPACT OF INTERNET ON LIBRARY AND INFORMATION SERVICES

Perhaps no other recent innovation has impacted the library profession to such a great extent as Internet. Not only is our world becoming an interconnected global community, but this early use of the Internet has changed the fundamental roles, paradigms, and organisational culture of libraries and librarians as well, which created profound impact on LandIS by offering new modes of information delivery and a vast information source.

There is a continuing evolution of the roles and functions of libraries and librarians, which appears to parallel the growth of acceptance and use of the Internet by library professionals. The innovative use of Internet technologies enable us to reach both local and distant users much more easily and effectively than hither to possible.

Technologies such as e-mail and Web provides tremendous opportunities for library and Inf. Scientists to deliver the information to the desktops of our users. Web offers significant advantage by integrating different library and information services with a common user interface offered by Web browsers. Realising the potentials, many libraries are rushing to getting the connectivity. The following listing will give an idea of which various functions of libraries may take advantage from Internet and Web technologies.

Acquisition:

- Correspondance with Book seller and Publisher.
- Reminders, Price verification
- Biblographic details and downloading of bib. records etc
- Ordering, billing
- Bookshops are on-line, *e.g.,* amazon.com

Classification:

- Network resources
  - Available on the net
  - Subscribed or free or trial basis
- Dewey Online
- Maths. Classification System
- Engineering Electronics Lib. Classification
- Search engines – such as yahoo use DDC.

Collection Development:

- Ownership vs Access
- Subscribe in print or e-form
- Subscribe in print as well as in e-form
- Pay-per-use
- Consortial approach

Cataloguing:

- Cataloguing of network resources
- Online Catalogues
- WorldCat (OCLC)
- WebOPAC – web sites
- MARC adds 856 field
- OCLC Scorpian project- MARC and AACR2
- Metadata standards - Dublin core

Circulation:

- Remote login
- Status check
- OPAC access
- Reminder to users
- User requests
- Direct borrowing
- ILL

Resource Sharing:

- Union Catalogue
  - Access, adding, downloading
- Access to databases over networks
  - Ohionet, ILLINET, WLN, OCLC, BID (UK)
  - Full text journals access, etc.

Services:

- ILL
- Document Delivery Service, *e.g.,* Ariel
- Reference/ Inf. Services
- CAS
  - Recent additions,
  - Contents pages
- SDI
  - From library collection
  - Databases
  - Internet Sources
- OPAC
- Database access
  - Bibliographical
  - Full text

- Many vendors and organisations are moving to Internet (web) access

Subject Lists/ Gateways:

- Internet Public Library
- *EEVL* – Engineering
- *SOSIG* – Social Science
- *OMNI*- Medical
- *ADAM* – Arts, Design, etc.

User Education:

- Through E-mail
- Through Web
- Setting Intranet.

Preservation and Storage:

- The Internet is also a medium for the preservation and storage of information. In past, libraries were seen as the main storage facility of information. As society becomes increasingly more digital and more information resides on the Internet, the focus on storage and preservation is shifting. For example, some academic libraries are now faced with the problem of whether or not to purchase serials that can be just as easily accessed on-line. Preservation of these same media also becomes an issue of economics, not the 'just in case' preservation ideology of the past paradigm. Co joined to the function preservation is the destruction of information. Because the Internet can be seen as a medium for preserving information, the process of destruction of information also is affected. As more and more information is created and stored on the Internet, the capacity to store this information is also decreasing.

RETRIEVAL OF INFORMATION

Directories, Search Engines, Meta Search Engines and Information Gateways/Virtual Libraries etc are widely used to retrieve relevant information from Internet.

Search Engines:

- They are also called Meta crawlers or multi search engines
- Do not crawl the web compiling their own searchable databases
- Search the databases of multiple sets of individual search engines simultaneously from a single site and using the same interface.
- They function as intermediary
- Present the results of their searches in two ways
  - Single lists
  - Multiple Lists.
- There are three types of meta search engines,

  - Listing
  - Options
  - Automatic
- While you query, options less
- Cover all major search engines
- Do not return all results retrieved, they take only top ones from the list.
- They are very fast.
- Use them when you are in a hurry
- Helpful when you want to have quick overview on a subject and/or unique term.
- Use them when you are,
  - Conducting a relatively simple search
  - Not having any luck pulling up documents in your search.

RESOURCES AVAILABLE ON THE INTERNET

The advent of IT and other communication technologies changed all means of information services and sources. The Internet has given the world numerous easy-to-use and inexpensive research tools. Internet is changing the way we view information sources. Information bundled in World Wide Web in the form of structured and Non-structured sources create huge problem for professionals who are dealing with information. The shift in publication process takes place as individuals, institutions, publishers, professional associations, business houses and many others are publishing information on Internet.

Electronic publishing is considered as the speedy, accurate and effective way of communication among academia and research community, and becoming a favorite idea among information professionals to experiment with. The library and information professionals have a vital role to play in organising the information and bridging the *information gap*. Internet has become a part of library environment today. Internet for reference work in the library is gaining popularity.

It can be successfully utilised for providing short-range and long-range reference service because various primary and secondary sources of information are available online from many sites. As information professionals, we can arrange the sources on net as we come across, in a structured manner.

These can be:

- E-journals
- E-books
- Standards
- E-TDs
- Preprints
- Library catalogue
- Bibliographical Tools

- Share wares
- Old books
- News papers
- Dictionaries
- Magazines
- Encyclopaedias
- Databases
- Directories
- Films
- Maps
- Technical reports
- Audio/Video
- Proceedings
- Patents
- Web sites of Companies, Institutions, Organisations, Associations, etc.

EVALUATION OF INFORMATION SOURCES

When we access or retrieve something on the Web, we need to decide whether the information is useful, reliable, and appropriate for our purposes. The resources identified can also occasionally contain inaccurate and misleading information. The nature of the Internet and WWW makes it easy for almost anyone to create and disperse information.

People also have considerable freedom and variety in the formats with which they publish information on the Web. We have to double -check the facts before giving it to users. Here we need to use some general guidelines or criteria when evaluating information sources.

We should ask the following questions about whatever information we found:

- Who is the author or Institution?
- How current is the information?
- Who is the audience?
- Is the content accurate and objective?
- What is the purpose of the information?
- How easy to use it?

More than that, we can consider coverage, presentation and arrangement of information in the sources to find out its value. The tremendous increase in online information sources made the searching difficult, where organising skill is required for library and information professionals. Libraries role is also enhanced where they will have to adapt to changing environment.

The scope is only limited to the imagination of information professionals, where they have to acquire thorough understanding of changes in their profession. Willingness to take up the challenges in information resource management is the need of the hour for us.

WEB SITE FOR A LIBRARY

The roles of libraries and the Internet in providing information in the 21st century are firmly intertwined. It behooves any librarian working today to understand not only how to find things on the World Wide Web, but to have a basic understanding of how it works. Librarians will be called on to become information architects, to be able to create Web sites with clearly stated goals, that are aesthetically pleasing and filled with relevent content and functionality.

As more and more libraries set up comprehensive Web sites, there becomes an increasing demand for librarians who have an understanding of HTML, as well as other types of Internet programming skills such as javascript, SQL, CGI, ASP, and Cold Fusion. Librarians should know the principles of setting up an efficient information resource. As the Internet becomes more interactive, there is a push Towards making databases accessible online; the best example of this is the library card catalog. Other interactive options include e-mail and bulletin board service, and moving from CD-ROMs to online subscriptions.

A library Web site is not merely establishing a presence on the Internet. It can be a virtual addition to the existing library structure, reaching out to patrons around the clock and providing valuable information resources. Additionally, a library's Web site is an important source of information about the library. The library's Internet policies, special programming, and new materials can all be made viewable at any time from the Web site. Libraries, too, should be designing their own Web sites that serve as portals to interesting sites that have been reviewed and annotated by professional librarians. Librarians will continue to play an important role as information professionals in the Information Age, well into the 21st century.

DIGITAL LIBRARIES OF THE FUTURE AND THE ROLE OF LIBRARIES

Research on digital library (DL) systems started in Europe in the mid-nineties. At that time DLs were seen essentially as repositories of digital texts accessible through a search service which was operating by indexing information stored in a centralised metadata catalogue. The construction of a DL was very resourceconsuming since, for each new DL, both the content and the software providing the DL functionality were built from scratch. As a result of this development approach, only powerful user communities or user communities with in-house computer science technical skills could afford the building up of DLs. These DLs were created to serve end-users only as consumers of information. They did not provide any functionality for submitting the documents.

The submission was usually performed either by the author or by a librarian operator by means of specific procedures residing outside the DL. Today, the requirements imposed on DLs are very different from that early time. A novel notion of DLs, also referred to as "knowledge commons" has recently emerged, whose fulfilment requires new technologies and new organisational models. This paper focuses on such new DLs by first discussing the motivations for their introduction, then presenting an innovative DL technology, called DILIGENT, and, finally, illustrating the role that libraries can play in this new scenario.

DIGITAL LIBRARIES OF THE FUTURE

According to the most recent understanding, the DLs of the future will be able to operate over a large variety of information object types - far wider than those maintained today in physical libraries and archives. These information objects will be composed of several multi-type and multimedia components aggregated in an unlimited number of formats. These, for example, can mix text, tables of scientific data and images obtained by processing earth observation data, or they can integrate 3D images, annotations and videos. These new information objects will offer innovative and more powerful means to researchers for sharing and discussing the results of their work. In order to be able to support these objects, the DL functionality has to be appropriately extended far beyond that required to manipulate the simple digital surrogates of the physical objects. In order to support these objects the DL may need considerable resources.

For example, the creation and handling of the new documents may require access to many different, large, heterogeneous information sources, the use of specialised services that process the objects stored in these sources for producing new information, and the exploitation of large processing capabilities for performing this tasks. New DLs are also required to offer a much richer set of services to their users than in the past. In particular, they must support the activities of their users by providing functionalities that may range from general utilities, like annotation, summarisation or co-operative work support, to very audience-specific functions, like map processing, semantic analysis of images, or simulation. The availability of this new DL functionality can, in principle, change the way in which research is conducted.

By exploiting such types of DL, for example, a scientist can annotate the article of a colleague with a programme that extracts useful information from a large amount of data collected by a specific scientific observatory. This programme, executed on demand when the annotation is accessed, can complement the content of the paper with continuously refreshed information. In the new DLs users are not only consumers but also producers of information. By elaborating information gathered through the DL they can create new information objects that are published in the DL, thus enriching its content. The new DLs are thus required to offer services that support the authoring of these new objects and the workflows that lead to their publication. In parallel with the evolution of the role of DL systems, we are now observing a large expansion in the demand for DLs.

Research today is often a collaborative effort carried out by groups belonging to different organisations spread worldwide. Motivated by a common goal and funding opportunities, these groups dynamically aggregate into virtual research organisations that share their resources, *e.g.* knowledge, experimentation results, or instruments, for the duration of their collaboration, creating new and more powerful virtual research environments. These virtual research organisations, set up by individuals that do not necessarily have great economic power or technical expertise, more and more frequently require DLs as tools for accelerating the achievement of their research results. This new potential audience demands less expensive and more dynamic DL development models.

They want to be able to set up new DLs that serve their needs for the duration of their collaborations in an acceptable timeframe and with an acceptable cost. The current DL development model cannot satisfy this large demand; a radical change is needed if we want to be able to address these new emerging requirements. A great contribution towards the satisfaction of all the requirements can certainly come from the introduction of mechanisms that support a controlled sharing of resources among different organisations. Sharing in this context is not only applied to repositories of content, as is usually meant today, but can be extended to any type of resource needed to build a DL, *i.e.* language and ontology resources, applications, computers and even staff with the necessary skills for supporting the DL development, deployment and maintenance.

Supporting this type of sharing requires the introduction of appropriate solutions at both the technological and organisational levels. These two levels are not independent; instead they strongly influence each other. In fact, the availability of a good technological solution favours the creation of an appropriate organisation, and vice-versa, a successful organisation stimulates the development of new supporting technologies. We present the Diligent infrastructure as an example of a technological solution for these new DLs. The organisational aspects stimulated by the introduction of this technology are briefly discussed afterwards.

DILIGENT

Diligent (DIgital Library Infrastructure on Grid ENabled Technology) is a three-year Integrated Project funded by the European Commission under the 6th Framework Programme for Research and Technological a Digital Library Infrastructure that will enable members of dynamic virtual research organisations to create on-demand transient digital libraries that exploit shared resources. Resources in this context are multimedia and multi-type content repositories, applications, and computing and storage elements. Following the understanding of DLs expressed in Borgman *et al.*, this project focuses on the development of DLs that "are not ends in themselves; rather they are enabling technologies for digital asset management, electronic commerce, electronic publishing, teaching and learning, and other activities".

From an abstract point of view, the Diligent infrastructure can be understood as a broker serving DL resource providers and consumers. The providers are the individuals and the organisations that decide to publish their resources under the supervision of the broker, according to certain access and use policies. The consumers are the user communities that want to build their own DLs. The resources managed by this broker are content sources (*i.e.* repositories of information searchable and accessible through a single "entrance"), services (*i.e.* software tools that implement a specific functionality and whose descriptions, interfaces and bindings are defined and publicly available) and hosting nodes (*i.e.* networked entities that offer computing and storage capabilities and supply an environment for hosting content sources and services).

Providers register their resources and give a description of them by exploiting appropriate mechanisms provided by the infrastructure. The infrastructure also automatically derives other properties of the resources that are used to enrich the explicit description. The infrastructure manages the registered resources by supporting their discovery, monitoring and usage, and by implementing a number of other functionalities that aim at realising the required controlled sharing and quality of service. A user community can create one or more DLs by specifying a set of requirements. These requirements specify conditions for the information space (*e.g.* publishing institutions, subject of the content, document types), for the operations that manipulate the information space (*e.g.* type of search, tool for data analysis), for the services for supporting the work of the users (*e.g.* type of personalised dissemination, type of collaboration), for the quality of service (*e.g.* configuration, availability, response time) and for many other aspects, like the maximum cost, or lifetime.

The broker satisfies the community's requirements by selecting, and in many cases also deploying, a number of resources among those accessible to the community, gluing them appropriately and, finally, making the new DL application accessible through a portal. The composition of a DL is dynamic since the DL broker continuously monitors the status of the DL resources and, if necessary, changes them in order to offer the best quality of service. By relying on the shared resources many DLs, serving different communities, can be created and modified on-the-fly, without big investments and changes in the organisations that set them up.

In order to support the transactions between the providers and the consumers, the DILIGENT infrastructure exploits the virtual organisations

(VOs) mechanism that has been introduced in the Grid research area. This mechanism models sets of users and resources aggregated together by highly controlled sharing rules, usually based on an authentication framework. VOs have a limited lifetime, are dynamically created and satisfy specific needs by allocating and providing resources on demand. Through the VOs mechanism the DILIGENT infrastructure glues together the users and the resources of a DL.

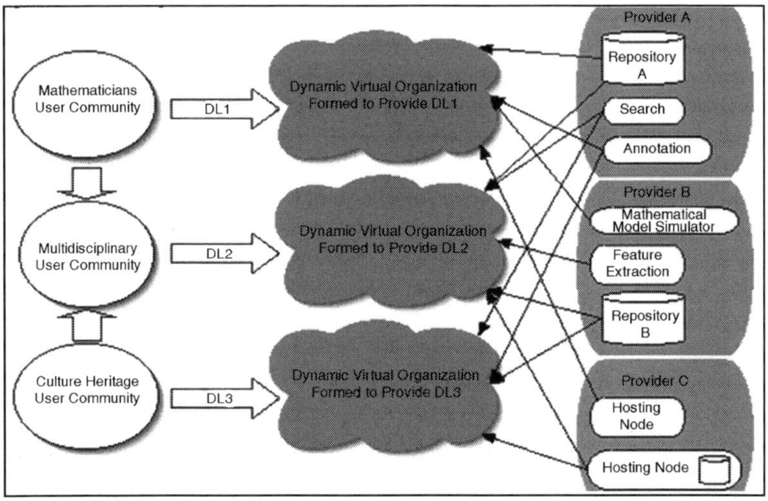

Fig. The Role of Virtual Organisations in DILIGENT.

Figure 1.1 graphically illustrates the role of VOs in supporting the brokerage model. The consumers, *i.e.* the user communities that require DLs to support their needs. The providers, each of which makes a number of resources available, are on the right. The infrastructure acts as a mediator by maintaining a framework where multiple virtual organisations, active on the same shared resources, can co-exist. The DL development model proposed by DILIGENT is radically new. Within the described framework each DL consumes the required resources only for the time it needs them.

This opens a lot of new opportunities for the creation of the functionalities required by the new "knowledge commons" environments. In particular, the exploitation of more effective, but also very computationally expensive algorithms becomes viable at an acceptable cost for many communities. For example, thanks to sharing, the use of the high processconsuming algorithms that automatically extract features from multi-media objects can be exploited in a large number of DLs. Moreover, in the framework established by the new development model, the user communities can easily, and in a timely manner, create and maintain their own DLs with limited resources since the management of the DL is automatically and transparently carried out by the infrastructure. The system that implements the functionality of the DILIGENT infrastructure is being built by integrating DL and Grid technologies. The motivation for this design choice relies on the similarity between many of the problems encountered through our new notion of DLs and the issues addressed by the most recent research in the Grid domain.

From the functional point of view, the DILIGENT system is divided into five functionality clusters:

- *DL Creation and Management:* is responsible for the dynamic construction and maintenance of the transient DLs and for the controlled sharing and management of the resources that are used to implement them. The functionalities offered by this cluster allow users to express the requirements that the DL must fulfil. Moreover, they automatically identify and arrange the pool of resources needed to satisfy these needs.
- *Content and Metadata Management:* implements the handling of DL content and related metadata, the consistent and distributed management of annotations, and the integration of external content and metadata sources.
- *Process Management:* manages the creation of user processes composed of existing services, the validation of their correctness, the automatic optimisation of their definition according to the resources available and the service characteristics, and their reliable execution. Thanks to this feature, the DILIGENT system can easily be enriched with additional operational workflows to meet new user requirements.
- *Index and Search Management:* is responsible for enabling cost-efficient search and retrieval of information in DLs, while satisfying the level of quality required for the overall data retrieval and delivery operations.
- *Application Specific Functionality:* provides the functionality needed to support user-specific scenarios, like portals, document visualisation, or features extraction.

From the architectural point of view, the DILIGENT system is designed as a Web Services Resource Framework (WSRF) application built on top of the gLite Grid middleware released by the Enabling Grids for Escience in Europe (EGEE) project. gLite hides the heterogeneous nature of the computing elements (*i.e.* services representing a computing resource) on the one hand and storage elements (*i.e.* services representing a storage resource) on the other hand by providing an environment that facilitates and controls their sharing. The DILIGENT services are being initially deployed on a project-proprietary gLite infrastructure. Architecturally, this infrastructure is completely interoperable with the EGEE infrastructure. EGEE is currently the largest European Grid infrastructure ever built.

A number of other recently funded projects will extend this infrastructure to other geographic regions, like Mediterranean countries, Latin America, or China. The interoperability with the EGEE infrastructure will allow any authorised virtual community that wishes to create DLs to also exploit the resources made available by this vast Grid infrastructure. During the project timeframe, the DILIGENT infrastructure will be populated with a number of important archives and software applications provided by the two communities that are participating in the experimentation with the results of the project, one from the environmental e-science domain and one from the cultural heritage domain.

The first community is ImpECt (Implementation of Environmental Conventions) and includes leading players in the environmental sector. This community will use DILIGENT to support the organisation of conferences and the preparation of projects and periodical reports. Through DILIGENT this community expects to improve accessibility, interoperability and usability of environmental data, models, tools, algorithms and instruments, integrating the distributed data sources with specialised data handling services. The second community, ARTE, is a community of scholars located in different parts of the world, working together to establish a new discipline that merges experiences from research in medicine, humanities, social sciences and communication.

In order to achieve their objectives, these researchers require instruments to ease the construction of multimedia artefacts and to improve support for education. At the time of the writing of this paper initial experimentation with the features of a DILIGENT DL has already been conducted by implementing simplified services for preparing environmental reports, as required by the ImpECt environmental agencies. Through the exploiting of rich information sources, ranging from raw data sets to maps and graphs archives, these agencies periodically prepare reports on the status of the environment. Currently, this task is performed by first selecting the relevant information from each of the multiple and heterogeneous sources available, then launching complex processing on large amounts of data to obtain "products", like graphs, tables and other summarised information and, finally, producing the required report by assembling all the different parts together.

This process, which is repeated periodically, requires a lot of work due to the complexity of interfacing the different sources and tools. Despite the effort expended, the resulting reports do not completely fulfil the requirements of their readers, who would like to have a picture of the environmental status which is updated at the time the report is accessed. A DILIGENT DL offers a more effective framework for the creation and maintenance of these reports. In our experimentation, for example, we have built a DL which exploits content maintained in both repositories including textual documents and archives of Earth observation raw data provided by the European Space Agency. In this

DL, which is accessible through a single user interface, all the different kinds of information necessary for creating the reports can be found.

By combining this information and by defining how to derive the associated "products" (images, tables, or graphs) from raw data, the users can create their reports much more easily. Moreover, a specialised user interface allows authorised users to access these composite reports by choosing static or dynamic generation. The selection of dynamic generation triggers associated process workflows which, by combining appropriate applications, generate the required products on demand by processing both the raw data and other intermediate products stored in the DL repositories. The dynamically generated products are obtained by running those applications that are computationally intensive on the Grid.

In this way the complex processes required to generate the products are executed in few minutes at a limited cost to the community that is exploiting them. In order to obtain the same performance without the Grid, an institution would have to equip its digital library with a great number of computers, while in the case of DILIGENT the institution can also exploit computer capabilities made available by third party organisations. The same is true for storage capacity. Maintaining raw data, intermediate products and high resolution images requires a large amount of storage capacity. By exploiting the Grid technology, part of this information, especially the temporary part, can be maintained in third-party storage systems.

THE ROLE OF LIBRARIES IN FUTURE DLs

In the framework envisaged by DILIGENT, libraries play an important role at the organisational level. In particular:

- As providers of resources, they can help to enhance the amount of available resources by making stakeholders aware of the importance of sharing. In particular, as far as the sharing of content is concerned, they can operate by promoting digitisation campaigns and the Open Access approach. These actions may result in a vast amount of new digital information accessible online which can be exploited by advanced services.
- Also within a digital framework, libraries are certainly the best candidates for carrying out content description, maintenance and preservation of resources. By exploiting their large experience acquired in the past, they can contribute to the long-term availability and to the quality of the resources disseminated by the DLs.
- Long-term availability also requires the implementation of models able to support the sustainability of the resources provided. Libraries, either alone or as members of library consortia, can also act as the organisations deputed to define and put in place these models.

- As main resource providers, libraries can work jointly on the definition of common policies and standards. An agreement on these aspects would strongly contribute towards facilitating the design and development of the new complex services required to fulfil the emerging user needs.
- In the future envisaged by DILIGENT, libraries can also play an important role as mediators between the infrastructure and the user communities. In particular, they can proactively promote and facilitate the creation of DLs that respond to the needs of the user communities. They can also assist users by providing, if necessary, the skills required to select, update and exploit the DL content and services.

INFORMATION TECHNOLOGY-BASED LIBRARY SERVICES

New information technology can potentially support a range of traditional and Non-traditional library services. Most of the library services generated using information technology resemble closely to those generated manually with improvements and modifications to suit the requirements of automated services.

OPAC AND WEBPAC

Remote access to the Library catalogues (OPAC) was possible only through a telnet connection before the Web was launched. The web-based interfaces are now available for most of the integrated library software packages including Libsys. Web sites are increasingly providing links to their webPAC instead of telnet links to their Library OPAC.

Exploiting the provisions of hyperlinking that the web provides, various searchable elements of a bibliographic record in a webPAC are hyperlinks to other records in the database. For example, an author is a hyperlink to all records in the database for that author, a series is an hyperlink to all serial title under that series; a keyword for a record is a link to all records in database having that keyword, ,etc.

In effect, a web PAC adds softwarebased functionality to a conventional OPAC. A user has additional incentives to visit the library web page hosting webPAC.

With web-based resources and services in place, many libraries are phasing out their dumb terminals. The library web sites are increasingly becoming a more logical gateway to the catalogue and other web-based library resources. The acceptability of web-based interfaces to the Library OPAC is much greater because web interfaces are familiar to the users with its graphical and navigational interfaces. The users can click complex subjects instead of typing them or remembering complex commands.

INFORMATION ALERTING SERVICES

As the name implies, information alerting services or Current Awareness Services (CAS) are produced by the libraries for their users to alert them about new developments in a given field of study. Information alerting services are issues periodically by the libraries either for internal distribution amongst staff and employees or externally to other users.

The alerting service may be issued as a newsletter reporting new developments, programmes, forthcoming seminars and conferences, events, training programmes, ,etc. It may also consist of recent additions of books and other documents in the library for a specified time period. Most library integrated system facilitate generation of such a service organised according to subject category for a given time period.

Alerting service may also consist of an indexing service issued by a library or a commercial publisher or a society that regularly indexes the contents of periodicals and some other publications systematically in a specified subject field. Such indexing services are issued at a regular interval. Abstracting services are essentially indexing services wherein an abstract of articles are included in addition to its bibliographic details. Index India and Reader's Guide to Periodical Literature are examples of indexing services. Biological Abstracts, Chemical Abstracts and Index Medicus are example of abstracting services. Most indexing and abstracting services are now available as web-based databases with sophisticated search interface.

Selective dissemination of information (SDI) is a personal form of Current Awareness Service (CAS). It refers to the mechanism of selectively directing new items of information from primary or secondary sources to individuals based on their current interests in a particular subject. SDI is delivered based on a user interest profile which is matched with updates on databases for finding the items of interest for a given user. Push technology or personalisation are more recent terms that are used in place of SDI.

DIGITAL REFERENCE SERVICE

Reference service and imparting instructional training to the library users are key areas of activities for any library. The technology now allows reference librarians to reach out to the users using the network instead of waiting at the reference desk for users to come by. Besides, imparting instructions on mechanisms of using a library, a reference librarian is also involved in delivering reference service that require deep intellectual understanding of subject.

Although automated libraries are not yet sufficiently advanced to offer interactive reference services, electronically-mediated reference services are increasingly available through libraries and information centres. Digital reference service, also called 'Ask-An-Expert' or 'Ask-A-Librarian' services are Internet-based question and answer service that connect users with individuals who possess specialised subject knowledge and skill in conducting precision searches.

As opposed to static web pages, digital reference services use the Internet to place people in contact with people who can answer specific question and instruct users on developing certain skills. The people who serve as digital reference experts (also called volunteers or mentors) are most of the time information specialists, affiliated to various libraries.

LIBRARY CHAT ROOMS

Several libraries have started experimenting with offering real time digital reference service, using chat software, live interactive communication activities, call counter management software, web contact software, bulletin board services, interactive customer assistance system or related technologies. Many libraries are experimenting with Internet chat technology as an innovative method to extend and enhance traditional and remote reference service.

While digital reference service is asynchronous method of information delivery, the Internet chat providing the benefit of synchronous communication between a user and a reference librarian (or mentor). Interactive reference services facilitate a user to talk to a real, live reference librarian at any time of day or night from anywhere in the world. Unlike with e-mail reference, the librarian can perform a reference interview of a sort by seeking clarifications from the user.

The librarian can conduct Internet searches and push Web sites onto the patron's browser, and can receive immediate feedback from the patron as to whether his or her question has been answered to his satisfaction. Most libraries currently involved in real-time reference service are part of a collaborative network so that they can share staffing and work around the clock to truly provide reference service any time. Library of Congress Collaborative Digital Reference Service is one of such services.

Several institutions including Cornell University, Internet Public Library, Michigan State University and North Carolina University are offering Internet chat-based services using software like LivePerson, AOL Instant Messenger, Conference Room and Netscape Chat. The librarians have observed that their relatively new chat-based service logged significantly more questions in a relatively short time than their well-established e-mail digital reference service. LiveRef(sm) maintains an online registry of real-time digital reference services.

ELECTRONIC DOCUMENT DELIVERY SERVICES

The term 'electronic document delivery systems' implies delivery of electronic version of a document that might involve reproduction of an electronic copy of a document if it is not available in electronic format. The libraries had been using fax machines for immediate delivery of photocopies of articles via telephone lines.

The first use of electronic document delivery was based on scanning technology. With maturity of scanning equipment and technology, document supply services started scanning the documents as bitmap page images. Applications are built in such a way so as to automatically produce a hard copy together with a header page containing the address of the applicant which can again be send by snail mail or facsimile. A software package known as 'Ariel' is used in several libraries in developed countries for delivery of scanned articles via Internet.

The Ariel software is loaded on an Internet-enabled computer, can receive and send electronic information to other libraries which have installed Ariel. Availability of most of the peer reviewed research journals in electronic format, inexpensive technology to scan articles and improved electronic delivery mechanisms are some of the enabling factors that have contributed to well-established electronic document delivery system now available commercially. More recently most of the secondary services that were available on CD ROM or through online search services are now available on the Internet where the bibliographic references are linked to their full-text on the publisher's site.

The technology has now been perfected and there are several electronic document delivery services that allow a user to download an article in full-text from their site or deliver them electronically as attachment to e-mails. Most electronic publishers and aggregators like OCLC, OVID ,etc., are offering full-text of articles through their web sites. Different vendors have various payment options; some charge each time the journal is used, whereas others provide open access for a set annual fee. A user who wishes to have the item delivered can enter a credit card number and specify a delivery method (postal, UPS, fax, e mail, ,etc.,) and indicate whether it is a rush item (with a rush order fee attached.) The ADONIS (Article Delivery Over Network information Systems) can be considered as a landmark development in electronic document delivery system. The project was launched by a consortium of five major publishers - Academic Press, Blackwell's Scientific Publications (merged with Wiley InterScience), Elsevier Science Publications, and Springer Verlag.

The project uses combination of laser scanning, printing and digital optical storage technology for storage and retrieval of complete pages of over 650 scientific, technical and medical journal articles. The issues of journals are available on CD ROM with weekly updates for distribution to each centre in various countries licensed to use the system for document delivery.

LIBRARY WEB SITES

Libraries are using web technology to create home pages as starting points or as gateways for searching information about the library. A home page reflects characteristics of an academic institution.

It provides an opportunity to the library to propagate its services and facilities to the academic community worldwide. The home pages of libraries are increasingly used as an integrated interface designed to deliver detailed information about a library as well as to provide access to all computer-based servicces offered by a library.

Several library web sites facilitate virtual guide to the physical facilities including collections, services and infrastructure available in the library through their web sites. Most library web sites provide library layouts and floor plans to guide users to physical location of facilities and services along with link to relevant information. Besides offering information, the library web sites of academic institutions invariably hosts subject gateways or subject portals that contains links to web resources for subjects of interest to the institution. Most of the IT-based library services mentioned in this article are offered through the web sites of libraries. The library web sites can have features like have Frequently Asked Questions (FAQ) along with their answers, library calendar listing events or show information for forthcoming events, Web forms for inviting feedback. Moreover, libraries may also use bulletin boards, threaded discussion forum and listservs to help promote and evolve web-based library services.

WEB-BASED USER EDUCATION

The www provides a dynamic environment for distributing information over a large network and web-based instructions is a suitable tool to do so. Web-based guides and teaching tools can be easily updated, accessed, and printed on demand. They may include colour graphics and screenshots. The web-based user education provides a high degree of interactivity and flexibility to the users offering them the benefit of self-pace, graduated to teach from basic to highly advanced levels and designed in a wide range of formats that accommodate diverse learning styles.

The proliferation of digital resources will generate greater demands on reference and instructional services. With availability of digital resources that can be used anywhere at any time, requirement for instructional and reference services would also grow. Failure to develop both the technological aspects and required service components would lead to under utilisation of digital resources. The library web sites can use web-based user education for imparting training to users in the following areas:

- Basic library skills along with glossary of library terms;
- Using Library OPAC/ webPAC, locating books, magazines and other library materials;
- Instructions for searching CD ROM and web-based databases and other electronic resources; and
- Instructions on subject searching training, using Boolean operators and searching Internet resources through search engines.

The web technology provides for incorporating both synchronous and asynchronous interactivity in the web-based user education.

CONCLUSION

So we can expect to see a shift from a service *provided* to a community to one in which *local people are more active and involved* in its design and delivery. Libraries will be recognised as connecting individuals, communities and organisations to innovate, create and provide new library based services and ideas. People will be using libraries to do more with each other and this activity will cross over between physical and virtual spaces. They will be creating new content, having conversations and using new technology for their own benefit, for their community or their business. Those working in libraries will be less occupied in straightforward transactions and more involved in linking people and organisations together in using library spaces and resources for new activities.

There will be a greater emphasis given to community, digital and entrepreneurial skills. In this context, volunteers offer new ways to add capacity and skills. Libraries' role out in the community, reaching vulnerable and excluded people, will extend to popping up temporarily as local circumstances demand and allow. This might involve using vacant spaces, or being invited in to other community services or workplaces to meet particular needs. If the library of the future will look different from those of the past and present, their enduring role and purpose means that some things will feel familiar. A high value will continue to be placed on the importance of quality leadership, professional skills and experience.

Books will sit comfortably alongside digital and other cultural resources in a rich and diverse library collection. Finding the information to answer any question, books to satisfy the never-ending desire for pleasure, learning and knowledge, and the practice of literacy as one of life's basic skills, will remain at the heart of what makes a library, and what will place the library at the heart of the community. Our national role means that we are well-placed to stimulate debate and offer support to the development of public libraries, and we want to work with our partners based on the thinking that has emerged in our research.

How that is reflected locally will be determined by each council based on their own priorities and the needs of their communities. It is this combination of enduring values, new thinking, collaborative leadership and flexibility that will equip public libraries to create economic and social benefits for this country and its communities long into the future.

7

Development of Public Libraries in India

Public libraries arose worldwide along with growth in education, literacy, and publications. Every country has its own public library history with influential leaders. Monarchs, wealthy people, and philanthropists have all made a contribution to society in the form of public library development. India is no exception. Libraries were established in ancient India mainly by the patronage extended by emperors, major capitalists, and scholars. Indian emperors and kings were supported scholars and scholarship. There is evidence of well-developed libraries even in the sixth century A.D. The famous Nalanda University in Bihar had its own magnificent library with a massive collection of manuscripts covering the universe of knowledge. Admission to library was restricted to scholars.

Other ancient universities, such as Taxila and Vikramashila, also had valuable libraries. Muslim influence in India during the 13th century A.D. marked the dawn of another era of learning and scholarship. The Mughal period gave a further stimulus to the growth of libraries. Mughal rulers attached considerable importance to libraries and appointed scholars as librarians.

The Mughal emperors were patrons of art and literature. In the period of Emperor Babur, Humayun, and Akbar many new libraries were established and existing ones further developed.

Mughal libraries featured magnificent buildings, rare manuscripts, and scholar librarians. The names of Maharaja Sawai Man Singh of Jaipur and Maharaja Ranjit Singh of Punjab will be remembered with appreciation in the history of library services in India.

The Maharaja of Tanjuar started the famous Saraswati Mahal Library in 17th century A.D. It remains a unique institution in its nature of collection and services Libraries established by the kings and capitalists functioned like private institutions and the admission was limited. Service to the general public had to wait for the British. Unfortunately, the arrival of the British and resulting political disorder also brought chaos to the Indian way of life. This was a severe blow to the cultural heritage of India, which had arisen from the Indus valley civilization. When libraries began developing in India during the early nineteenth century, they were a western product. In 1808, the Government of Bombay proposed to register libraries, which were to be given copies of books published from the "funds for the encouragement of literature". According to the "Sinha Committee", this was the beginning of the first phase of public library development in India. During the first half of the 19th century, the three presidency towns of Bombay, Calcutta, and Madras had public libraries. These libraries were mostly financed by Europeans residing in these towns.

Of these, the establishment of the public library at Calcutta in 1835 was the most significant. This was the library which later developed into the National Library of India. Almost simultaneous, subscription libraries were started in many Indian cities.

These were, of course, not public libraries in the true sense of the term, and did not provide free books for all. Founded in imitation of their western counterparts, the use of these libraries was confined to small, affluent portion of society.

The first three decades of the 20th century can be looked on as the golden age of the Indian library system. On January 31, 1902, the Imperial Library Act was passed and Lord Curzon transformed the Calcutta Public Library into the Imperial Library in 1906.

Developments in Baroda were also notable. Espranza sums them up:

- The development of public libraries in Baroda was unique. Baroda developed a network of public libraries to serve the entire Princely State. Maharaja Sayaji Rao Gackwad III of Baroda who traveled all over the world was deeply impressed by the role played by public libraries in the promotion of education in the United States and thought of extending such benefits to his own subjects. In 1910 he invited an American expert, William Alson Borden to organize the public library system for his state. The public library movement that flourished in Baroda was a glorious one. But that was not a general trend of that period because in no other part of India, a parallel development occurred.

Yet another development during the period was the organisation of a host of conferences such as:

- The first conference of library workers and persons interested in the library movement was held at Beswada, Andhra in 1914.
- The first All India Library Conference of Librarians was held in 1918 at Lahore.
- The first All India Library Conference was held at Calcutta in 1933.
- The first All India Public Library Conference was held at Madras in 1934.

With the existence of democratic governments in several provinces beginning in 1937, another phase of the library movement began. Between 1937 and 1942, a number of village libraries and travelling libraries sprang up in Assam, Bihar, Punjab, and Travancore.

It was estimated that there were about 13,000 village libraries in India in 1942. Another remarkable development was the appointment of the 'Library Development Committee' by the Government of Bombay, with A.A.A. Fyzee as its chairman. The Committee ambitiously recommended a comprehensive library system to be implemented in three successive stages. Because of financial constraints, the government could only implement part of the recommendations.

AFTER INDEPENDENCE

After independence, the growth of libraries in general has been remarkable, although not as remarkable as that of academic and special libraries. At the time of independence, India was facing a host of challenges. Those in the rural population, 88 percent of the total, were nearly all illiterate. Transportation was poor and mass media merely nominal. Nevertheless, the public library scene in India improved considerably during the post independence period, though it is still lacking on several fronts.

Verma and Agrawal argue that to compare our public libraries with those of the developed nations on equal footing, we have to go a long way. The 1951 census, the first conducted after independence, found 2,843 local governments in the urban and rural areas in India, of which 320 were rural district boards.

Only about one third of local governments maintained public libraries, about 950. In addition, there were about 1,500 subscription libraries. So-called public libraries were primarily reading rooms with a few hundred books for reading on the premises. The Delhi public library deserves special mention. It was founded in 1951 as the first UNESCO Public Library Pilot Project under the joint auspices of UNESCO and Government of India. The purpose of the library was to adapt "modern techniques to Indian conditions" and to serve as a model public library for Asia. The establishment of Delhi Public Library, the involvement of union government in the public library movement, and the enactment of public library legislation in some states are the main factors which contributed to the improvement of public libraries after independence. Although the government of India allotted funds for public library development in its five-year plans, this funding was not connected to effective planning.

ADVISORY COMMITTEE FOR LIBRARIES

The Government of India appointed a committee in 1957 to report on the status of public library development in the country. It is also called the Sinha Committee, after its chair, the late Dr. A.P. Sinha, who was at that time Director of Public Instruction in Bihar.

The Sinha Committee's charge included:

- Determining present reading needs, how they are met, and what part existing library systems play in meeting the needs;

- Determining reading tastes, what agencies provide suitable literature, and how reading taste can be improved;
- Recommending future library structure in India;
- Recommending areas of cooperation between libraries and education systems;
- Considering the training of librarians and the conditions of their service;
- Recommending the administrative and financial measures necessary to support public libraries in India.

The committee submitted its report to Dr. K.L. Shrimali, who was Minister for Education, on the 12th of November, 1958. The Committee described the situation as dismal and called libraries in most cases, "a stagnant pool of books," because new books were not added regularly. The committee at the same time observed that wherever large collections did exist, they were not fully used because of rigid rules. Library users were not trusted and were required to deposit large sums of money as a kind of insurance, which lower income people could not afford.

As of March 1954 there were 32,000 libraries in India, with a little more than 7,100,000 books and a total circulation of about 37,700,000. The report observed that genuine public library service was rarity, and that public library service throughout the country was unsatisfactory. The committee recommended creating state library networks based on uniform library legislation.

The chief recommendations of the report were:

- Library service should be made free to every citizen of India;
- The hierarchy of public library service in the country should begin with National Library, and proceed to State Central Library, District Library, Block Library, and Panchayat Library;
- An independent Director of Social Education and Libraries should be set up in every state, with a fulltime senior class-1 officer of the rank of Deputy Director of Education to plan, organize, and administer library services;
- An All India Library Advisory Council should be constituted as a central agency to review and assess the work done at the state level;
- Library Associations should actively assist the development of libraries in the country;
- University libraries should cooperate with public library systems by allowing selected public readers to use their collection;
- State governments should accept responsibility for public library services in their states;
- Librarians and social education workers should cooperate to promote literacy;

- A library cess of six paisa for each rupee of property tax should be levied with the permission of local bodies.
- The Government of India should match the amount collected in the states. State governments should also give matching grants to local bodies over the succeeding 25 years, their contribution should be raised to three times the cess collected.
- State and national governments should enact comprehensive state library laws incorporating the right of every citizen to have free access to libraries. The Government of India should provide necessary financial assistance to the state governments for this purpose.

PUBLIC LIBRARY

A public library is a library that is accessible by the public and is generally funded from public sources and operated by civil servants. There are five fundamental characteristics shared by public libraries. The first is that they are supported by taxes; they are governed by a board to serve the public interest; they are open to all and every community member can access the collection; they are entirely voluntary in that no one is ever forced to use the services provided; and public libraries provide basic services without charge.

Public libraries exist in many countries across the world and are often considered an essential part of having an educated and literate population. Public libraries are distinct from research libraries, school libraries, and other special libraries in that their mandate is to serve the general public's information needs.

Public libraries also provide free services such as preschool story times to encourage early literacy, quiet study and work areas for students and professionals, or book clubs to encourage appreciation of literature in adults. Public libraries typically allow users to take books and other materials off the premises temporarily; they also have non-circulating reference collections and provide computer and Internet access to patrons.

SERVICES OFFERED

In addition to print books and periodicals, most public libraries today have a wide array of other media including audiobooks, e-books, CDs, cassettes, videotapes, DVDs, and video games, as well as facilities to access the Internet and inter-library loans. Readers' advisory is a fundamental public library service that involves suggesting fiction and non-fiction titles.

Public libraries may also provide other services, such as community meeting rooms, storytelling sessions for infants, toddlers, preschool children, or after-school programmes, all with an intention of developing early literacy skills and a love of books. In person and on-line programmes for reader development, language learning, homework help, free lectures and cultural performances, and other community service programmes are common offerings.

One of the most popular programmes offered in public libraries are summer reading programmes for children, families, and adults. In rural areas, the local public library may have, in addition to its main branch, a mobile library service, consisting of one or more buses furnished as a small public library, serving the countryside according to a regular schedule.

Public libraries also provide materials for children, often housed in a special section. Child–oriented web sites with on-line educational games and programmes specifically designed for younger library users are becoming increasingly popular. Services may be provided for other groups, such as large print or Braille materials, Books on tape, young adult literature and other materials for teenagers, or materials in other than the national language.

California and Nevada now offer a new service called Link+. This new programme links county libraries across the two states, allowing patrons access to books their library may not have in their collection.

Librarians at most public libraries provide reference and research help to the general public, usually at a reference desk but can often be done by telephone interview. As online discussion and social networking allow for remote access, reference is becoming available virtually through the use of the Internet and e-mail.

Depending on the size of the library, there may be more than one desk; at some smaller libraries all transactions may occur at one desk, while large urban public libraries may employ subject-specialist librarians with the ability to staff multiple reference or information desks to answer queries about particular topics at any time during regular operating hours. Often the children's section in a public library has its own reference desk.

Public libraries are also increasingly making use of web 2.0 services, including the use of online social networks by libraries. Public libraries in some countries pay authors when their books are borrowed from libraries. These are known as Public Lending Right programme.

DIGITAL DIVIDE

As more commercial and governmental services are being provided online, public libraries increasingly provide Internet access for users who otherwise would not be able to connect to these services.

Part of the public library mission has become attempting to help bridge the digital divide. A study conducted in 2006 found that "72.5 per cent of library branches report that they are the only provider of free public computer and Internet access in their communities". A 2008 study found that "100 per cent of rural, high poverty outlets provide public Internet access, a significant increase from 85.7 per cent last year".

The *American Library Association* (ALA), addresses this role of libraries as part of "access to information" and "equity of access"; part of the profession's ethical commitment that "no one should be denied information because he or she cannot afford the cost of a book or periodical, have access to the internet or information in any of its various formats."

In addition to access, many public libraries offer training and support to computer users. Once access has been achieved, there still remains a large gap in people's online abilities and skills. For many communities, the public library is the only agency offering free computer classes and information technology learning.

As of 2008, 73.4 per cent of public libraries offered information technology training of some form, including information literacy skills and homework assignment help. A significant service provided by public libraries is assisting people with e-government access and use of federal, state and local government information, forms and services.

Internationally, public libraries offer *information and communication technology* (ICT) services, giving "access to information and knowledge" the "highest priority." While different countries and areas of the world have their own requirements, general services offered include free connection to the Internet, training in using the Internet, and relevant content in appropriate languages. In addition to typical public library financing, *non-governmental organizations* (NGOs) and business fund services that assist public libraries in combating the digital divide.

ORIGINS AS A SOCIAL INSTITUTION

The culmination of centuries of advances in the printing press, moveable type, paper, ink, publishing, and distribution, combined with an ever growing middle class, increased commercial activity and consumption, new radical ideas, massive population growth and higher literacy rates forged the public library into the form that it is today. Public libraries are not a new idea; Romans made scrolls in dry rooms available to patrons of the baths, and tried with some success to establish libraries within the empire.

Naturally, only those few that could afford an education would be able to use the library, where those less than rich or without control of money; women, children and slaves could not. In the middle of the 19th century, the push for truly public libraries, paid for by taxes and run by the state gained force after numerous depressions, droughts, wars and revolutions in Europe, felt mostly by the working class.

Matthew Battles states that:

> "It was in these years of class conflict and economic terror that the public library movement swept through Britain, as the nation's progressive elite recognized that the light of cultural and intellectual energy was lacking in the lives of commoners."

Libraries had often been started with a donation, an endowment or were bequeathed to various, parishes, churches, schools or towns, and these social and institutional libraries formed the base of many academic and public library collections of today.

Andrew Carnegie had the biggest influence in financing libraries in the United States of America, from the east to west coast. From just 1900 to 1917, almost 1,700 libraries were constructed by Carnegie's foundation, insisting that local communities first guarantee tax support of each library built.

The establishment of circulating libraries by booksellers and publishers provided a means of gaining profit and creating social centers within the community. The circulating libraries not only provided a place to sell books, but also a place to lend books for a price. These circulating libraries provided a variety of materials including the increasingly popular novels.

Although the circulating libraries filled an important role in society, members of the middle and upper classes often looked down upon these libraries that regularly sold material from their collections and provided materials that were less sophisticated. Circulating libraries also charged a subscription fee, however the fees were set to entice their patrons, providing subscriptions on a yearly, quarterly or monthly basis, without expecting the subscribers to purchase a share in the circulating library.

Circulating libraries were not exclusively lending institutions and often provided a place for other forms of commercial activity, which may or may not be related to print. This was necessary because the circulating libraries did not generate enough funds through subscription fees collected from its borrowers. As a commerce venture, it was important to consider the contributing factors such as other goods or services available to the subscribers.

Many claims have been made for the title of "first public library" for various libraries in various countries, with at least some of the confusion arising from differing interpretations of what should be considered a true "public library". Diffi-culties in establishing what policies were in effect at different times in the history of particular libraries also add to the confusion.

The first libraries open to the public were the collections of Greek and Latin scrolls which were available in the dry sections of the many buildings that made up the huge Roman baths of the Roman empire. However, they were not lending libraries.

The "halls of science" run by different Islamic sects in many cities of North Africa and the Middle East in the 9th century were open to the public. Some of them had written lending policies, but they were very restrictive. Most patrons were expected to consult the books on site. The later European university libraries were not open to the general public, but accessible by scholars.

PUBLIC LIBRARIES IN INDIA

Public library is largely regarded as the People's University. It has tremendous developments in India from the early period to till date at various stages. Most of the Indian states now have free public library services to develop the people of India at different levels.

ANCIENT PERIOD

"The history of the development of the public library may be said to be as old as that of education in India". During Vedic times, the pupils stayed in the *guru-gruha* for several years for education. Since ancient times, India is being very much pertinent in search of knowledge and wisdom. Oral communication was the best means amongst the people of India and writing was not available. "The earliest written and recorded materials found in India are the inscriptions on stone pillars of King Asoka; these inscriptions could be called the first outside open libraries". Later, *Ashrams* came into existence in India and students study under the supervision of well-known teachers. They kept many manuscripts for use of the teachers and students as well as for the visitors. Many students joined ashrams and such big ashrams were known as *vidyapeeth*, where numbers of teachers are engaged to teach the students. These educational institutions collected many different manuscripts and other materials which can help in their teaching and daily routine. They kept and preserved carefully. "The reading materials, of course, related to many subjects formed the source material for transmitting knowledge in different streams of education and culture. The collections might be likened to modern libraries since they were carefully maintained and extensively used by students and teachers alike". Such *ashrams* or *vidyapeeths,* where manuscripts and other reading materials were reserved, may be regarded as a kind of library as they serve information and knowledge to the students and community in different ways. Pandey S K Sharma stated that; "In India, since the ancient times libraries have been functioning as light houses for those who wanted to read and to extend the boundaries of various disciplines. References are available to prove that Nalanda University had its own multistoried library in AD 600 with massive collection of manuscripts. The collection of the library was housed in three buildings, each having nine floors and three hundred rooms. This library was opened by the then Emperor of India, King Davapal. The library was open for any body that was known scholar and took interest in reading, interpreting and even copying the documents kept in the library. Chinese traveller Whuen Sang is known to have consulted this library in the seventh century and to have taken from here hundreds of treatises to China and Japan. This library was completely destroyed by Bakhtiar Khilaji, who invaded India in AD 1205. And burnt the library. The library kept on burning for about six months".

Libraries in ancient India also developed at other famous centers of learning, such as *Vikramshila* and *Odantapuri.* Universities of ancient India, like Taxila and Vikramshala also have valuable collection on *tantras* and manuscripts in their libraries.

MEDIEVAL PERIOD

Muslims mostly rule the Medieval Period of India. Historically, it is also known as Mughal Period. There were great changes not only in social and political, but also on education and library system during this period. The Muslim rulers made great contributions to Indian culture and libraries played a significant role in the sociocultural development of the nation. "The period of Mughal is considered as the golden period of Indian history for its educational, literary, and library activities". Babur, king of Kabul invaded India and annexed Delhi to his kingdom. "He established the first Mughal Imperial Library in 1526".

Babur inherited manuscripts from his father and kept in his library and also collected books from different sources of his kingdom. Babur died in 1530 and was succeeded by his son Humayun. Humayun much lived in Agra and established library in his palace. He set up a library at Agra Fort, which was managed by Lal Beg.

In his library, he kept books, gilded pen cases, portfolios, picture books and beautiful works of calligraphy. After the death of Humayun, his son, Akbar, succeeded him in 1356. Akbar is regarded as one of the greatest Mughal king. Akbar improved the management of library with some technical works. He appointed Sheik Faizi to manage and control library services.

Akbar was very interest in manuscripts and appointed calligraphers to copy good manuscripts. He established a separate library for women at Fatehpur Sikri and made great improvement to the library. At the time of his death in 1605, the Imperial Library has twenty-four thousand books.

Jahangir, another rule of Mughal period, made a law that when a wealthy man died heirless, the property should be used for building and repairing schools, monasteries, libraries, and other institutions. Some wealthy and scholars, like Abdul Rahim Khan-i-Khanan, Shaik Faizi, Gulbadan Begum and ruler of Mysore and Jaipur also have their private libraries.

Some Hindu learning centers also have libraries. "The libraries of these centers contain huge collections of manuscripts on religion and philosophy as well as other subjects like medicine, science and history". Christian missionaries have also contributed for the libraries since the coming of Vasco da Gama in India.

During the Mughal period, library technical works, *viz.* Accessioning, Classification and Cataloguing were also carried out in some ways. The head librarian was known as *"Nizam"* and the assistant librarian *as "Muhatin"* or *"Darogha"*. Other staff of libraries during Mughal period is Scribes, Book

Illustrators, Calligraphers, Copyists, Translators, Bookbinders and Gilders.

THE BRITISH PERIOD

The Britishers came to India primarily to establish trade and commerce. Some of them were very interested for the upliftment of rich cultural heritage of India. "A number of Academic institutions were established during the British period by the East India Company and by the Christian missionaries".

The University of Calcutta was established in 1857 and its library was opened in 1873. Other Universities, University of Bombay and University of Madras were established in 1879 and 1907 respectively. There were only nineteen Universities in India before 1947. Universities were equipped with libraries in accordance with the Indian University Act of 1904.

The Bengal Royal Asiatic Society set up library in 1784, Bombay Royal Asiatic Society in 1804 and Calcutta Public Library in 1835. Establishment of these libraries enlightened the community and may be regarded as the foundation of the concept of public libraries to the Indian people.

Some of the important libraries set up in 19th. Century in India are Andrews Library, Surat in 1850, Gaya Public Library, Gaya in 1855, Long Library, Rajkot in 1856, Connemara Public Library, Madras in 1860, Government Library, Janagarh in 1867, Adyar Library, Adyar in 1886 and Dahi Laxmi Library, Nadiad in 1892.

Apart from these, other libraries, like Gujarat Vernacular Society along with a library, in Ahmedabad 1848 and Barton Library, Bhavnagar in 1882 were also established. Some of the Indian states also established public libraries.

Such as Baroda established Baroda State Library in Baroda in 1877, Cochin established Public Library and Reading Room in Trichur in 1873, Dhar established Victoria General Library in Dhar in 1856, Indore established General Library in Indore in 1852, Jaipur established Maharajah's Public Library in Jaipur in 1899. Others states also established such kind of libraries, *viz.* Jammu and Kashmir in 1879, Kahtiawar, in 1886, Kolhapur in 1850, Nizam's Dominion in 1891 and Travancore in 1829.

The first significant date in the development of public libraries in India is 1808 when the Bombay Government initiated a proposal to register libraries, which were to be given copies of books published from the 'Funds for the Encouragement of Literature'. The contributions of His Highness the Maharaja Sayajirao III, Gaekwar of Baroda towards library movement in India cannot be overlooked. He is remembered today as the Father of Library Movement in India. At the age of 18, in 1881, he was entrusted with full power of the government of Baroda in the Gujarat speaking region of the Bombay Presidency and the Peninsula of Kathiawar.

Baroda's population was predominantly rural, the main occupation was agriculture. The people in general were economically poor and socially backward. Education was the foundation to reconstruct a new social and economic life and education should be the right of the humblest villager.

He introduced free and compulsory education in his princely states. Baroda became the first territory not only among the native states but also in British India to have compulsory free primary education. He opined that primary education was to be the very base and decided to preserve it by means of libraries, which were the only agencies for perpetual universal self-education.

He decided to establish library as an experiment in one of the towns of a *taluka* and in order to implement his idea immediately; he issued orders to his ministers. "In conformity to his ruler's instructions, the Minister of Education prepared a detailed plan to open Circulating Libraries in the State, which was approved in March, 1907. Every public library instituted through the State's financial assistance was to be named as Circulating Library".

In 1906, he went to America as "an observer, a student desirous of acquiring all the knowledge and experience that could enable him to make his own State a model one in India". He was very much impressed by the library services of America for the development of the people in their social, economic and educational life. He then invited an American, William Alanson Borden, a pupil-assistant of Charles A Cutter, who is working as Librarian of the Young Men's Institute, New Haven, Connecticut to come and established library services in India.

In response to his invitation, Borden reached Baroda on November 6, 1910, and became the Director of State Libraries. It can be traced back that public library movement started since 1910 in India. Borden makes a survey of libraries in Baroda and concludes that there were over 241 libraries, holding a little over 100000 volumes. But he did not find any of those libraries adequately housed, nor did he find them shelved in such a manner as to make them most attractive to readers or convenient to those in charge.

He then make proposal for the best services of libraries in the State as:

- Should Your Highness feel disposed to grant me the necessary authority, I propose to organize a Department of Public Libraries, to rank with the other Departments of Your State, with the necessary equipments of officers and clerks, etc. and to bring all the libraries under its control and management;
- To unify all the collections of books in Baroda City into one Central library;
- To add to this Central library, general and technical books;
- To erect a suitable library building of fireproof construction, with reading grooms, study rooms, Women's Library, Children's library, Lecture hall, Library school, and executive offices;
- To make that library to be Free Public Library of Baroda City, and also the main storehouse for all the valuable historical documents

and papers now in private hands in the State, but which the owners would probably be glad to have stored in a safe place;

- To make it also the center from which traveling libraries should start and from which the books, new and old, could be distributed to the various branch libraries in the different towns, cities, and villages of the State.

The Maharaja apparently accepted Borden's proposals, and ordered that the whole scheme might be implemented in parts. The Library Department was created under Order No.9/19, January 30, 1911, for organizing libraries in Baroda.

As the Director of state libraries, he planned a network of free public libraries consisting a state central library, four district or divisional libraries, forty-five town libraries, and more than a thousand village libraries-all integrated into one chain system.

Borden played a leading role for the establishment, management and organization of public libraries in India. As a result of system, within two decades 85 per cent of the Baroda urban and rural population had access to libraries.. Borden developed library classification scheme to suit Indian libraries.

Another great contribution of Borden was the establishment of the first library school in India, in which he trained his own assistants and successors. Borden conducted the first formal library-training programme in India at Baroda in 1911. He was instrumental in the foundation of the Baroda Library Club and its journal, "Library Miscellany", published quarterly in three languages between 1912 and 1919.

University of Madras created the post of University Librarian in 1923 and Dr. S R Ranganathan joined the post on 4 January 1924. Ranganathan published his Five Laws of Library Science in 1931, Colon Classification in 1933 and Classified Catalog Code in 1934.

He also prepared Model Public Library Bill and drives to legislate library bill in Indian states. He made a tremendous contribution for the development of libraries in India. Scholars, educationists and people of library bent of mind founded Calcutta Public Library in 1835 and the same was opened on 21 March 1836 for the public.

In 1944, Calcutta Public Library was shifted to a new and spacious building, constructed in honour of the Governor-General of India, Lord Metcalf. Indian War of Independence broke out in 1857 resulted in to Europeans of Calcutta withdrew their support for the library management in 1899. Consequently, the management and establishment of the library were gradually waning and by the end of the century, the activities of the library came into standstill.

Lord Curzon, the then Viceroy and Governor-General of India visited Calcutta in 1899 and found a miserable condition of Calcutta Public Library. He bought the rights of the Library from the proprietors and later merged it with the Official imperial Library consisting of government departmental libraries of the East India Company. He then declared open of a new Imperial Library of India on 30 January 1903 in the Metcalf Hall. In 1948, one year after the independence of India, Imperial Library was transformed into National library of India and was housed to the Viceroy's Palace in Calcutta, namely, the Belvedere Palace.

POST-INDEPENDENCE PERIOD

Public libraries in India made a tremendous growth after the independence of India in 1947. The central and the state governments took a number of steps forward for the development of the nation from the point of education and considered library as essential part of it.

The programmes executed by provincial and central governments since 1910 for the social and adult education of the populace paved the way for the enactment of library laws and rules for grants-in-aid in the country. Hence public library became part of the education budget.

To enhance the level of literacy of 16 per cent in 1941, the government undertook some programmes such as extension services, continuing education, social education, non-formal education and adult education. The government further initiated steps for the development of community and organized some projects in this regard. Libraries were considered to be an essential part of the Community Development Project that was launched during the first plan period.

In order to accelerate the pace of socioeconomic development, the government considered public libraries to be an integral part of development projects.. The Connemara Public Library in Madras became the State Central Library in 1950 under the provision of Madras Public Libraries Act 1948, and became one of the three depository libraries in 1955.

Delhi Public Library was established in 1951 as the first UNESCO Public Library Pilot Project under the joint auspices of UNESCO and Government of India to adopt "Modern Techniques to Indian Conditions" and to serve as a model public library for Asia.. In 1954, the Delivery of Book Act was passed to include newspaper.

The act obligated every publisher in India to deposit one copy each of its publications to the National Library in Calcutta, the Asiatic Society Library in Bombay, Connemara Public Library in Madras, and Delhi Public Library in New Delhi The Advisory Committee for Libraries as constituted in 1957 by the Government of India, with K P Sinha as the Chairman.

The Committee submitted its report in 1959 with a drafted Model Library Bill. The Planning Commission constituted a Working Group on Public Libraries in 1964 and the Commission submitted its report in 1965 with a Model Public Libraries Act. The model bill was sent to all the states/UTs, which do not have Public Libraries Act.In 1972, the Government of India, Planning Commission constituted Working Group on Development of Public Libraries to make recommendations for library development. Raja Rammohun Roy Library Foundation, an autonomous body under the Department of Culture, Ministry of Education, was established in 1972.

The main objective of the Foundation was to assist state library services in developmental works. In 1979, a library section was established in the Department of Culture under the Ministry of Education, which section was under the charge of an Under Secretary. The objective was to promote the development of public libraries in India.A Working Group on Modernization of Library Services and Informatics was appointed by the Planning Commission in 1983 and submitted its report in 1984 with the formulation of National Policy on Library Services and Informatics. Delhi Public Library became a copyright library in 1982.

National Literacy Mission was adopted in 1986, which emphasized education for women and also establishment of rural libraries. Library networks and systems were strengthened at the national level institutions in the development of literature in neo-literates. Fourteen states namely, Tamil Nadu, Andhra Pradesh, Karnataka, Maharashtra, West Bengal, Manipur, Kerala, Haryana, Mizoram, Goa, Orissa, Gujarat, Uttaranchal and Rajasthan have enacted Public Libraries Bills during 1948 to 2006.

The Government of India, Department of Culture, appointed a Committee on National Policy on Library and Information System in 1985. The National Policy on Education, 1986 states that a nationwide movement for improvement of existing libraries and the establishment of new ones will be taken up, provision will be made in all educational institutions for library facilities, and the status of librarianship improved.

The National Book Policy, 1986 also had an impact on libraries, as:

- Provision of reading material for children by all the agencies involved;
- That 10 per cent of the annual education budget of the governments be used to purchase books for libraries.

These goals are to be achieved by using formal, non-formal, and open channels of learning.. Rural libraries should become the focal point for postliteracy and continuing educational programmes. Publishers, voluntary organizations, and school library programmes undertaken as part of the "Operation Blackboard Scheme" of the National Education Policy on Education, 1986 were given assistance. The following five libraries were regarded as national importance and may be stated in a very brief manner.

National Library, Kolkata

National Library, Kolkata was established in 1836 in the name of Calcutta Public Library. It was not a Government institution running on a proprietary basis. The then Governor General, Lord Metcalf transferred 4,675 volumes from the library of the College of Fort William to the Calcutta Public Library.

This and donations of books from individuals formed the nucleus of the library. Prince Dwarkanath Tagore was the first proprietor of the Calcutta Public Library. Both the Indian and foreign books, especially from Britain, were purchased for the library. In the report of 1850 we find that the library started collecting books in Gujarati, Marathi, Pali, Ceylonese and Punjabi.

The Government of Bengal and North Western Provinces regularly made by individuals as well as donations. The Calcutta Public Library had a unique position as the first public library in this part of the country. Such a well-organized and efficiently run library was rare even in Europe during the first half of the 19th century. Because of the efforts of the Calcutta Public Library, the National Library has developed rare books and journals in its collection.

The Imperial Library was formed in 1891 by combining a number of Secretariat libraries. Of these, the most important and interesting was the library of the Home Department, which contained many books formerly belonging to the library of East India College, Fort William and the library of the East India Board in London.

But the use of the library was restricted to the superior officers of the Government. Lord Curzon, the then Governor General of India, was the person who conceived the idea of opening a library for the use of the public. He noticed both the libraries, Imperial Library and Calcutta Public Library, were under-utilized for the want of facilities or restrictions. So, he decided to amalgamate the rich collection of both of these libraries.

He was successful in effecting the amalgamation of Calcutta Public Library with the then Imperial Library under certain terms. The library, called Imperial Library, was formally opened to the public on 30th January 1903 at Metcalf Hall, Kolkata.

The aims and objectives of the Imperial Library, well defined in a Notification in the 'Gazette of India' *as 'It is intended* that it should be a library of reference, a working place for students and a repository of material for the future historians of India, in which, so far as possible, every work written about India, at any time, can be seen and read.

Librarian of the British Museum, London, was appointed as the first Librarian of the Imperial Library. After his death, the famous scholar and linguist Harinath De took over the charge of the library. After his death J. A. Chapman became the librarian. Mr. Chapman showed keen interest in the affairs of the library and worked hard to improve its status. After his retirement, Khan Bahadur M.A. Asadulla was appointed as the librarian and he continued as the librarian till July 1947.

The policy of acquisition broadly adhered to by the Imperial Library was enunciated by Lord Curzon in his speech at the opening ceremony of the library, "The general idea of the whole Library is that it should contain all the books that have been written about India in popular tongues, with such additions as are required to make it a good all-round library of standard works of reference."

After the independence the Government of India changed the name of the Imperial Library as the National Library, with an enactment of the Imperial Library Act 1948 and the collection was shifted from the Esplanade to the present Belvedere Estate. On 1st February 1953 the National Library was opened to the public, inaugurated by Maulana Abul Kalam Azad. Sri B.S. Kesavan was appointed as the first librarian of the National Library.

The reviewing Committee in its report of 1969 suggested that the following should be the basic features of the National Library; Acquisition and conservation of all significant printed materials produced in the country to the exclusion of ephemera:

- Collection of printed materials concerning the country wherever published and also acquisition of photographic record of such materials that are not available within the country;
- Acquisition and conservation of manuscripts having national importance;
- Planned acquisition of foreign materials required by the country;
- Rendering of bibliographical and documentation service of retrospective materials, both general and specialized;
- Acting as a referral centre purveying full and accurate knowledge of all sources of bibliographical activities;
- Provision of photocopying and reprographic services; and
- Acting as the centre for international book exchange and international loan..

Khuda Bakhsh Oriental Public Library, Patna

Khuda Bakhsh Oriental Public Library, Patna was open for the public in October 1891 with 4000 Oriental manuscripts. Maulvi Khuda Bakhsh donated his entire collection to the nation by a deed of trust.Acknowledging the immense historical and intellectual value of its rich and valued collection, the Government of India declared the Library as Institution of National Importance by an act of Parliament in 1969. The Library is now fully funded by the Ministry of Culture. This autonomous institution is being governed by a Board with the Governor of Bihar as its ex-officio Chairman and Director is carrying the responsibility of dayto-day management of Library affairs.

Rampur Raza Library, Rampur

Rampur Raza Library, Rampur was founded by Nawab Faizullah Khan in AD 1774. It was brought under the management of a Trust till the Government of India took over the library on 1 July 1975 under the Act of Parliament, which declared it as an institution of National importance.

It contains very rare and valuable collection of manuscripts, historical documents, specimens of Islamic calligraphy, miniature paintings, astronomical instruments and rare illustrated works in Arabic and Persian languages besides

80,000 printed books. Nawab Faizullah Khan who ruled the state of Rampur, from 1774 to 1794, established the library with his personal modest collection kept in the Tosha Khana of his Palace.

Now the Library occupies the position of an autonomous institution of national importance under Department of Culture, Government of India and is fully funded by Central Government. The Library has now attained an International status of higher studies.

Thanjavur Maharaja Serfoji's Sarasvati Mahal Library, Thanjavur

Thanjavur Maharaja Serfoji's Sarasvati Mahal Library, Thanjavur is one among a few medieval libraries existing in the world. It contains very rare and valuable collections of manuscripts, books, maps and paintings on all aspects of Art, Culture and Literature.

The *Encyclopaedia Britannica* in its survey of the Libraries of the world mentions this as "the most remarkable Library in India". The Library houses a rich and rare collection of manuscripts on art, culture and literature. Conceived and christened as the Royal Palace Library by the Nayak Kings of Thanjavur. And the Maratha rulers nourished it for intellectual enrichment.

In 1918 this library was made as a public library. A body constituted by the Government and financed by the Central and State Governments now administers the library. During the reign of Nayaks of Thanjavur, "Sarasvati Bhandar" was formed and developed. The Maratha rulers who captured Thanjavur in 1675 A.D. patronized the culture of Thanjavur and developed the Royal Palace Library till A.D. 1855.

The Sarasvati Bhandar was situated within the Palace campus and the Manuscripts used for the purpose of reading by the Royal personages. Among the Maratha Kings, King Serfoji II, was an eminent scholar in many branches of learning and with great enthusiasm he took special steps for the enrichment of the Library.

It is a fitting tribute to the great collector Serfoji that the Library is named after him. Till the survival of the last Maratha Queen, the Library was the Palace property. After that, the Library together with the Palace properties formed the subject of litigation in Civil Courts.

The Royal Family members voluntarily came forward to delete this Library from the suit properties formed an Endowment and dedicated this Library to the public with one lakh rupees for its maintenance and upkeep. The Government of Madras in their G.O. Ms. No.1306 Home dated 5th October 1918, took possession of the Library under the Charitable Endowment Act and framed scheme for the Library management.

In 1983, the Library was declared as an Institution of National Importance. The Government of Tamil Nadu abolished the Five Member Committee of administration and made it as a Registered Society as per G.O. 209 (EST) dated

1-2-83. The Society was constituted and got registration on 9-7-1986 under the Tamil Nadu Registered Societies Act of 1975.

The Society consists of ex-officio members of Central and State Governments, nominated Scholars, Member from the Royal family and the Director of the Library. The Hon'ble Education Minister of the Government of Tamil Nadu is the ex-officio Chairman of this society.

Harekrushna Mahtab State Library, Bhubaneswar

Harekrushna Mahtab State Library, Bhubaneswar was conceived during 1st Five-year Plan under the advice of Government of India and was completed in 1959, enshrined within a beautiful land of 3 acres in a prime location of Capital City of Bhubaneswar.

In 1967, it was named as Gandhi Bhawan commemorating birth centenary of Mahatma Gandhi, the father of the nation. In 1987 it was renovated and entire space of the four storied building was utilized for the functioning of two Libraries *i.e.* State Library for the entire State of Orissa and another Public Library for Bhubaneswar City.

In 1987, Government decided to rename the State Library and the Public Library as Harekrushna Mahtab State Library and the Bhubaneswar Public Library respectively. The former is a Reference Library and lending of books is not permitted whereas the latter is a Lending Library for the public of Bhubaneswar City. These two Libraries have managed to function over the limited space. Total readers seats available are about 350 against the present demands of 600-700 readers per day.

LIBRARY LEGISLATION IN INDIA

Since the beginning, the public libraries served as the local information centers making the source of knowledge readily available to the public. The local community from the local fund or individual munificence could not achieve the services of a public library. Public leaders, scholars and learned societies have realised that the only way to establish and develop a public library system is through legislation. The UNESCO Public Library Manifesto, 1972 stated that, "The public library should be established under the clear mandate of law", which is substantiated by the IFLA/UNESCO Public Library Manifesto 1994 as;

> "The public library shall in principle be free of charge. The public library is the responsibility of local and national authorities. It must be supported by specific legislation and financed by national and local government. It has to be an essential component of any long-term strategy for culture, information provision, literacy and education".

Libraries are recorded under the Article 246 of Indian Constitution, Seventh Schedule List II of State List No.12 and the Indian Constitution Act, 1956, "Libraries, museums and other similar institutions controlled or financed by the State; ancient and historical monuments and records other than those to be of national importance." Provision of public library service is the responsibility of the State Government as the subject matter of libraries is relatable to entry 12 of the State List in the Seventh Schedule to the Constitution of India.

Dr. S R Ranganathan regarded as the pioneer of library legislation in India. "The concept of legislation for libraries is a contribution of S R Ranganathan to Indian public libraries". He made library legislation obligatory for the implementation of the second law of library science, "Every reader his/her book". Ranganathan the second law can be properly carried out only by legislation.

Dr. S R Ranganathan strived a lot for library legislation and prepared different library bills for the Indian Union and constituent states; such as;

- Model Library Act for constituent states of India;
- Bengal;
- Bombay;
- Central Province and Berar;
- Old Madras state which later became Act in 1948;
- United Province;
- Cochin;
- Travancore;
- Union Government;
- Madhya Pradesh;
- Union and Constituent States;
- Constituent States;
- Union;
- West Bengal;
- Kerala;
- Uttar Pradesh;
- Mysore which became Act in 1965;
- Assam;
- Gujarat and Model Library Bill.

Public libraries also considered as community information centers providing access at local level to a wide range of knowledge and information for the benefit of the individual and society as a whole. To ensure sustained development and information network services public libraries should be based on legislation.Public library legislation may be in various forms depending upon the government structure. It can be simple, allowing the establishment of public libraries but leaving standards of service to the level of government directly responsible for the library, or more complex, with specific detail on what services should be provided and to what standard.

But no British Government passed library Act for creation of public library system in Indian states.. There have been different efforts to work out library legislation models in India. In the pre-independent and post-independent of India, there have been five models of public library bills suggested by experts and national level professional associations and organizations.

MODEL PUBLIC LIBRARIES ACT OF DR. S R RANGANATHAN

The first Model Public Libraries Acts was prepared by Dr. S R Ranganathan in 1930 and revised in 1957 and 1972. It was discussed at the First All Asia Educational Conference held at Banaras during 26-30 December 1930. It was introduced in West Bengal Legislature in 1931 and in Madras Legislature in 1933. The Bill could not be passed due to financial clauses on library grant, library cess etc.

Salient features of final version are:

- Establishment of public libraries in city, rural and other areas;
- Constitution of State Library Authority *i.e.* Minister of Education;
- Constitution of State Library Committee as an advisory body of the State Library Authority;
- Constitution of Local Library Authority for each city and one for each district;
- State Library Authority, Government and Local Library Authority may determine library rate in such a manner and may determine collection of library cess from time to time.

MODEL PUBLIC LIBRARIES BILL OF MINISTRY OF EDUCATION

The Government of India, Ministry of Education appointed an Advisory Committee for Libraries in 1957, under the Chairmanship of Shri K P Sinha, former Director of Public Instruction, Bihar. This committee recommended the need for library legislation for each state. As a follow-up action of the Advisory Committee, the Ministry of Education, Government of India appointed a committee under the Chairmanship of Dr. M D Sen. The Committee drafted Model Public Libraries Bill in the year 1963.

The salient components of this Bill are:

- Constitution of State Library Authority as an apex body to advise the Government in the matter of library developments;
- Constitution of State Library Directorate for direction and controlling of library services;
- Constitution of District Library Committee in each district;
- Treatment of employees as government servant;
- Collection of library cess at the rate of 6 paise per rupee on house tax and property tax.

MODEL PUBLIC LIBRARIES BILL OF THE PLANNING COMMISSION

The Planning Commission, Government of India, constituted a 'Working Group on Libraries' in 1964 to plan and advice on the development of Libraries during the Fourth Five Year Plan. The Working Group recommended a Library Development Scheme to be implemented during the Fourth Plan period with a financial commitment of ₹.309 million, which was appended by Model Public Libraries Bill and submitted its report in 1965. Bill was not considered even by a single state.

The Bill included the following features:

- Establish, maintain, develop and integrated adequate public library service in the state;
- Constitution of Committee of Experts to prescribe the standards of service;
- Constitution of State Library Council to advise the government for the promotion and development of library service;
- Establishment of State Library Directorate to control, direct and supervise library system in the state;
- Establishment of State Central Library, State Regional Libraries and District Libraries;
- Treatment of employees in the system of State Government Servants
- Government shall be the financial source and shall maintain the public library system in the state.

MODEL PUBLIC LIBRARIES BILL OF INDIAN LIBRARY ASSOCIATION

The Indian Library Association (ILA) formed in 1933, has keen interest in library legislation. The ILA discussed library legislation at its various seminars organized in 1964, 1978 and 1981. Consequently, ILA Council at its meeting held on 23 June 1989, keeping in view of the developments and experiences gain from the existing Acts, resolved to prepare a Model Library Bill. Accordingly, as asked by ILA, Dr. Velaga Venkatappaiah, Chairman, Central Sectional Committee on Public Libraries of the ILA prepared a Model Public Library Bill. ILA accepted the draft Bill with minor changes at its National Seminar on Public Library Legislation in 1990 at the final product of the Model Public Libraries Bill was published in 1991.

The Bill was circulated to all the states and union territories but few states reacted favourably to the Bill. This Model Bill was again discussed in a National Seminar on Library Legislation and revised as the Model State Public Library and Information Service Act in 1995. In view of emergence of Information Technology at all levels, the model act was again revised in 2000.

The important components of this Bill are:

- State Library and Information Service, based on a State Policy;
- Constitution of State Library Authority at the apex level with Minister of Libraries as Chairman as policy making and executive body;
- Establishment of Directorate of Public Libraries for directing, controlling and supervising;

- Constitution of City, District Library Authority for rendering service from district to village level;
- Provision for network of Public Library and Information Services from state to village level;
- Constitution of State Library and Information Service;
- Collection of Library cess on house tax and property tax, entertainment tax, professional tax, vehicle tax, etc.;
- Constitution of State Boards for education, book production, co-ordination, etc.;
- Accountability of public expenditure and services.

MODEL UNION LIBRARY ACT

The Government of India appointed a committee to explore the possibilities to establish a National Central Library at New Delhi in 1948. Dr. S R Ranganathan, a member of the committee drafted a Library Development plan in 1950 with a 30-year programme and a draft Library Bill for the states and Union Public Library Act.

This was revised in 1959 and again in 1972. However, libraries falls under the state list of the constitution and it may not be possible to pass Bill as a Union Act, unless and until the constitution is suitably amended for this purpose.

The main features of this model Act are:

- Constitution of a National Library Authority;
- Establishment of national central libraries;
- Constitution of National Library Committee as an advisory body to the National library Authority;
- Constitution of National library fund;
- Amendment to the delivery of Books and Newspaper Act, 1954.

The IFLA/UNESCO Public Library Manifesto 1994 reads that, "The public library is the local center of information, making all kinds of knowledge and information readily available to its users". Public libraries, to become an enthusiastic source of information and knowledge for the local community, needs certain forms of developments in terms of infrastructure, collection and the trinity of library as well. It cannot survive by the local contributions and dedication alone, but through the support of government.

"The pubic library, as a democratic institution operated by the people for the people, should be established and maintained under the clear authority of law; supported wholly or mainly from public funds; open for free use on equal terms to all members of the community regardless of occupation, creed, class or race". Efforts have been going on well under the initiatives of professional associations and learned societies in this context. "In India, the post independence era was favourable to the establishment of public libraries based on legal basis"..

FOUR PRIORITIES FOR THE 21ST CENTURY PUBLIC LIBRARY SERVICE

- Place the library as the hub of a community.
- Make the most of digital technology and creative media.
- Ensure that libraries are resilient and sustainable.
- Deliver the right skills for those who work for libraries.

The key issues emerging in this research are similar to those we handle with the wider arts and cultural sector. It is because there is such a close fit with the Arts Council's five long term goals that we will be able to develop solutions to these challenges from which both libraries and arts organisations can benefit.

Place the Library as the Hub of a Community

We know that, in future, many people are likely to lead more isolated lives. More will work from home and more will live alone. Opportunities to meet in free public spaces for a wide variety of purposes will be increasingly important. Our findings show that libraries will continue to be valued as trusted, safe, democratic places that offer valuable resources and expertise to support the activities of the people who use them.

Libraries' physical space will be more flexible and integrated with a virtual presence that includes web-based reading groups, social networking and links to other online resources. People will engage in creative and cultural activities as well as reading and learning, exchanging ideas, conversation and knowledge.

Space shared with community based services (such as council, health, business support, and learning organisations) will be better for local people, and will bring benefits such as skills exchanges, reaching more people and cutting costs.

The challenge: the use of a library's space:

- Re-think the way library spaces are used to encourage shared and creative activity while continuing to welcome those who want to explore on their own
- Integrate the library's physical and virtual spaces
- Sustain enough spaces offered by libraries to meet the needs of their communities

Make the most of Digital Technology and Creative Media

Digital technology is developing rapidly and will continue to have a major impact on the way we obtain and consume information, culture and the written word. Beyond the library building, people will expect a more interactive experience and to be able to gain access to library services all day, every day, particularly while on the move. Libraries should be at the heart of digital innovation. They should develop their role in actively connecting communities and helping people to experience, experiment with and master new technologies. Digital technology will be the key to future library service delivery but our research points out that its true potential will not be achieved unless the principle of an open, enabling ICT infrastructure is agreed by local authorities and library services.

This would allow libraries to innovate, and to share or jointly adopt services more efficiently. By making it easier to develop national services and enable local innovation, people will get access to more resources, information and support. Many assume that digital information sources and online services are accessible to everyone. But a digital divide still exists because a significant number of people lack the confidence, the necessary skills or the desire to make effective use of technology. Some who do, are held back by poor digital connections or can't afford them. Public libraries will ensure that no-one needs to be left behind or excluded.

The challenge: using technology:

- Improve the quality and consistency of the virtual library experience
- Develop an open ICT infrastructure that encourages innovation and better service
- Enable libraries to lend the full range of e-books, including remotely

Ensure that Libraries are Resilient and Sustainable

Our research, along with reductions in public expenditure, makes clear that libraries will need to reduce costs and find other sources of funding to supplement local authority support. Alongside this, communities are becoming more involved in the design and delivery of library services. To find the right solution, councillors in local authorities are considering whether they should change the way their library service is governed, or whether they can share aspects of their service with others.

Our research indicates that, as with many other public services, this trend will continue and grow, and the debate about community involvement in public libraries needs to be seen in this wider context. We do not suggest that any one approach is the right one in all circumstances but we have published guidance, based on experience to date, that we suggest should be taken into account. Some library services are already doing this and we believe that they could be role models, not just among libraries, but for all public services. This kind of community involvement will become seen not as a cost-cutting tool but as a normal way of working, with staff and users developing ideas and creating services together.

The challenge: cutting costs, finding new sources of funds and new ways of working:

- Create a positive environment for communities and individuals to become actively involved in the design and delivery of their library services

- Encourage the development of new approaches to governing and managing libraries that make it more likely that they will survive and succeed
- Equip libraries to be commissioned to deliver other public services, and to commission other organisations to deliver library services

THE FUTURE OF PUBLIC LIBRARIES IN AN INTERNET AGE

With the Internet reshaping so many aspects of our lives, it has become common for prognosticators to speculate about the ultimate demise of all sorts of institutions that many of us have come to take for granted. So when Public Agenda set out to investigate public and civic leaders' thinking about public libraries today, we were not at all certain what we would hear. The first message that came was loud and clear: there is a future for public libraries in the Internet age. Even with the vast and growing amount of information available on the Internet and more competition for public funding, Americans say that public libraries will continue to play a vital role in communities.

A strong majority say that if their public library were to shut down, they would feel "that something essential and important has been lost, affecting the whole community" (78 per cent). The feeling that libraries are central to healthy communities is even more common among those who are most actively engaged in communities: the voters, volunteers, and contributors who make communities strong and can usually be counted on to raise a ruckus when things go wrong. In our recent report on the research, "Long Overdue: A Fresh Look at Public and Leadership Attitudes About Libraries in the 21st Century", Public Agenda documents the strong beliefs people have that their communities must have wellfunctioning public libraries in order to be healthy and strong. Large majorities said that all children should have a good, safe, appealing library in their neighbourhood; that libraries play a crucial role in preserving permanent and unalterable records; and that government should support the wiring of libraries so that low-income people can have access to the Internet.

AMERICANS SAY LIBRARIES ARE A GOOD PUBLIC INVESTMENT

At a time of broad concern about wasteful public spending, and as we hear of communities refusing to pay more taxes for public education or "essential services", 71 per cent say that libraries spend public money well. Fifty-two per cent say that if their local library needed additional funding, they would favour a tax increase to generate the necessary resources— significantly more than the number who favour charging users (32 per cent) or reducing services (16 per cent) as options for solving a financial shortfall. In many ways, people believe that libraries are more essential now than ever before. Americans say that since so many businesses are selling information, we absolutely need public libraries to provide vital information free of charge to anyone who needs it.

They also strongly agree that libraries are an important, quiet oasis from fast-paced, stressful lives. In an age when people are often deeply cynical about the performance of all sorts of public services, from public education to the police to cultural institutions, public libraries are rated A more often than any other public service we asked about. Indeed, public libraries seem almost immune to the distrust that is associated with so many other institutions. More than one hundred years ago, the philanthropist Andrew Carnegie saw the potential of the public library to be the center of enlightened learning in every community. He offered to build libraries if communities would contribute land, furnish money for annual maintenance, and exercise governance and oversight.

He gave communities the incentive to participate in a national movement and between 1881 and 1917 invested the equivalent of $3 billion to build 1,689 libraries across the nation. The result of Carnegie's investment and the involvement of communities helped educate generations of Americans. His commitment helped fix the library in the American consciousness as a significant public institution that needed and deserved broad public support. A century after this compact with American communities, nearly 90 per cent of library funding derives from local public dollars—which can be seen as either a curse or a blessing.

LIBRARIES FOR TODAY, LIBRARIES FOR TOMORROW

When people think about their expectations of libraries today, they generally think about the traditional services that most libraries carry out so well. Topping the public's list of priorities is that the basic services they have come to expect from libraries remain free of charge to the public. They also expect libraries to have enough current books for children; numerous reference materials; and friendly, knowledgeable librarians available. Libraries should offer convenient reading hours and special programmes for children, and they should have well-maintained buildings along with books and information that are organised for easy self-service. The top-ten list of public priorities for libraries also includes making available safe and productive gathering places for teenagers, being open on evenings and weekends, and having plenty of current books for adults.

For the most part, these public expectations are matched by libraries' performance, the public told us. People give especially high grades to their public libraries for having buildings that are well maintained; comfortable places to read; and enough friendly, knowledgeable librarians to supply help when needed. Although people clearly want libraries to ace the basics—materials, hours, and service—they also expect more and more from libraries in this age of the Internet. "Long Overdue" reveals a great deal about libraries and technology. Libraries are anything but relics of the past. They are viewed as key players in our digitised future.

Two-thirds of survey respondents say that having enough computers and online services for people should be a high priority for their local library. Seven in ten favour wiring libraries so that those who might not be able to afford a computer in their home can learn computer skills and get online. Those who think that libraries are merely becoming "information resources of last resort" for those who can't afford a home computer seem to be mistaken. Advanced computer users and families with higher income are even more likely to use public libraries and the technology services they offer. But, not surprisingly, people with few computer skills are the most likely to say wiring libraries to provide for "have-nots" should be a high priority.

WHERE IS THE LOVE

Public libraries are beloved institutions, but they can't survive on accolades alone. With the advent of computers and search engines, digital libraries, and the Internet, some question if libraries are essential and whether they should command priority in the competition for public dollars. Public Agenda's research shows public libraries are not seen as objects of nostalgia, but rather as essential community players in the effort to increase equity, opportunity, and community development in the information age. A growing number of communities are determined to keep their libraries at the leading edge of technology: affording small businesses the resources to compete globally; giving residents access to credible, current health information; and making libraries vital information access points for everyone.

These communities reveal the vast potential of libraries for the future. But only a small percentage of communities invest in public libraries to the extent necessary to produce maximum dividends. In those communities where the case for libraries is less clear and competition for public funds is high, there are disturbing indicators that support for libraries is slipping. The precarious financial condition of the nationwide public library system (to the extent that there is a cohesive system at all) that we heard about from library advocates was reinforced in our interviews with civic leaders across the nation.

Civic leaders do see the great strengths of the public library as being an information center in the digital age, an important resource for those who have the fewest resources available to them, and the "go to" place for all manner of public functions (including health information, job services, immigrant acculturation, and adult literacy training). But they also see challenges for libraries that need to be addressed by library supporters. Many civic leaders pointed to public libraries' seemingly infinite variety in governance structure as a major stumbling block. Public libraries' lack of marketing, impassive advocacy, and isolation from the community were also cited as shortcomings in library performance. Our research identified four specific areas where civic leadership, public citizens, and library leaders all seem to agree that there is a major opportunity for public libraries to step in and address community needs:

- Developing better programming and services for teens,
- Addressing illiteracy and poor reading skills among adults,
- Offering ready access to information about government services (including making public documents and forms quickly and easily available), and
- Permitting much greater access to computers for all.

Yet venturing into these areas would likely require financial resources that many libraries do not currently have. The civic leaders we spoke to questioned whether a groundswell of citizen support for public libraries would emerge in their communities. "Long Overdue" suggests that there is, in fact, strong potential for vocal support from activist citizens who could argue effectively for consistent and reliable financial support for public libraries. But library supporters, especially leaders with governance responsibility, must take the steps necessary to harness this potential and make it a reality.

LEVERAGING PUBLIC GOODWILL FOR FINANCIAL SUPPORT

There are people in every community who make things happen but don't necessarily hold any official post. These are the folks we refer to in our research report as "community soldiers", because no battle can be won without them. The good news for libraries is that these citizens—who nearly always vote in local elections and involve themselves in community organisations and activities—are heavy users and big fans of libraries. But even though they may be considered champions of libraries, currently they are not very aware of the potential financial vulnerability of their local libraries. Although 45 per cent of the civically engaged think their local government has not furnished enough money and assistance to the public libraries in their communities, 42 per cent think they have, and 13 per cent say they simply do not know. It appears that those citizens who can be counted on to rally to the cause if libraries are in financial peril are no more likely than the general population to be aware of the challenges facing libraries today.

Public lack of awareness of the financial challenges libraries face aside, there are other reasons everything is not milk and honey in the land of libraries. Libraries face real challenges today. Only 35 per cent of survey respondents say their local library gets an A when it comes to having convenient hours so people can use the services; only 28 per cent give libraries an A for offering access to catalogues and databases through the Internet; 26 per cent give an A for having enough computers and online services in the library for the people who want to use them; and just 24 per cent give an A for making available reading hours, homework help, and study space for children and teenagers. These are services that the public rate among the highest priorities for libraries. Clearly there are opportunities to improve service delivery on the part of local libraries.

Library leaders would like to do much more in the way of customer service and innovative programming. But as our interviews with public leaders attest, finances are always a challenge. The civic leaders we interviewed generally share the public's high regard for libraries but are more conscious of the tenuous financial condition of many public libraries. Some public libraries are comfortable with the funding they receive, but the vast majority are not so well supported. Though the public remains largely unaware of the fiscal pressures on libraries today, civic and business leaders believe that public libraries are often first on the chopping block when state and local budgets are cut.

Recent history in Salinas, Calif., a community that closed almost all of its libraries (and is profiled in our study), points to the passion for libraries that can emerge when a funding crisis imperils a treasured institution. But since the vast majority of the public do not sense that their own libraries may be at risk, most people do not see a reason to raise their voice in concern. It is simply not something on their radar screen today. The "canary in the coal mine" metaphor has a place here. Leaders have pricked up their ears to the distressed calls of the canary, but the public seems to hear only a sweet song and no hint of impending trouble.

LIBRARIES: ESSENTIAL COMMUNITY PROBLEM SOLVERS

To identify the most favourable potential opportunities for libraries to strengthen public support, Public Agenda asked the public about their priorities for urgent action in their communities and in which areas they think government should be more effective because current performance is relatively poor. Researchers explored the same terrain in the interviews with national and local leadership.

Four areas of opportunity resonated most with the public and leaders alike:

- *Providing stronger services for teens*: The public is greatly concerned about teenagers and feels (72 per cent) that offering safe and productive activities for teens should be a high priority for their communities. This is also an area where the public potentially holds local government accountable, believing local government both can and should do more for teens. In the public's reckoning, libraries can potentially fill the gap: three out of four Americans (74 per cent) believe providing services for teens should be a high priority for libraries.
- *Helping address illiteracy and poor reading skills among adults*: Another major opportunity for libraries to fill community needs is with supplying literacy and reading programmes for adults, which many civic leaders tied to strengthening workforce skills and economic development. Sixty-eight per cent of the public said adult literacy programmes should be a high priority for the community, very few said it was something their community was doing a very good job of

providing, and a large majority (68 per cent) said it should be a high priority for their local library.

- Affording ready access to information about government services, such as making available government forms or information on literacy programmes.
- Ensuring even greater access to computers for all. Almost two-thirds of Americans say having enough computers and online services for the people who want to use them should be a high priority for libraries.

For public libraries today, the greatest challenge is not in convincing the public of their worth—in the present or for the future. People clearly see many valuable roles for libraries to play. Our research yields ample evidence that libraries are highly valued public institutions serving multiple needs that, the public notes, will certainly continue to be needed with changing times.

A TIME OF RECKONING

America's public libraries are facing a pivotal time in their history. There is a rich tradition of public service that infuses citizens with great respect for the mission of libraries. Libraries have received significant public and private financial support over the years, ranging from local property tax support to state budget funding and a high level of private philanthropic funding. But funding level and mechanisms vary tremendously from one community to the next—and that's part of the problem. During the past several decades, there has been a major effort to upgrade technology and Internet access to bring the benefits of these new technologies to all citizens, regardless of economic circumstances. This has added further to public approval of the allimportant contributions of libraries.

Of course, libraries have also long held a position of special importance in educating schoolchildren and older students. The kind of action required for libraries to position themselves securely in the future will demand active and engaged governance. When change happens in communities, it is often a product of the passion of engaged citizen leaders who demand change from elected officials. But our research into a variety of library environments would suggest that libraries may suffer in some cases from a kind of "benign neglect" on the part of those who are most civically engaged. The reasoning here may be a variation on the theme that if it ain't broke, don't fix it. Although the public's strong feelings about how well libraries are doing their job make clear that libraries aren't broken, this doesn't mean there aren't cracks in the foundation.

Those who are most passionate about the importance of libraries in communities, if they are to secure their future, must make certain that the local and state governance structures that determine funding understand all that libraries are able to do for citizens and just how successful their constituents perceive them to be.

8

Society Literacy, Library Legislation and Public Libraries

After Independence, India has experienced growing population of literate and educated citizens due to various efforts in universalisation of elementary education through programmes like:

- Sarva Shiksha Abhiyan (SSA),
- District Primary Education Programme (DPEP), and
- National Literacy Mission and so on.

On the other hand, for the facilitating educated citizens with the adequate documentary and knowledge resources, government and other agencies have established public libraries. The community information centres and village knowledge centres are the recent additions to this effort that would transform India into an information society, where information and knowledge resources are considered as critical ingredient for development. But problem is with the effective and efficient use, consumption and evaluation of information resources, so that informed citizen can take right decisions.

Here information literacy can play a vital role in educating the users of libraries on various information and documentary resources, where to start searching of information, what where and how to access them, how to assess and compare retrieved information, how to communicate their information or findings to the general masses and experts, and so on. In addition to borrow books for entertainment and leisure, public libraries can also disseminate information on community development, best practices, literature, culture, trade, education, etc. which may be further elaborated when needs arise.

Information seekers may want consolidated or exhaustive information. To provide right information to the users, public librarians should be trained to develop information literacy competency and should able to educate the user that will make user information literate. Before going into depth, we would like to know what is 'information literacy' and who are 'information literates'.

'Information literacy' is "the ability to recognize when information is needed and have the ability to locate, evaluate and use effectively the needed information". Information literacy embraces related concepts like 'user education', 'library instruction', 'bibliographic instruction' and 'library research', although 'information literacy' has broader perspectives and wider applications than these concepts. Information literacy competency development programmes and standards are designed to produce information literate. American Library Association Presidential Committee on Information Literacy defines 'information literates' as:

- "...ultimately, information literate people are those who have learned how to learn. They know how to learn because they know how knowledge is organized, how to find information, and how to use information in such a way that others can learn from them. They are people prepared for lifelong learning, because they can always find the information needed for any task or decision at hand."

ROLE OF PUBLIC LIBRARIES IN E-GOVERNMENT

The E-Government Act of 2002 states the goal of E-Government as enhancing "governmental functions and service," achieving "more efficient performance," and increasing "access to Government information, and...citizen participation in Government". Since the passage of the E-Government Act, E-Government has quickly become an increasingly popular element of service delivery at the federal, state and local levels. If E-Government services are planned and executed well, they allow government agencies to increase effectiveness and efficiency, and can increase citizen trust in government.

The challenges that libraries encounter in providing E-Government vary geographically, as planning and execution of E-Government service varies between states, municipalities, and counties. Even different agencies within county governments approach E-Government in a number of different ways, and with varying levels of success. In addition to increasing effectiveness and efficiency of services, governments have increased their use of E-Government in an effort to cut operating costs. The Florida Department of Children and Families' (DCF) eliminated almost ten thousand staff positions between 1999 and 2007 with the introduction of its ACCESS Florida E-Government programme, three thousand of which are attributable directly to the ACCESS Florida initiative. The DCF ACESS programme is a "modernized public assistance service delivery system... based on streamlined workflows, policy simplification, technology innovations and partnership with local community organizations".

This programme largely eliminates DCF offices, instead, funneling applicants and programme participants to a network of Community Partners for assistance with applications and administration of accounts. DCF now counts public libraries among its Community Partners – agencies and organizations willing to provide Internet access and service assistance applicants. A close examination of the DCF Community partners list reveals that, in most counties, libraries are the only partners charged with providing free Internet access to any citizen who enters requesting service. Other partners are limited to specific constituencies. Since 1994, the Information Use Management and Policy Institute at Florida State University has conducted a national survey of public library internet connectivity. Between 1994 and 2007, Internet availability in libraries grew from approximately 21 per cent to over 99 per cent. Bertot, Jaeger, Langa and McClure write, "...by meeting user information needs through public access computing and Internet services, public libraries were able to serve a larger community need for access to e–government services and resources".

The 2008 national survey found that approximately 95 per cent of public libraries provide asneeded assistance to patrons with understanding and using E-Government resources, while 69 per cent help with E-Government applications and services. Sixty three per cent of respondents indicated that the public library was the only free public internet access point in the surrounding community. Thus, public libraries provide substantial E-Government service and resource support. One can view Government to Citizen EGovernment as a three-part system comprised of the public, the government agency involved and the networks and points of access that allow citizens to participate in EGovernment with that agency. By seeking EGovernment information at the library and requesting assistance from librarians, citizens have added a fourth component to the system: the local librarian as a surrogate agency service provider. In this capacity, the librarian facilitates what ideally develops into discourse around the design of the E-Government implementation in question. As library activities write:

"To develop citizen-oriented EGovernment services that achieve cost savings implies that governments...actively seek to discover what citizens want from E-Government"

Some provides a useful framework for understanding the implications of this "fourth party" service provider. The object outlines a four-part chain of interaction in E-Government development that includes developers (agencies), local designers (developers), service providers (libraries) and citizens.

The framework proposed by the library activities it is in the best interest of all parties to collaboratively develop effective ways to collect and channel patron feedback for successful, iterative development of the E-Government system. Citizens in need of government services do not bear sole responsibility for involving librarians in EGovernment service. Some agencies refer citizens to public libraries to access web-based forms or applications that are not available in their offices.

The DCF Access web site encourages applicants to "apply for public assistance (food stamps, temporary cash assistance, and Medicaid) using the internet wherever it is available including home, a library, or a school". Because they are, in many cases, the only organizations offering free Internet access in their communities, the public library plays an instrumental role in leveling out differences in citizen access to personal computers and the Internet, moving the E-Government system away from exclusion of segments of the population, and towards "design for all".

In this role, many libraries have begun to evolve into "one-stop shops" that now include assistance with government service programmes, access, and delivery. This is a substantive departure from a longstanding role of public libraries that serve as access points to government information and forms (*i.e.*, tax forms during tax season). For example, though librarians provided tax forms in the past, they did not serve as tax accountants who assisted patrons complete and file their taxes.

Now, citizens come to the library seeking government programme and services assistance, not simply access to information. This shift seems to occur in direct relation to government agencies cutting back in their provision of programme support services due to the adoption of E-Government technologies.

PURPOSE AND OBJECTIVES

The purpose of this exploratory study was to identify the E-Government related needs of citizens who access government related information at the library, and to identify current library E-Government practices in order to provide practical guidance to public libraries in meeting the needs of local community members they serve.

Specifically, the study addresses the following questions:

- What E-Government services and resources do public libraries typically provide?
- What types of E-Government assistance and/or resources do members of libraries' community members request?
- Why do citizens seek E-Government services and resources at the public library?
- What barriers and issues do librarians face in providing E-Government services and resources?

Answers to these questions can help ascertain EGovernment needs from a user perspective, but also foster understanding the impacts of E-Government on community-based support organizations such as public libraries.

The study was exploratory and used an iterative multi-method approach. Limited to public libraries in the state of Florida, the study used:

- Interviews with public librarians. The interviews explored and identified the E-Government services public librarians provided, and the issues encountered by public librarians in providing EGovernment services and resources.
- E-Government workshops. The study team conducted five E-

Government workshops in key geographic regions to explore E-Government service provision by libraries in the regions.
- Survey of workshop attendees. The survey asked librarians to identify the most frequently provided E-Government services, and to identify issues encountered by patrons seeking E-Government assistance in local libraries.
- Librarian-maintained reference log files. The log files captured specific E-Government service and resource transactions provided to users in libraries.
- User survey. The survey explored the reasons why users came to the public library for E-Government services and resources, library services requested and used to engage in E-Government services, and issues encountered while engaging in E-Government services. The survey was available in English, Spanish, and French Creole. The survey was primarily in print format, though a web-based Survey Monkey version of the survey was available in English.

The interviews and workshops informed the development of the log file and user surveys. User surveys and log files were pre-tested to ensure their usability and ability to capture valid and reliable data.

STATE LIBRARY AGENCIES

Continuing education for professional and support staff in all the professions has been receiving increasing emphasis in recent years. The need to update current practice through new knowledge and insight of societal conditions and client needs has had its impact in the library and information science fields.

The advances in automation and technology, the proliferation of knowledge, and the growing recognition of the need to provide access to the rapid delivery of information in many formats have given priority emphasis to continuing library education as a means of responding to the changes taking place in our society. State library agencies have a continuing responsibility for a planned approach to the development of library and information services in each state. This planned approach includes the need for the continuing education of library personnel to meet changing service demands.

This object reviews the background for the continuing education role of the state library agency, the development of continuing education for libraries, the implications of these developments, current programmes in progress, and trends which may indicate future change. Historically, state library agencies have had the responsibility for statewide library development, particularly public library development. The provision of advice, assistance and consultant services has been one of the primary means employed. Included in the advisory activities were the conducting of workshops and other educational and staff development programmes. State library agencies having responsibility for school library development as units of state departments of education carried on similar programmes and activities to improve school libraries.

Following the enactment of the federal Library Services Act (LSA), state library agencies moved into a new era of growth and influence. The requirement to develop state plans and the attendant emphasis on establishing libraries, creating library systems and extending library services created the need for staff development and continuing education activities as a major component in the achievement of desired objectives.

A U.S. Office of Education study of state library extension resources and services compares the data from 1955-56 prior to LSA with the re- sources and services of state library agencies in 1960-61. For the purposes of this chapter, the report of consultant activity and training programmes during this period is of interest. Forty-eight States reported 16,466 field visits compared to 6544 in 1955-56; 44 states held or sponsored some 1600 training programmes for over 56,000 persons from 1956 to 1961. These pro- grams served professional (36 per cent) and non-professional (22 per cent) personnel and public library trustees (26 per cent).

The responsibility of state library agencies for the planning and administration of federal funds under the Library Services Act of 1956 and the Library Services and Construction Act (LSCA) of 1964 gave added impetus to national documents and conferences concerned with improving the capabilities of state library agencies. These reports emphasize a stronger focus on goals, purposes and long-range plans with the attendant need for highly skilled consultants and related staff development activities in the field in order to implement the statewide programme.

All state library agencies view continuing education and consultant services as a major responsibility of the agency. In a recent survey, about one-half of the state library agencies considered the continuing education responsibility to be a shared responsibility and not solely the responsibility or of the state library agency. In recent years national activities of major importance have contributed to an increased awareness of continuing education responsibility and to an increase in planned activities of state library agencies.

In the regional hearing conducted in 1972 by the National Commission on Libraries and Information Science (NCLIS), one of the identified priorities was the availability of continuing education for the development and maintenance of competencies which are needed to deliver the library and information services required by the nation. Subsequently, NCLIS funded a study in 1973 to recommend a nationwide programme of continuing education which culminated in Continuing Library and Information Science Education. This report made recommendations which eventually led to the formation of the Continuing Library Education Network Exchange (CLENE). The NCLIS report outlines the develop-ment of library continuing education and comments on the necessity for continuing life- long learning.'

Based on responses from the field, an operational definition of continuing education was developed which includes the following:

- The implication that lifelong learning is necessary to keep the individual up to date,
- Assurance that the individual carries the basic responsibility for his/her own development,
- Diversification to new areas of interest, and
- Involvement in educational activities beyond those considered necessary for entrance into the field.

In comparison with other professions, the librarians felt that continuing education should be pro- vided for all levels of personnel, not solely professional, and that it not be limited to improved competence for the job held now or aspired to in the future. In its plan for continuing education, the report suggests roles and responsibilities of the individual agencies and organizations in order to coordinate efforts, including those of the individual employee, the employing library, the state library agency, the library schools, and state, regional and national associations.

Major responsibilities outlined for the state library agencies include coordination of continuing education programmes on a statewide basis, identification of continuing education needs of the state, provision of a link between librarians in the state and national and regional plans, and the appointment of a continuing education coordinator on the state library agency staff. The other major responsibility is three- fold: the planning, implementation and evaluation of statewide continuing education programmes based on identified needs.

These initial efforts to provide a suggested outline of responsibilities continued to receive attention through CLENE as a newly formed national organization. State library agencies which joined CLENE as sustaining members, as well as the state library agency directors and continuing education staff members, influenced some of the priorities of CLENE. In 1976 CLENE received a USOE, Title II-B grant to provide an "Extended Institute to Train State Library Agency.Personnel to Implement and/or Strengthen Statewide Systems of Continuing Education for Library/Information/Media Personnel." The workshop phase of the institute was held November 7-13, 1976, at the Illinois State Library. Continuing education personnel from twenty-five state library agencies met to develop planning and implementation skills in continuing education. For participating states the institute spurred development of statewide coordinated planning among providers of continuing education in the state.

During this period several regional consortia of states were formed with a primary concern for continuing education. CELS grew out of a survey of members of six state library associations where the need for Continuing education was strongly expressed. State library agencies are major financial contributors to this programme. The Western Interstate Commission on Higher Education (WICHE) had a major continuing education component funded in large part by five state library agencies. The Western Council of State Libraries has succeeded WICHE in this regional effort.

State library agencies were asked to report on activities in needs assessment, programmes in continuing education, the extent of cooperation of other agencies in planning and implementing continuing education programmes, recent changes and improvements in state library agency continuing education programmes, and trends and new developments in continuing education. Forty responses to the questionnaire were received. State library replies indicate that all state library agencies have a responsibility for continuing education. Several have stated that the agency statutes define this responsibility but most suggest that agency planning documents cover these functions.

Cooperation with other continuing education agencies is extensive; 63 per cent of the respondents work closely with state library associations, and 34 per cent with library schools. State universities, higher education commissions, state departments of education, and other agencies were also listed. State staff are active participants on the continuing education committees of other agencies, and either library associations or the state library agency has formed a continuing education committee for coordinated planning and programmes. The formation of continuing education planning committees representing all types of libraries is a recent development in many states.

These committees are in various stages of the development of guidelines, policy statements or state plans for coordinated continuing education programmes. Examples of plans underway can be found in Illinois, Michigan, Ohio and Louisiana. Oklahoma reported the formation of a state committee in 1978, Maryland in 1977. Pennsylvania is planning a special project in 1978 with a director and task force to develop continuing education coordination. States participating in the Western Council of State Libraries and CELS are the primary planners for the continuing education programme of the regional consortia. Coordinated planning appears to be one of the more significant activities now underway.

Continuing education needs were identified by the majority through surveys and questionnaires at state, regional or local levels;consultations with local staffs and "perceived changes in the library climate," evaluation of current programmes and of new national library trends and programmes were also cited. The responses did not indicate the types of libraries involved in the needs assessment process. The influence of continuing education committees and recently formed task forces has not yet been felt to any great degree in the development of continuing education programmes as reported.

The continuing education programmes sponsored by state library agencies are directed primarily to public library staffs, although programme offerings to reach a broader group were listed. All respondents listed public library directors and public library professional staff as participants; twenty-six listed non-professional public library staffs. However, twenty- one listed academic librarians;twelve, school librarians;twelve, multi-type participants; and two listed institutional and special library staffs.

Principal topics in continuing education programmes covered a wide range including copyright, networking, automation, planning, management, public relations and audiovisual materials. However, over one-third of the respondents offered basic or refresher courses to public library staffs in such areas as reference, children's services, storytelling, and young adult services. A few states mentioned law materials, oral history, censorship, and government documents. Workshops on community needs and development of special services to disadvantaged, senior citizens and other groups reflect the outreach programme priorities of some states.

Wisconsin reported a continuing education programme for public library and staff through the University of Wisconsin using the Education Telephone Network (ETN). Once a month for about two hours, several topics are discussed by a group or panel. Local libraries may purchase sets of materials related to the programme.

Topics covered in the last two years include:

- Networks,
- Censorship,
- School-public library cooperation,
- The independent adult learner,
- Deaf awareness, and
- Service to special groups.

Alaska and Hawaii reported the use of video cassettes to bring continuing education programmes to remote areas, and West Virginia reported that the capability now exists there to provide this form of continuing education programming.

Frequently, continuing education programmes sponsored by the state library agency are executed by contract with a university or other educational organization. Some states do this extensively; others use this method for institutes in such areas as management.

Recent changes and improvements in the continuing education activities of state library agencies reflected the increased emphasis and direction given a planned and coordinated programme. The establishment of a new position of continuing education coordinator was listed by five states; assignment of this responsibility to an established position was listed by many states.

Several states were engaged in "train the trainer" programmes with the shift to local library systems of responsibility for staff development and training in their own institutions, particularly for non-professional staff. State programmes will provide for more advanced and intensive training and attempt to ensure continuity in programme offerings. At least two states - North Carolina and Maryland -provide reimbursement to public library staffs for attending out-of-state institutes.

The responsibility of the continuing education coordinator for developing and disseminating information on continuing education offerings in-state and nationally; for maintaining a master calendar; for providing continuing liaison with library schools, library associations and other educational agencies; and for assuring a programme of needs identification and developing plans to meet needs were mentioned. These activities reflect to a marked degree the influence of the CLENE report and subsequent programmes and activities of CLENE. It should be noted that state library agency personnel active in CLENE are frequently those most active in continuing education development in their respective states.

Several states commented that NCLIS and CLENE had provided the impetus for renewed continuing education activity at the state level; one saw CLENE as the key to noteworthy, effective state library agency work in continuing education. The continuing education programmes of CLENE itself provide state library agency personnel the opportunity to gain knowledge, exchange information, and encourage the further coordinated development of continuing education activities of state library agencies.

Changes and trends seen as important and needed for further development of continuing education include the development of more non-traditional methods for the delivery of continuing education programmes, as well as education techniques more suitable to adult learners. States ex- pressed the need for improved needs assessment and evaluation skills and techniques.

At least one-half the states were interested in a recognition system for continuing education. This seemed to be the national trend of greatest interest. Some states are currently using the continuing education unit (CEU) in institutions of higher education for library programmes. CEUs are directly related to certification in several states. South Dakota State Library provides voluntary certification for public libraries based on CEUs. Michigan and North Carolina have proposals for recertification of public librarians through approved programmes in continuing education and the CEU. The "college without walls" programme in New Hampshire and Vermont has prompted library staff to indicate that continuing education programmes should provide some academic credit.

A nationally recognized CEU programme for librarians was specifically cited by several respondents. The study recently completed by CLENE, Model Continuing Education Recognition System in Library and Information Science, was first discussed in January at a CLENE meeting and is to be further examined and discussed at a national convention sponsored by NCLIS in June 1978. State library agencies will need to give the proposal and comments from the field serious study, since it has implications for an increased state library agency role.

This object has attempted to provide a summary of the development of continuing education responsibilities in state library agencies as viewed in the literature and reported from the agencies themselves. A few other points and issues need to be raised. State library agencies have a continuing responsibility for the improvement of the quality of library services in the state. In that respect they are in a unique position to assess the impact of continuing education programmes on library services in the state, and have a responsibility to do so. There is no documentation to determine whether this is being done, but the need to develop the evaluation and performance criteria for this purpose is evident. In the author's opinion this would lead to fewer programmes of longer duration, involving participants in more appropriate learning situations and plans for implementation in their libraries.

Another issue is the responsibility of the individual for his own continuing education and for the pursuit of programmes that satisfy individual needs and interests. State library agency programmes are geared primarily to the perceived needs of the institution and to the priorities of the state library plans and objectives. To the extent that these coincide with individual needs and interests and that participation is voluntary and encouraged, the interests of both can be served.

By publicizing continuing education programmes at state, regional or national levels, state library agencies are helping individuals to become aware of other opportunities. Each state library agency needs to define its own role in continuing library education in relation to those of library schools, library associations and other providers of continuing education programmes.

State library agencies should continue efforts to make possible situations in which innovators and practitioners can reach each other, invent ways to be mutually instructive and supportive, define steps by which to strengthen the drive towards improved continuing education programmes, and undertake cooperative endeavours that ultimately may matter greatly in the capacity of library personnel to deliver the library and information services needed in today's society.

LIBRARY LEGISLATION

The Nature of the Problem

It would appear at first sight that provision and public maintenance of a system of public libraries would be an obvious step in any country where education and the promotion of literacy were considered important. Education, after all, is not an end in itself; the individual must not only have access to the printed word during his period of formal education, he must have the means of enlarging his experience after school and university, and this necessarily implies organized collections of printed materials. If a library is an essential adjunct to school or college, it is an essential adjunct in the world outside.

One would also think that the legislative base for such a system of public libraries would be a comparatively simple matter, and that those libraries would automatically be free for all to use. It is almost universally recognized that education should be compulsory, and that it should be free up to a certain level. True, cost can be a limiting factor but few countries today do not devote a large proportion of their resources to educational provision. Neither of these assumptions is in fact correct. Systems of public libraries, as against individual public libraries, have only recently been recognized as essential, even in advanced countries, and many countries, some with a secure basis of culture and education, do not have generally applicable public library legislation. Examples are France, Belgium, the Netherlands and Italy. Even where public library legislation has been long established, it can be seen from the examples studied here that, in the framework of the modern State, public library law is noticeably defective. The development of public libraries has probably been hampered by the paradox that they were in fact recognized as instruments of popular education and social welfare long before the conception of compulsory education and before the legal framework of the modern State was established. The concept of the public library has been essentially that of a local community project.

All countries have public libraries, buildings where books are provided for general reading, either free of charge or for a small subscription. They have been provided in thousands all over the world by charitable bodies, educational, social and religious organizations, by philanthropic individuals, as memorials to a person or to commemorate an occasion. The public libraries in England and the United States in the early nineteenth century were typical, but they are not always a passing phase of development. The traveller interested in the phenomenon will come across examples almost anywhere: in Asia, for example, the Hardinge Library in Delhi, the Connemara Library in Madras, the Raffles Library in Singapore; in Africa, the King George VI Memorial Library in Tanga, the Connaught Library in Nairobi. Some become moribund. Some are being or have been incorporated by good fortune into a national or local public library system. Some operate even today with some success. But they are not public libraries in the modern accepted sense, nor were they, for that matter, in the nineteenth century.

Edward Edwards, pioneer of the public library in Great Britain, summed up their built-in failure over a hundred years ago, in evidence to the Select Committee on Public Libraries of the House of Commons in 1849:

- Without some assured provision of the means of continued increase, as well as simple preservation-no man ever secured to posterity the

> true advantage of a public library. To those persons, therefore, who took thought of such matters, two principles to start with seemed plain. The one that new libraries should be formed in a catholic spirit. The other, that they should be freed from all dependence either in gifts or in current 'subscriptions', for their permanent support. The first principle involved the corollary that the new institutions and their management should stand entirely aloof from party influences in politics or religion. The second principle involved the corollary that the maintenance must be by rate, levied on the whole tax-paying community, and administered by its elective and responsible functionaries.

This statement quite obviously implied that a legal basis was necessary, if the public library was to be a permanent institution and on the implications of this statement most of the public library legislation of the nineteenth century and early twentieth century was founded.

In 1949, Unesco issued the first international declaration on the need and the functions of the public library, and in it was contained the same principle:

- This manifesto, by describing the potentialities of the public library, proclaims Unesco's belief in the public library as a living force for popular education and for the growth of international understanding and thereby for the promotion of peace.
- The public library is a product of modern democracy and a practical demonstration of democracy's faith in universal education as a lifelong process.
- Though primarily intended to serve the educational needs of adults, the public library should also supplement the work of schools in developing the reading tastes of children and young people, helping them to become adults who can use books with appreciation and profit.
- As a democratic institution operated by the people for the people, the public library should be: established and maintained under clear authority of law: supported wholly or mainly from public funds: open for free use on equal terms to all members of the community, regardless of occupa-tion, creed, class, or race.

The manifesto goes on to define the purposes and list some of the services of the public library. It did not, however, attempt to deal with a problem that was already engaging the attention of public librarians and those concerned with the spread of education and literacy, that there must not only be a legal base, but that that base must give equal opportunity to all citizens to use the services of public libraries. In other words, the legislation must be mandatory and cover the whole of the area falling within the scope of the legislation. The legislation must also provide for something more than opportunities for voluntary co-operation between libraries-it must provide for a nation-wide service, even though the public library remains a locally rooted institution. In 1953, Unesco organized its first seminar on public libraries in developing countries, at Ibadan, in Nigeria. Eighteen countries were represented, mostly in West Africa. Legislation was one of the primary subjects discussed, and in the general report of the seminar, the following statement of principles was included:

- Only legislation can empower the appropriate authorities to provide the service and ensure adequate financial support and efficient administration according to a national standard. Only legislation can define the functions of the providing authority, create the conditions in which it may fulfil those functions, and ensure development.

Library law for national schemes should include the following elements:

- General authorization of expenditure without fixing a maximum.
- Compulsory implementation whenever conditions become favourable. The basis of favourable conditions, it is suggested, is the possession of necessary finance and all requisite material by the providing authority, the existence of a tested organization and the presence of trained and experienced personnel. Compulsory provision is never likely to precede compulsory primary education.
- The obligation to employ only qualified and trained personnel as librarians, and to authorize development only when professional librarians are available to administer the service.
- Service for the entire population in some form or other.
- The inter-lending of books between libraries so that the book resources of the whole territory shall be available to all.
- The book stock shall embrace every shade of opinion, without prejudice to anyone.
- The national scheme in all its parts shall aim at free service.

An addendum to this statement pointed out that there was great difficulty in arriving at a conclusion regarding compulsory legislation, since it was recognized that permissive legislation might well allow for a high standard to be set by enthusiastic authorities, which would act as an inspiration to others. This, and other proposals of the Ibadan seminar, were an act of faith at the time they were published, in view of the conditions of West Africa at the time, just beginning to emerge from colonial rule, with very few African librarians. But the statement was the beginning from which can be traced the rapid development of public library services in Ghana, Eastern Nigeria and Sierra Leone, based on simple but mandatory legislation. In 1955, the Public Libraries Section of the International Federation of Library Associations published a memorandum on the development of public library services, of which one section was devoted to legislation:

Each State should adopt library laws which will include the following provisions:

- Appropriate local authorities must be empowered to expend public funds for public library purposes.
- The amount of local expenditure should not be limited: local authorities should be able to expend as much as they are willing and able.
- The public library purposes for which funds may be expended shall be so defined as not to restrict development.
- Local authorities should be empowered to enter into arrangements with other local authorities for joint schemes for providing the whole or any part of the service, and to contribute to the cost of schemes for cooperation and mutual assistance.
- Each local authority should appoint a library committee directly responsible to the local council.
- Each local authority should have power to appoint staff who shall be employed in accordance with the conditions and regulations applicable to other local government officers.
- The use of all the services provided must be available to all inhabitants free of any charge whatsoever.
- Though each local authority provides services primarily for the use of its own inhabitants and those who work or study in its area, other persons living outside that area should be able to use those services if they wish... when adequate library services are provided generally in a country or region, however, they should be available to all, regardless of place of residence, without payment.

As soon as practicable, all appropriate local authorities should be legally obliged to maintain adequate public library services. The document was adopted as a statement of policy, with the recommendation that it be sent for study to all governments and appropriate agencies concerned. One further example may be given of the continuing concern with the importance of library legislation. In October 1955, Unesco organized a further seminar on public libraries, this time at Delhi, India, where a successful demonstration project had been founded. The seminar was held in the Delhi Public Library and twelve Asian countries were represented by forty-six librarians and educators. Again, public library legislation and its nature were under discussion, and the following proposals were accepted:

Over-all control and co-operation of development, to provide for a permanent and progressive national public library service, can be obtained only by legislation, which should provide for the following:

- Opportunity for the development of public library service which will be available to all people on the basis of free and equal access.
- An independent service, and not one attached to another department.
- The constitution of a governing body, to be referred to in this report

as the central library board, or in a federal state a number of such bodies, subject to a national body with advisory functions.
- Provision for adequate public finance.
- The constitution of district library boards responsible for administration of units of public library service.

Other parts of the report pay tribute to the work done by private bodies in founding and maintaining public library services, but affirm that planned direction and control are now required, and that these cannot be achieved by subsidy to private organizations. On finance the report states: It is of fundamental importance that finance should be by public funds, whether national, state or local, or a combination of these... differences in the structure, powers and financial resources of government at local, state, and national level are such that a simple statement of general applicability cannot be made. It can be said however that sources of finance must be adequate for the support of the service established. The proportion of local funds to national or state funds is a matter for decision by individual governments.

On the unit of service:
- At an early stage in the establishment of a national public library service, the question arises of the convenient administrative unit. This may be defined as the smallest autonomous unit of public library service... the selection of this unit as the real basis for the development of public library service, is a matter of some importance. It should be a viable area as regards finance and administration, and should conform as for as possible to existing local government boundaries... for ideal development, the area chosen should contain both rural and urban districts.

It is illustrative of the complexity of the problem that these four authoritative statements on public library development, issued over a short period of time, should vary so greatly in their emphasis. The Unesco Manifesto concentrated on the value and use of the public library, but said nothing about its financial or legislative base. The Ibadan seminar defined as a first principle that only legislation could provide the necessary secure and permanent foundations. It said nothing about the administrative unit on which implementation must depend, or financial problems, but it did prescribe mandatory legislation under favourable conditions.

The IFLA statement, though it defined the nature of public library service, proposed what was in fact permissive legislation, and it did not make any proposals about central control, the size of the administrative area, or financial viability of local authority areas. Although it said there should be no upper limit on expenditure, it did not mention the vital problem of minimum expenditure. The Delhi seminar proposals, with the previous statements before it, went much further, and proposed legislation which would provide for over-all control, viable areas and financial support at national and local level. But it found itself in difficulties when it attempted to define the nature of the viable area. Any acceptable general statement must be vitiated by the enormous differences between countries in national administrative and executive structure, local government and its relationship to central government, the powers existing at different levels of government, and above all, the financial capacity of these different levels.

The stage of educational and technical development of a country must also be taken into account, but this is possibly not quite as important as it may appear. While literacy is obviously a primary requirement of public library use, most countries now have an extensive programme of primary and secondary education, and in many countries, too, advanced technology exists side by side with primitive standards of living in some areas. It should also be remembered that in the last century, in some countries, notably the United Kingdom, public library legislation actually preceded general legislation on education. It would be a mistake, also, to assume that the problems of public library legislation are confined to the developing countries. If there is one thing that emerges quite clearly from this study of public library law, it is that the problems of an adequate and effective library law are just as great in the more advanced countries as in the developing ones, apart from the fact that some advanced countries do not yet have a general public library law.

In some countries, such as the United Kingdom, the United States and Canada, the problem is primarily one of reshaping law which is defective and inadequate to meet the need of the user of the public library in the twentieth century, who requires access to the enormous and increasing flood of printed material, numbered in books by the hundred thousand, and periodicals by the thousand. These requirements create in their turn a need for more and more specialized and trained personnel. The search is for a legislative base for viable units which can meet the readers' needs, and provide not only the material, but the technical services, equipment and staff required.

In other advanced countries, such as Norway and Denmark, the problem is not one of the viable unit, which in fact cannot be provided, but of compulsory co-operation to give the same results. The problems facing the developing countries may be different, but not so very different. It has often been stated that in social legislation, some African and Asian countries are at the stage others had reached in the nineteenth century. This is only superficially true. We are all living in the twentieth century. If the legislation of the nineteenth century is to be repeated, there is a long road to travel. Not only long, but unnecessary. The example of the past is to be learned from, not repeated.

Basic Principles and Practical Considerations in the Framing of Legislation

Assuming for the purpose of this chapter that new legislation is being considered, the first consideration in the framing of legislation is, of course, the nature of the State itself and the place that legislation takes in its structure. Particularly in social legislation such as the establishment of public libraries, which has primarily a local impact, account must be taken of the nature of the authority by which national government passes on its responsibilities, the basis of taxation at local and national level and in a federal State, the constitutional rights of established organisms within the State. Even where there is no general legislation, in countries where the doctrine of ultra quires does not apply and organs of local government may establish any service they are not specifically forbidden to do, public libraries may exist perfectly legally by local legislation, and this in turn will cause difficulties in framing a general law.

This is the case in the Federal Republic of Germany, and to some extent in the Netherlands and Belgium. Apart from this, there are patterns in the relationship of local government to national government which must be taken into account. H. F. Alderferl in his study of local government in developing countries, identifies four basic patterns, which are established in developing countries either through adoption or by passing on of previous colonial development. The French pattern, which exists in a large part of Africa, carries the doctrine of ultra vires much further than in England or the United States. Local government has no powers not granted to it by constituted authority.

Local government also is subject to executive jurisdiction which is independent of the administrative and legislative branch to a great extent. Generally, he states, French local government is characterized by centralization, chain of command, hierarchical structure, executive domination and legislative subordination. The English pattern, as defined by Alderfer, is characterized by decentralization, with local decision-making bodies with more or less independent powers, as against concentration, in the French pattern, where all power lies with the central government with local units acting as agents.

The English pattern generally implies also legislative dominance, the committee system and voluntary citizen participation. The Soviet system is one of 'democratic centralism', with all organs as links in one continuous chain of governmental power. Communist Party direction and leadership exist at all levels, and local agencies are not law-making or executive bodies in their own right, but subject to correction not only at the next higher level but at other levels. The 'traditional' form of local government is non-Western, though in Western forms there are traditional residues. The pattern is one of a chief or local leader, or a group of people, having jurisdiction over a village or group of villages. Essentially the form is non-urban, but it has deep roots and cannot be ignored as a working unity.

The Indian panchayat system of local government is an example of a traditional form being incorporated into the local government system of a modern State, organized generally on the English system. The clash between two systems, and the different types of law that may be produced, was illustrated in Africa when, at a UNESCO seminar at Enugu in 1961, the question of a model Act for African countries was discussed. The Act proposed was on the English model. This was simple and mandatory, giving almost unlimited authority to an independent board, subject to central government control. It was this type of legislation which has been successful in practice in Ghana, Eastern Nigeria and Tanzania.

The delegates from the French-speaking countries could not accept this since it was not an acceptable type of legislation for their countries, and they proposed a different model Act for their purposes. Without quoting this in full, it can be said that it was at once more detailed and less specific. Though it set up a directorate attached to the Ministry of Education, and advisory bodies, it could be said to be rather a statement of intention than a legislative instrument. Subsequent decrees in the various territories have similar structure. Thus, the decree for the Ivory Coast goes into some detail on expenditures and staff required, but does not provide for means of raising the necessary funds or an organization charged with continuous development.

The differences may be more apparent than real, given a determination to create a public library service, but it does seem that in Europe, the Scandinavian countries, the United Kingdom and Ireland have been more successful, through planned co-operation between local and national government, than for instance, in France. A recent survey in Le Monde of the public libraries of Paris showed enormous variations in expenditure on libraries in the various communes, with seemingly no co-operation or standards imposed centrally. A generous system of subsidies for building is offered by the central government, but there does not appear to be any way of forcing local authorities to take advantage of them if they do not wish to provide their share.

There are other, important factors to consider in pre-consideration of legislation. Some investigation must be made of the practical problems, and a body of facts built up. While the survey is important, it must be a practical move towards action, and not an end in itself or a means of delaying action. One of the most successful librarians in charge of a library service in a developing country has said that until a service is provided it is impossible to say what sort of service is needed. A careful analysis at grass roots level involves a detailed statistical examination of a community-its growth rate, its educational levels, its literacy rates; it involves the testing of different types of reading materials and a survey of existing places for reading and studying.

Such an approach overlooks the complete lack of basic statistics on which to base the survey. And above all, it ignores the sense of urgency which permeates any developing country trying to pull itself into the twentieth century by its bootstraps. I am sure that these critics would produce a magnificent report. . . and that report would probably conclude that the contemplation of any form of library service was premature.

By the time it appeared it would have been overtaken by events, such is the speed of development of Africa today. This may be overstating the case against survey, but it is true that a survey should be made after decision-to discover specific problems and how they might be overcome.

These problems can be summarized as follows:

- *Educational Situation:* The provision of libraries depends on adult literacy, and is also concerned with the provision of primary education. Literacy rates based on averages are deceptive-for instance, the adult literacy rate in India is less than 20 per cent, but in Delhi in 1954 it was nearly 40 per cent and is now over 50 per cent. The Government of India report of 1959 did not consider that a literacy rate of 20 per cent was any barrier to a nationally organized public library service, but of course one would assume that a low average literacy rate would suggest concentration on urban areas. In terms of cost relative to use, there would be no point in providing for an elaborate system of mobile libraries to serve rural areas.
- *Language and Book Production:* The number of languages in use and their relative importance is a factor in pre-consideration. Allied to this is the matter of book production. Lack of book production in the national language is an extreme limiting factor, though the establishment of public libraries may well stimulate production and in fact has done so in some countries. But it must be observed that the success of public library development in some African countries has been due largely to the fact that English is the established language of communication, thus giving immediate access to an abundant source of material.
- *Population Density and Concentration:* It goes without saying that a rural and scattered population is more difficult to provide for than an urban one. The problem therefore is not one so much of over-all density as of concentration, and this can well affect the unit of administration
- *Communications:* This also affects the matter of the unit, and administrative arrangements. Decentrali-zation may well be necessary. This may be a problem of organization rather than legislation, but it must be considered.
- *Income and tax structure:* This affects the time factor during which legislation can be expected to come into effect, and also the proportion of cost to be met from various sources.
- *Existing Legislation:* This may exist nationally or locally, and consideration must be given to its possible incorporation in new legislation. In some countries, Ceylon is an example, effective public libraries exist in some areas through local legislation, and a new

library law must take into account their existence and their legislative base.

- *'Trained Librarians and Training Facilities:* While most countries will have trained librarians, though not in public libraries, pre-consideration must take into account the availability of trained librarians to implement legislation. Opportunities for training abroad must also be considered. While it is an important consideration, the availability of trained librarians is no more than a temporary limiting factor, since there is little point in training unless there are opportunities for employment. In India and Pakistan, facilities for training and qualification are in advance of employment possibilities in the public sector-not only bad planning but wasteful public policy.

These are some of the major items For pre-consideration and survey. The objective is to determine what a country can afford, how great is the need, what structure is required, and how legislation can assist rapid development, without placing too great a burden on financial ability or the administrative structure. None of them should be over-emphasized. The objective remains the same; the limiting factors affect how it is to be attained and at what speed. In this connation, the object by E. M. Broome repays careful study. Nearly all these limiting factors were present, but none of them deterred the Government of Tanzania from passing legislation and implementing it with determination and success.

As was reported at the Delhi seminar:

- In all countries represented at the seminar, public library service is already being provided in some degree, and the time is ripe for further development. In no country do the material difficulties appear to be unsurmountable, nor is a low literacy rate a decisive adverse factor. The rate of development may vary with the speed of overcoming these problems, but the basis for public library services should be laid now. The major deficiencies in present provisions are: lack of over-all control, and the existence of small unco-ordinated units; lack of, or deficiencies in, existing legislation; lack of sufficient funds and government interest; and lack of trained and experienced librarians.

Practical Considerations in Framing Legislation

It has been said that it is easier to pass a law than it is to change it, and this is a lesson to be learned from existing legislation. In the United Kingdom, for nearly seventy years only minor amendments were made to the enabling legislation, despite the fact that under the existing law there was no means by which county councils could set up public library services for rural populations.

Legislation should therefore be flexible and allow for changes in social conditions, in local-government structure and in the tax base. It should be capable of immediate application, but with progressive application. Study is made of the comparative merits and defects of existing legislation, but certain basic problems can be enumerated for primary consideration.

The Public Library as an Independent Service or Part of a National Library Service

In any country which can even consider the foundation of a public library service, there will already be in existence many libraries of high standard: university libraries, libraries of institutions, government departmental libraries, technical libraries and almost certainly a national and probably state libraries. It is tempting to think that there is an advantage in creating an integrated library service of which such libraries are a part. But it must be remembered that public libraries are for the whole community, whereas all other libraries are designed to serve a section of the community for a special purpose, and that purpose must be their prime consideration. Techniques are similar, but basic purposes are different. Uniting all libraries in one piece of legislation at an early stage is hardly practical, since not only would it tend to stifle the growth of the public library, but it would also entail bringing independent libraries under the legislation, and this would undoubtedly be resisted. At the same time, there is an obvious need for provision for cooperation and some co-ordination, probably best organized around the national library. Bibliographical and interloan functions should be of value to all libraries. The national library could therefore be usefully linked to the central public library authority.

The Central Authority

The need for a central authority charged with carrying out the provisions of legislation is clear. Should it be an independent body or one linked to, or subordinate to, a government department? This is a matter for decision at governmental level. There are advantages in making the central authority part of the department of education, with a department for libraries and controlling body, which should have more than advisory functions. The central board or authority is a modern device of government much used in developing countries, and experience of its past success in other circumstances will affect legislation for public libraries. But the implementation of legislation should not be left to any other body but education, and if education is chosen as the implementing and organizing department, then a section including trained librarians is essential, with advisory and inspecting functions.

Permissive or Mandatory Legislation

It has been shown that permissive legislation is of limited effectiveness, even when accompanied by financial inducements. Legislation should therefore require action to be taken, wherever the ultimate source of action. But provision should be made for progressive implementation at a rate to be determined by resources.

Relationship Between Local and Central Authority

It is generally accepted that the public library is a local community service. In fact, this becomes less and less true with the explosive growth in production of information material and technical developments in library organization. The answer must be sought in the local government structure of the country concerned. In some countries, a nationally controlled public library service has been created, with provision for some devolution to local government at later stages. The existence of federally organized states also presents some problems. But it must be stated that local interest is desirable and must be stimulated. This implies the passing over of some authority, or the creation of local advisory bodies.

The Size of' the Unit

Assuming that local authority interest is essential, the question then arises: what unit, what size and with what authority? The lbadan seminar, speaking for the situation in Africa, concluded that since recognition of local authority was only beginning, the sole public authority should be the national or state agency. At the same time, the appropriate local authority must eventually be given a responsible place in any national scheme of book service. The roots of the service must be in the local community rather than in the state, regional or national headquarters. The size and authority of the local unit are important questions, even when there is a suitable urban authority. An urban authority should never be the sole local unit, since its economic and social catchment area is equally important for public library purposes. The requirements for a viable unit, as we have seen, were well stated in the report of the Delhi seminar, but it is already clear, fifteen years later, that they are expanding. In developed countries for example, much larger units than previously thought necessary are now postulated, and the basing of a service on too small a unit can be disastrously hampering in later development. Apart from size, there are other considerations. Whatever the attachment at national level, it is generally conceded that at local level the public library service should be executively independent of other agencies, whether education or other departments such as cultural affairs or social education.

The public library serves all, but is not solely a part of any, SO it should remain independently governed and administered. The question of policy control is a matter of the form local government takes. There is much to be said for the board system, independent but responsible to the local-government system, but this is not always legally possible. But it should be possible at all times to bring into consultation persons of knowledge and goodwill.

Finance

It is generally now accepted that financial support for public libraries should come from public funds, that is, taxation. It is also generally recognized that the service should be free to the user, though this is not always the case in practice. In most developing countries, this means major support at national level, with assistance at local level so far as practicable, having regard to the limitations of local taxation in most developing countries. The acceptance of this principle has been a major limiting factor in public library progress, even in advanced countries, as will be demonstrated in study of existing legislation. It follows, therefore, that any unit at local level must be a tax-raising body, and provision for funds from taxation at a national level must be written in to any legislation. In a federal system, of course, another stage of financial support will be introduced. Various calculations of the cost of a public library service have been made, but they are of little value in view of changing needs, and could not sensibly be included in basic legislation. No one would expect a public library service to spring armed and ready from the ground, like Jason's dragons' teeth, and financial provision must depend on the rate of implementation of legislation. The Government of India report of 1959 postulated a period of twenty-five years for the creation of a full service, but its calculations as to cost are already completely out of date. Given progressive implementation, standards of service required are also a matter for progressive regulation, and not a suitable one for inclusion in legislation. The power to make regulations on standards and other matters should, however, be given.

Other Considerations

There are several other considerations which may have to be taken into account in framing legislation, but their importance will vary according to country. In some countries, there will be a problem of fitting in private or subscription libraries to the system. There must also be some provision for co-operation between libraries, but this again will vary with the primary decisions already taken. If a linkage with the national library, for instance, is envisaged, or if the unit of service is the whole country, then these provisions can be taken care of automatically under regulation. But if existing resources, as provided by various agencies, are to be fully utilized, then some provision for co-operation and inter-lending must be made. Although university and institutional libraries may not be fully integrated, their resources, after their first priorities are met, should be circulated generally. Whether library education, or the encouragement of library associations, should be incorporated in legislation is a moot point.

It could be fairly argued that if opportunity for employment of qualified people is given by the provision of a public library service, then educational institutions will provide the necessary further education facilities for training librarians and technicians, without any legal requirement to do so. Library associations, also, should not be too dependent on legislative assistance. Again, the provision of a service will itself exert the necessary stimulus for the creation of an active body of professional librarians. And if such associations are to encourage further progress and technical improvement, they should be independent. All these problems and others applying to particular countries will need to be closely considered before framing suitable legislation in terms which will create a permanent, expanding public library service available to all people, whatever their age, status or geographical situation.

The way in which the problems have already been approached and the answers embodied in legislation is the subject of the next stage. There are many lessons to be learned, and the gap between intentions and results is often a depressing commentary on how the goodwill of legislators can be frustrated by circumstances unforeseen or unsuspected. Government and legislation are, alas, by no means an exact science. But in the framework of the modern State, legislation as an instrument of authority is necessary. In the case of public libraries it can truthfully be said that no successful public library system can exist without legal authority, but that many devices have been necessary to get round defective legislation. Public libraries happen to be the subject of this study, but no doubt authorities on law and government could produce better examples of problems caused by legislation rather than solved by it.

The Pattern of Legislation Comparative Solutions

The main body of this study consists of summaries of the existing legislation in fourteen countries, and taking into account the federal countries, twenty Acts are considered, with others mentioned in passing. More could have been chosen, but in fact, not more than thirty countries have effective general library legislation, less than a quarter of the independent nations of the world. Of the countries chosen, four are developing countries, two are countries with centrally planned economies and three are federally organized.

This, therefore can be considered a reasonably representative sample, ranging from the most advanced countries, where coverage is complete and basic standards established, to a country which has only just become independent, Botswana. They all have one thing in common; in none of them is legislation, even now, entirely satisfactory and effective, in that it encourages development to the point of greatest efficiency and maximum results. All have problems to some degree, despite the fact that in most of the countries considered there has been revision of law in the last ten years. The advanced countries, most of which have had public library legislation in some form for many years, but with varying effectiveness, have no great problem of financial ability to provide a nationwide system of public libraries, if that ability can be brought to bear.

The problem is rather one of an inadequate and unsuitable local-government structure, and the supplementation of local resources, or in some examples, replacement of local initiative, by central-government intervention. A pattern clearly emerges in nearly all recent legislation, first of a search for a larger and more viable unit of service, which must be both geographically and financially able to deploy larger resources for public library service, and second of the creation of a central advisory body to encourage improvement of public library service. One can see similarities in the solutions adopted, but there are also wide variations. It is proposed in this chapter to show by comparison the major similarities and variations of the law as it stands in advanced countries. There are important lessons to be learned by the developing countries in framing their own legislation, and it appears that the advanced countries could also learn from their neighbours. In making these comparisons, it must of course be borne in mind that though public library law is evolutionary in character, it cannot be separated from the general body of law of a country, and it must be set in the executive, social and geopolitical structure of the country concerned.The fact that some countries with a high educational and cultural standard have not so far been able to enact general mandatory legislation on public libraries proves this to be the case. Permissive legislation has been replaced by mandatory legislation in most countries. The appropriate local authorities are now required rather than permitted to provide a public library service.

In some countries, notably the United Kingdom, Finland and Sweden, mandatory provision is not necessary, since coverage is already complete. In Norway, obligatory provision is laid down in the Act, and in Denmark a date is set for all communes to provide public libraries. In Canada and the United States, though provision is not mandatory, the problem is no longer one of provision but of viability, and this could be said generally of all the countries considered, except the countries having centrally planned economies, where the law has nothing to say on this. But it would appear that in Hungary, at any rate, there is complete coverage.

Central Government and Advisory Bodies

In all countries, the intervention of the central government, either at state or federal level, or both, has led to the setting up of a central body to guide future progress, and this is the most common feature in all recent legislation. These central bodies may take many forms, either advisory or executive. They may be independent, or responsible to a department of State. Their membership may be drawn from organizations or individuals. Their constitution and powers can be summarized as follows:

Czechoslovakia

The Central Library Council is an advisory body in the Ministry of Education and Culture. There are two bodies, one for Bohemia-Moravia and one for Slovakia. Membership consists of representatives of authorities and expert librarians. All proposals concerning libraries are submitted to them, and they have the right to initiate proposals themselves.

Denmark

The Library Council consists of sixteen members representing all sections of the Danish Library Service. They are appointed by the Minister of Cultural Affairs, are consulted in all matters of importance to the working of the Libraries Act, and have the right to initiate representations. The chairman is the Library Director, head of the State inspectorate.

Finland

The library delegation is an advisory body responsible to the Central Board of Schools. There are twelve delegates, representing the Department of Education, local authorities, library training and other organizations working for libraries and adult education. The delegation can take the initiative in submitting proposals to the Central Board of Schools.

Hungary

The National Council for Library Activity, responsible to the Ministry of Culture, has a section for public libraries. It has also a working organization, the State Institute of Libraries, similar in some respects to the State inspectorates of Scandinavian library systems. The functions of the National Council are advisory and technical, but being a direct organ of central government, it obviously has great prestige.

Ireland

The Library Council has as its main purpose the operation and supervision of the Irish Central library, and a secondary purpose of assisting local library authorities to improve their services. Its membership is by nomination, and a majority of the members are nominated by universities or the National Library. The powers of the Library Council are considerable, since it considers applications for grants from local authorities and its functions are much more than advisory. In view of the form of local government in Ireland, it can be said to be an executive body with potentially great powers. In fact, the original secondary function has become the primary one.

Qntario

The Provincial Library Council is an advisory body responsible to the Minister for Education, and it consists of nine members appointed by the minister, and one for each regional system. It has certain functions under the Act and may also make recommendations regarding development and co-ordination of library service.

Quebec

The Quebec Public Libraries Commission is responsible to the Minister for Cultural Affairs. Its membership is six persons nominated by the minister, whose qualifications shall be their interest in the development of public libraries, and the Director of Public Libraries of the Province. The powers and duties of the commission are wide, in that it is generally charged with the study of the best means of developing public library services, and it must report every three months on its findings regarding the working of the Public Libraries Act.

United Kingdom

The Library Advisory Councils, set up by the Minister of Education under the 1964 Act, one for England and one for Wales, have no set number of members, nor any stated qualifications for membership. They are nominated directly by the minister, and actually the representatives are drawn from local authority members, university and public librarians representing all the major interests of local government and various sizes and types of library. The function of the councils is purely advisory, and their main work is in connexion with the achievement of standards and the general working of the Act. But by their existence, they have become the advisory bodies for libraries in general, and on such matters as librarianship training.

Washington State

The State Library Commission is an executive commission appointed by the Governor, and responsible for administration of federal and state funds for improvement of public library services. It operates through the state library and appoints the state librarian, who acts as secretary to the commission. Though its main functions are executive, it also has advisory responsibilities. The functions of these bodies are mainly advisory, and as will be seen generally from their constitutions, are intended as a source of expert opinion on public library development. They are useful bodies, but equally important, their existence creates a secretariat, and that secretariat, whether clearly laid down in legislation as in Quebec, or not, as in England and Wales, inevitably assumes supervisory functions. Those functions can be of inspection and control, as in Finland and Denmark, or they can be limited to advice to the appropriate minister and the right to ask for regular reports and give advice to individual library authorities. Even where there is no central coordinating body, there is invariably a central coordinating government department.

In Norway, the State inspectorate is recognized by the Act, and the State Inspector is a direct appointment of the Crown, though responsible to the Ministry of Church and Education. In Sweden, there is a Library Section of the Central Board of Education, and its functions include supervision of State grants, approval of building plans, and supervision of the School of Librarianship. With the change in local government law, its functions are now more limited, being more advisory than supervisory. In the United States, in addition to the state departments concerned with public libraries, now established in most states, there is an office in the Department of Education in Washington charged with supervision of the very substantial grants under the Library Services and Construction Act. Except in Scandinavia, where they have been in existence for many years, the emergence of these bodies and the departments attached to them is comparatively recent, and their influence on public library development is bound to increase. It will be noted that the usual attachment of the library councils and their civil-service bureaux is to the Ministry of Education, in some cases to the Minister of Culture. But this attachment at central-government levels does not necessarily imply any attachment of public libraries at lower levels of government to any particular department.

Provision for Co-Operation

In most countries, legislation shows a marked preference for the provision of public library services within the existing local-government framework, and an equal reluctance to interfere with those existing agencies, even when they are clearly not viable. The only exception to this in recent legislation, where smaller authorities are required to give up their powers, is in England and Wales, where there is provision for the compulsory surrender of library powers by authorities of less than 40,000 population.

Even here, the clauses have not so far been used, since a major local-government reform is expected to make them unnecessary. Local-government reform in Sweden and Denmark is also making the problem less urgent, though it will still exist. Failing the forcible creation of larger public library authorities, the search for the larger unit must take the form of co-operation, and recent legislation is characterized by the creation of a superstructure of co-ordination, often at two or three levels, either mandatory or permissive. Library authorities are either to be persuaded to join with others in a library system, or a superstructure of co-operation is created above them, in which they have the opportunity, or are compelled, to take part. Financial assistance is usually given. Some examples of this kind of provision are as follows:

Denmark

A number of suitable libraries are designated as county libraries, serving a district. Their functions are to assist the local libraries in the district by lending or obtaining for them books and other suitable materials they cannot provide themselves, and by giving advice and technical assistance. In the present legislation, the Library Director recommends which libraries shall be recognized as county libraries, and the minister shall ensure that the district served is of a suitable size and that the county library is able to carry out its functions. In the past, it is thought, too many county libraries were designated, and the districts were too small. The provision is mandatory, that is to say, all libraries must join a district, and an advisory committee is formed to direct the work. National grants are made to the county libraries, and the county or counties must also contribute at rates laid down. The communes themselves do not contribute directly.

Norway

The system of regional central libraries is similar, except that the designated libraries have wider functions in super-vision of their local libraries. The problems of establishment, and suitable areas, are very great in Norway, and though nineteen regional libraries have now been established, they vary greatly in resources. Again the inclusion in an area is mandatory, and grants are made to meet the cost, with supplementary grants from the areas covered.

Sweden

In addition to the establishment of county libraries on similar lines to Denmark and Norway, a further superstructure has been added of three inter-library loan centres, which lend to the county libraries and receive grants for their services from the State. It must be emphasized that in the Scandinavian countries, the aid-giving libraries are the larger libraries in their area, and though they may establish special departments for their additional functions, in no sense, except in a limited way in Norway, do they administer or supervise the other libraries in their area.

Quebec

The regional libraries in Quebec are quite different from others, and serve a different purpose. They are intended, not to superimpose an additional system, but to encourage the provision of public library service in those sparsely populated areas which cannot provide for themselves, even with grant aid. The system is fully described in the appropriate section, but briefly, when a minimum area containing 25,000 inhabitants can be defined, an ad hoc committee is formed. The kind of service depends on the size of the area and other factors, but generally, grant is 85 per cent of the total cost. Such a system is only required under extreme adverse conditions, but the similarity to the Norwegian system in its northern area is obvious.

Ontario

The Ontario method of creating larger areas is in effect a three-tier system. In a county, a combined library system can be formed at the request of 75 per cent of the authorities in the county, then a county library service is formed, and a separate public library board set up. But it is only responsible for that part of the county which has asked for inclusion. The system has obvious defects, but it does have the effect of helping some at least of the smaller authorities to combine. Superimposed on this system of county libraries and independent libraries is provision for regional library systems, working roughly on the Scandinavian pattern, and having similar responsibilities. Substantial grants are available from state funds, but regions are not necessarily inclusive of all the libraries in their area since, throughout the legislation of Ontario, there are no mandatory powers.

United States of America

There are no mandatory powers in the United States, and most recent legislation, both federal and state, has written into it an injunction that the independence of the community library is to be respected and preserved.

The creation of the larger unit therefore is by the voluntary amalgamation of independent libraries into 'systems', in which service is often provided by contract between one library and another. It is interesting to note that current thinking puts the minimum viability of a system at 150,000 population.

United Kingdom

A voluntary system of co-operation has existed for many years, with member libraries paying subscriptions usually on a per capita basis. The country is divided into fourteen regions for this purpose. The 1964 Act legally recognizes this system, and provides for compulsory membership by all library authorities, and for amalgamation of the regions where necessary.

Two of the largest regions, comprising London and the south-east of England, have already amalgamated, with the authority of the Ministry of Education. The purpose of the regions is principally inter-library co-operation, and for this purpose provision is made in legislation for bringing into the system other than public libraries.

LIBRARY LEGISLATION IN INDIA

Public library development in the state is the responsibility of the respective state government. Ten states in India have enacted Public Libraries Act in their states. The library legislation ensures the smooth functioning of the public libraries in the state. A state may have three tiers of public libraries in hierarchy. The apex body would be a state central library, the next tier consists of district libraries in all districts of the state, and third tier consists of rural and urban public libraries spread all over the state. Public Libraries Act also ensures each village or city at least have one government-aided public library. This Act also makes provisions of finances, human resources and other resources for the development and functioning of public libraries. Some state governments provide grants for the public libraries; some other state governments collect Library Cess from the taxpayers.

The states that passed Public Libraries Act are shown along with the year:

- Tamil Nadu (then called Madras Public Libraries Act, 1948);

- Andhra Pradesh (Hyderabad Public Libraries Act, 1955; then Andhra Pradesh Public Libraries Act, 1960);
- Maharashtra (Kolhapur Public Libraries Act, 1945; then Maharashtra Public Libraries Act, 1967);
- West Bengal (West Bengal Public Libraries Act, 1979);
- Manipur (Manipur Public Libraries Act, 1988);
- Kerala (Kerala Public Libraries Act, 1989);
- Haryana (Haryana Public Libraries Act, 1989);
- Mizoram (Mizoram Public Libraries Act, 1993);
- Goa (Goa Public Libraries Act, 1994).

Although other states as such have no Public Libraries Act, these states have government funded public libraries at the state and district levels; government aided public libraries at the rural and urban areas are mostly absent or having in an unorganised manner. The Delhi Public Library is located in Delhi, which is fully funded by the union government, so Delhi state has no such Act. For getting into the profession, public librarians should have formal training, at least a Certificate in Library Science (CLS) or Diploma in Library Science (DLS) for the rural libraries and Bachelor's in Library and Information Science (BLIS) for the district libraries. There is also provision of training of public librarians in the Public Libraries Act in some states, in the forms of orientation training, refresher training.

The public librarians should be aware of recent development in information sources and information systems, especially in the digital environment, as many public libraries worldwide are providing web-based library and information services to their users. Digital divide in the India can reduce significantly if they use computers and Internet technologies in the public libraries at the grass-root level. The users of public libraries then access digital information available through Internet to keep abreast of recent development in their areas of interest. Information literacy competency development programmes for public librarians and users can be a part of provisions in the Public Libraries Act of the states.

Role of State Level Library Associations

Library associations exist in most of the states and union territories of India. State level library associations are very active in public libraries development in their respective states. Some library associations also conduct certificate and diploma courses in library science that help the learners get into the profession. Some library associations also conduct refresher courses for the in-service public librarians, mostly in the areas of library automation, ICT applications in libraries, and other contemporary issues. Most library associations observe Library Day and Dr. S.R. Ranganathan's birthday. On those occasions they organize one-day seminars or lectures. This way public librarians get informed about the recent development in the librarianship and public libraries movement in India and the states. Some library associations bring out their newsletters and bulletins for their member librarians and disseminate various professional information. Some library associations take up the issue of information literacy competency for the librarians and library users. Library associations in the state should come forward and develop information literacy competency of the public librarians through organizing training programmes, workshops and seminars. In December 2005, Indian Library Association had organized 51th All India Conference with the focus on "libraries, information literacy and lifelong learning", where many librarians felt the importance of information literacy in life-long learning and optimizing the usage of information in the libraries. In October 2005, an international information literacy workshop was held at the Punjabi University, Patiala, India to promote information literacy in South and South East Asia, with the support of UNESCO and other partners. In September 2003 at Prague, the International Alliance for Information Literacy was formed where India's Networking Alliance for Voluntary Actions, a network of NGOs, became a member. In India, a number of NGOs support public libraries and community information centres, where common people become users of these libraries. The state level library associations, NGOs and developmental agencies can collaborate amongst themselves to develop information literacy competencies of the librarians and library users.

Information Literacy (IL) Competency Development Programmes for Public Librarians and Library Users

Information literacy (IL) competency development programme for public librarians would be a kind of training course for the trainers. The public librarians would impart training to the end users of public libraries. Some of the skills required for the information literacy are already achieved by the public librarians through their formal degree or diploma courses; induction, orientation, and on-the job training programmes. Some librarians started their career before the introduction of information communication technologies (ICT) in library services and information handling. Such ICT skills, communication and teaching skills need to be obtained freshly through the refresher courses.

The aims of the information literacy competency development programmes for public librarians can be:

- The ability to apply the principles of scholarly communication to problems of information handling;
- The ability to locate, select and use appropriate information retrieval tools in order to obtain useful information in connection with studies or work of the end users, and when required;
- Confidence in using, and satisfaction in carrying out information searching;
- Confidence in communicating, instructing and educating the users.

Some of the objectives IL competency development programmes for public librarians are:

- Public librarians would be able to develop a systematic method of searching for information related to areas of studies of the users;
- They would be aware of wide range of sources available for finding information and select the sources which will best meet users needs;
- They would be aware of appropriate indexing and abstracting services and databases and understand the principles of their use;
- They would develop database searching techniques for accessing both web-based and CD-ROM databases;
- They would be able to use current awareness methods to keep up to date with the published literature;
- They would be able to use international academic networks for getting information;
- They would be able to use and create list servers, discussion forums, Internet chat services and bloggers for obtaining and disseminating information;
- They would be able to use local library network for sharing in-house resources and obtaining documents through inter-library loan and document delivery services;
- They would be able to compare and critically evaluate information obtained from various sources;
- They would be able to cite bibliographic references in the papers, objects, reports or theses;
- They would be able to construct an institutional bibliographic system;
- They would be able to motivate library users in accessing library resources and availing user services;
- They would be able to communicate, instruct and educate library users;
- They would be able to prepare learning and assessment modules both printed as well as web-enabled for the learners;
- They would be able to make strategies for influencing stakeholders; and prepare action plans.

Some of the aims and objectives of the IL competency development programmes can be considered for public library users, as some of the components of the programmes are common. These aims and objectives of the IL competency development programmes are not exhaustive; and some elements may be altered whenever needs arise. Public library authorities in India, like Raja Rammohun Roy Library Foundation, Delhi Public Library, state central libraries and library associations can introduce IL competency development programmes for public librarians objectives and aims. The changing library scenario, present and future public library systems in India should be considered when designing such courses.

9

Computer and Library Networks

LIBRARIAN'S COMPUTER AWARENESS AND USE OF IT APPLICATION IN COLLEGE LIBRARIES

Dramatic changes in information tcchnology and society are having a considerable impact on educational institutions and their libraries. Information is a vital and indispensable product of the modern society. Availability of right information accurately, precisely and timely is of critical importance.

IT is the synthesis of computers and communication. Rapid advances in computer and communication technology enable storing, processing and transmission of huge amount of information easily, quickly and inexpensively. Develop-ments in science and technology have brought about reduction in size and cost of IT and tremendous increase in its capabilities. The use of IT enables provision of specialised, user oriented library and information products and services effectively and efficiently.

INFORMATION TECHNOLOGY

Information Technology (IT) can be defined as those processes and technologies which are used in acquisition and dissemination of information based on some electronic technology. Somerville has stated 'Information technology has resulted from a convergence of computing technology and communications technology'.

This means it is essentially the result of advances in the three important areas of computing, telecommunication and microelectronics. Information Technology is the application of a wide variety of electronic technologies to the information-handling activities.

In the domain of library information service, information technologies such as computer, telecommunications, word processing, micro-graphics, reprographics, video recordings and other electronic devices for the storage, retrieval, reproduction and dissemination of information are used.

APPLICATION OF IT IN COLLEGE LIBRARIES

The main functions of a library are acquisition, technical processing, storage, retrieval and dissemination. The traditional methods of doing these result in slow, laborious and repetitive manual routines. With the advent of modern technologies and their applications, manual routines have transformed into machine oriented ones.

The application of modern technology has allowed access to and storage of information quickly. The availability of computers has gradually changed the library scene. The convegence of computers with new developments in telecommunication techniques and equipment is considered as new information technology. The new information technology has a wide range of services which libraries can avail themselves of and offer to supplement the existing ones to users. Some of the areas to which the modern technology could be applied in day to day activities of the libraries are acquisition, cataloguing, circulation, indexing and abstracting of articles ,etc.

NEED FOR IT

Twentieth century has been the century of explosions. It has witnessed the population explosion, socio-cultural explosion, and nuclear explosion. The information explosion is due to the fact that information generation is a continuous process.

The interdisciplinary research and multidisciplinary research has led to the creation of new ideas, new knowledge and unprecedented growth in information particularly in science and technology. In this era of information explosion, in which large amount of information needs to be processed, application and use of new technology , *i.e.,* information technology is essential.

COMPUTER AWARENESS

Nowhere has the impact of the computer been felt greater than in the field of library and information services. Already most of the libraries are flooded with documents and records that they simply can not handle efficiently without computers. Computers are changing the way in which libraries collect, store, retrieve and disseminate information. The libraries that can not adjust to these trends will not survive. So computers will come and stay forever in all the library and information centres that wish to function efficiently here after.

ROLE OF COLLEGE LIBRARIAN IN IT ERA

The problem we face today is not of dearth of information, but of excessive information. The developing countries are making an earnest effort to concentrate more on developing and using new electronic gadgets to provide better access to information. With the use of new information technology, the libraries can provide nascent information quickly in great volume.

Today, the librarian plays a significant role in information handling and information transfer. He is rightly known as the information officer and is supposed to provide an active service for maximum use of information with minimum cost and time. Information technology demands trained personnel to handle information storage and retrieval in libraries. A modern librarian has to play a very important role in the process of communication in the contemporary time, for which he must be well educated, highly qualified and professionally competent.

DEVELOPMENTS IN COMPUTER AND MICROPROCESSOR TECHNOLOGY

Dramatic reductions in the size and cost of computer components and equally impressive gains in the speed, storage capacity and reliability of hardware components have expanded their use rapidly in all activities and functions of a library and information centre. Notable reductions in the size of microprocessors combined with dramatically enhanced capacity have added new dimensions to the computer new hardware technology.

Initially, small silicon chips contained only few components and circuits, but the average number of components has doubled each year Since, 1965. Early small-scale integration efforts first gave way to large-scale integration (LSI) chips that contained thousands of components, very large-scale integration (VLSI) chips that contained hundreds of thousands of components and circuits, and now ultra large-scale integration (ULSI) chips come with millions of components and circuits.

A microprocessor, also known as Central Processing Unit (CPU) of a computer, is a complete computation engine that is fabricated on a single chip. Microprocessors are manufactured by different companies like Intel, Advanced Micro Divices (AMD), Motorola, ,etc. However, most widely-used microprocessors are manufactured by Intel. The first microprocessor used in a PC was Intel 8080. Introduced in 1974, it was a complete 8-bit microprocessor on a single chip. Intel 8088 used in the IBM PC in 1979, was the first microprocessor that made its presence felt in the market.

The PC market moved from the 8088, 80286, 80386, 80486, Pentium, Pentium-II, III, IV and now to Intel Dual Core and Quad Core. The new Intel Dual Core can execute any piece of code that ran on the original 8088, but the Dual Core runs about 3,000 times faster. The capacity of a microprocessor is measured in terms of the number of bits it can send or receive and the number of bits it can process internally.

The 8088 was an 8/16 bit processor, indicating that it can send or receive 8 bits of data and internally process 16 bits of data at a time. The 80286 was a 16/16 bit processor and 80386 chip had a 32-bit processor with a 32-bit data path and, as a result, was much faster than either the 8088 or the 80286 chip. The 80486 chip, introduced by Intel in late 1989, had a 32- bit processor.

It has architectural enhancements, Hence, it performed better than the 80386 chip. The Pentium is a 32-bit processor with a 32-bit data path. It is three times faster than the 80486. The Pentium II and III had a 32-bit processor with a 64-bit data path. It was three times faster than the Pentium. The Pentium IV is a 32-bit processor with a 64-bit data path, and was introduced in 2000.

It is four times faster than the Pentium. Currently, PCs and laptops are equipped with Dual Core which is a 64-bit processor with 64-bit data path and processing speed of 3.0 Ghz. Like microprocessor technology, digital storage devices have also witnessed notable reductions in its size and cost with dramatically enhancement in capacity of storage.

There are two types of data storage devices, *i.e.,* removable data storage devices and Non-removable data storage devices. The data storage devices come in many sizes and shapes. The storage devices can also be categorised based on media used for storage, for example magnetic storage media, optical storage media, metal-oxide semiconductors or flash memory devices (popularly known as Pen drives or USB drives). Magnetic storage media are commonly used for large volumes of data (*e.g.,* video, image, or remote sensing data). Large amounts of data are stored through tape drives because the capacity on the drives is huge - three billion (or three gigabits) of data per square inch can fit on a single magnetic disk.

Hard discs, floppies, tapes, cartridges, ,etc., are example of magnetic media. CD-ROMs and DVD ROMs are example of optical storage media which can again be of two types, , *i.e.,* i) write-once, read-many: data once written cannot be erased; and ii) Rewritable: the data that is once written can be erased completely and the same storage device can be used again for storing different data. A typical disc used in a computer-based CD drive stores 650 MB.

Digital Versatile Disk or DVD, initially stood for Digital Video Disc. Like a CD, DVD is an optical storage system for read-only, recordable and rewritable applications. The DVD format provides several configurations of data layers, moving from 2D storage to 3D storage. Each configuration is designed to provide additional storage capacity. The similarity between the DVD and the CD gets smaller with each upgraded configuration, however, DVDs in contrast to CDs has storage capacity of 4.7 GB.

Metal-oxide semiconductors-based storage devices, popularly known as pen drives or USB drives or flash memory devices, is Non-volatile computer memory that can be electrically erased and reprogrammed. It is a technology that is primarily used in memory cards and USB flash drives for general storage and transfer of data between computers and other digital products. Flash memory stores information in an array of memory cells made from floating-gate transistors.

In traditional single-level cell (SLC) devices, each cell stores only one bit of information. Some newer flash memory, known as multi-level cell (MLC) devices, can store more than one bit per cell by choosing between multiple levels of electrical charge to apply to the floating gates of its cells. Flash drives are now available with 8 GB storage capacity. Digital collections that are too large to store entirely on a disk use hierarchical storage mechanisms (HSM). In an HSM, the most frequently used data is kept on fast disks while less frequently used data is kept in nearline such as an automated (robotic) tape library.

An HSM can automatically migrate data from tape to disk and vice-versa as required. Intelligent storage networks and snap-servers are now available in which the physical storage devices are intelligently controlled and made available to a number of servers.

A number of RAID (Redundant Array of Inexpensive Disks) models are also available for greater security and performance. The RAID technology distributes the data across a number of disks in a way that even if one or more disks fail, the system would still function while the failed component is replaced.

DEVELOPMENTS IN COMMUNICATION AND NETWORK TECHNOLOGY

Communication technology, with its ability to transmit data and information from one location to another, serve as a tool to exploit potentials and ability of computer to store and process vast amount of information. A computer communica-tion network is an interconnection of a collection of several computers from which the user can select the service required and communicate with any computer as a local user.

A computer communication networks can be viewed as a collection of nodes with computing resources and nodal-switching computers that facilitate communication through a set of transmission links. Developments in communication technology have made it possible to interconnect geographically dispersed computing resources of different kinds and makes.

Users can access the network through PCs and terminals attached to a node and messages traverse these networks through the switching nodes. Since, computer communicates using digitised signals instead of electric signals, it requires different transmission facilities than those used for transmitting analogue electrical signals. It is, however, a common practice to use conventional telecommunication links for data transmission by converting digital signals into analogue signals using a process called 'Modulation' and the device that performs the conversion is called the MODEM (MOdulator - DEModulator).

Currently, terrestrial, satellite-based data networks, Integrated Service Digital Network (ISDN) and wireless networks are available that can handle all kinds of communication requirements (, *i.e.,* voice, data, telemetry, facsimile and video) without discrimination.

The computer networks can be grouped into four categories based on geographical locations of its computer terminals, , *i.e.*,

- *Local Area Network (LAN)*: interconnection of many computers within a given local area, more often premises of a single organisation building. A very high speed of data transmission can be attained within a limited geographic area. LANs are typically configured in a star, bus or ring. Low speed LANs use telephone wires or copper cables, optical fibre cables are used to achieve high-speed transmission of data.
- *Wide Area Network (WAN)*: WAN is used to interconnect a number of widely dispersed computers in various cities of a country or different countries. WANs use communication media maintained by telegraph or telephone companies. These networks usually have land telephone lines, underground coaxial cables, microwave communication and satellite communications.
- *Metropolitan Area Network (MAN)*: MAN refers to inter- connection within geographical limits of a city or town.
- *Gateways*: Gateways consist of software and hardware that are required to interconnect networks amongst themselves. Gateways contend with any differences in packet sizes, protocols and addressing methods between the two networks it connect. Gateways are also used to connect LANs to WANs and WANs, in turn, can be linked through gateways to create national and international data communication networks.

The communications networks can be grouped into the following three categories based on the technology and communication media used by them:

- *Public Switched Telephone Network*: PSTN are managed by common carriers usually telephone companies/departments the world over. The PSTN generally provide two basic services, the normal dial-up connections to the subscribers and permanent leased connection between two subscriber's points. The permanent leased connections provide single traceable line between two subscriber points. The leased lines are generally less prone to noise than dial-up lines.
- *Public Data Network*: Analogous to the public telephone network, many domestic common carriers provide data communications services via a specialised network called a Public Data Network (PDN). Most Internet Service Providers (ISPs) use combination of PDN and PSTN for providing Internet connectivity.
- *Integrated Services Digital Networks* (ISDN): An ISDN is a network that provides end-to-end digital connectivity to support a wide range of services, including voice and Non-voice services.

Computer networks use physical channels through which information is transmitted between computers in a network. Media may be classified as bounded , *i.e.,* wires (twisted pair telephone wires or UTP CAT 5), cables (co-axial) and optical fibres; or unbounded , *i.e.,* radio waves or microwaves. Data communication is an integral part of the modern information storage and retrieval systems in terms of their online access. Today, network technology works on client server architecture with middleware used for connecting software components or applications on clients and servers.

Technique of packet switching, evolved in 1960s, is used for transferring data between computer systems with an objective to facilitate networked computers to communicate seamlessly across multiple, geographically dispersed locations. The Transmission Control Protocol (TCP) and Internet Protocol (IP), called TCP/ IP suite, is the backbone of Internet and other TCP/ IP based networks.

With developments in communication technology, institutions have options to set-up fibre optic-based gigabit LAN or wireless LAN. Depending on the geographical location, institutions have options to buy terrestrial or satellite-based Internet bandwidth its combinations from a number of Internet Service Providers (ISPs).

LIBRARY NETWORKING

The world has been witnessing a knowledge and infor-mation explosion during the past few decades. Over 10 million journal articles are published every year besides news items, editorials and articles that are appearing in popular print media. Information professionals who would be the leaders in the twenty-first century depend on information for their work.

Access to information holds the key to development. Libraries which are store houses of knowledge and information, and information centers which disseminate knowledge and information, form two important components of present day society.

While there is a deluge of information on one hand, the cost of collecting, processing, storing and disseminating information has been spiraling up on the other hand. This calls for heavy budgets for libraries even to maintain a reasonable level of acquisition of journals, books and reports. Estimates show that a three to fourfold rise in library budgets will be needed by AD 2000 to maintain the same acquisition level as in 1990.

Information buying power of libraries has been declining year after year. Because of this, resource sharing and cooperative functioning through networking have become inescapable for libraries and information centres worldwide. India is no exception; for that matter, it is even more necessary to network libraries in newly developing countries like India than in the developed nations.

Efficient resource sharing can be achieved by using the recent advances in information technology for realising a network of libraries. Information technology signifies the coming together of the disciplines of electronics, computer hardware and software, communications, artificial intelligence and human/machine interface.

During the last six to seven years, library and information activities in the country have entered a new era. Individual libraries are coming out of the proverbial "Berlin Wall"around them. They are trying to form a larger community in an effort to tackle the ever increasing demands for better services, quantitatively and qualitatively, in an environment already over strained by financial pressures. Forced, motivated, or logic driven, the librarians are coming out of their shell in large numbers.

This has resulted in discernible change in the information scenario. Now a large number of library resource sharing networks like the Metropolitan Area Networks, such as Calibnet (Calcutta), Delnet (Delhi), Bonet (Bombay), Punenet (Pune), Malibnet (Madras), Mylibnet (Mysore), Hylibnet (Hyderabad), Adne (Ahmedabad), and countrywide ones like ERNET (Educational and Research Institutions), Sirnet (CSIR Laboratories), Inflibnet (Universities and Research Institutions) and Desinet (Defence Laboratories), and sectoral ones like BTISNET (Biotechnology) and TIFACLINE (Technology *per se*) are under various stages of conceptualization, design and development.

A host of agencies, like the National Information System for Science and Technology (NISSAT), Dept. of Electronics, INSDOC/CSIR, DESIDOC/DRDO, DBT, NIC, and TIFAC/DST, are involved. Looking from the participant's side, it is common to find an institution participating in more than one network.

The ultimate goal of information/library networks is to interlink information resources in a metropolitan area, so that that users could access information irrespective of its location, format, medium, language, script etc.

Further, the development of such networks requires actions in several areas such as training, rationalization of information resource acquisition, diffusion of standards, preparation of union lists, generation of database services apart from setting up hardware, software and communication facilities. The concept of library networking to aid information resource sharing and support activities in libraries has become a real necessity.

The shortcomings observed are mainly related to two aspects:

- Non-availability of materials and services, and
- Efficient administrative control.

In India, the need for resource sharing has been well recognized but the technology options available until now were limited. NISSAT has taken up networking of libraries in Calcutta (Calibnet), Delhi (Delnet), Madras (Malibnet), Mysore (Mylibnet), Hyderabad (Hylibnet), Ahmedabad (Adnet), Pune (Punenet), and Bombay (Bonet). The present study highlights only some of the major library networks in India.

Towards library networking activities in India NISSAT has taken the initiative for promoting resource sharing activities. These initiatives are aimed at ensuring better utilization of science and technology information resources, minimization of functional load of information centres and encouragement of motivational factors to a large extent by better means of communication.

NISSAT only goes to the extent of setting up general infrastructural facilities like network service centres including hardware, software, manpower and other organizational requirements, communication facilities etc. With a change in the development and implementation strategy, the participating institutions in a network are to arrange their own terminal hardware, software, manpower and data conversion.

DELNET

The limitation of financial resources and space for housing library collections in the libraries in Delhi led to the promotion of sharing of resources by automation and networking and establishment of the Delnet in 1988. NISSAT took the initiative in setting up Delnet. It has emerged as an important resource centre for the libraries in Delhi.

In Delhi the libraries have been growing very fast in number and site during the last four decades. They cater to specialized and general clientele and are of various types which include institutional libraries, research libraries, government libraries, public libraries, departmental libraries and libraries of the universities, colleges and schools. During the recent years, cumulative information has been increasing at a very fast pace and with it the increase in demands of the users. It has been noticed that in the era of information explosion the libraries in India are generally ill equipped to handle and retrieve information effectively.

The financial resources and the space for housing library collections are limited in almost all of the libraries. The option left with the forward looking librarians has been to promote the sharing of resources by automation and networking. Initially, 40 libraries were directly linked to the DELNET host system through e-mail to promote library mailing, interlibrary requests, transfer of files, exchange of messages, interlibrary services, etc. Side by side with the automation of participating libraries, the functions and services have also started.

Presently about 90 libraries are members of DELNET. Almost all participating libraries are now computerized by means of acquisition and fund accounting, cataloguing, circulation, serials control and local users services. Users are able to locate books and serials through Online Public Access Catalogue (OPAC). A union catalogue of current periodicals available in Delhi libraries, and a union list of current serials available in Indian libraries are available on online for Delnet participant libraries. A central database of Delnet has been created and made operational. This central database includes the library holdings of Delnet member libraries used as union catalogues of books/ monographs.

Delnet provides access to the central union catalogue for books and monographs, efficient electronic mailing facilities to access databases of member libraries. It also proposes to develop a network for accessing CD–ROM databases available at member libraries in the near future. Delnet also provides CAS and SDI services, consultancy in library computerization, training and H.R.D. and assistance to libraries on standardization, local automation, retrospective conversion etc. Delnet is likely to emerge as a co–operative network incorporating all disciplines of science, technology, social sciences and humanities.

CALIBNET

The Calcutta Library Network (CALIBNET) was inaugurated on 21 December 1993. NISSAT, Department of Scientific and Industrial Research (DSIR), Government. of India, took the initiative in setting up CALIBNET, which has adopted a two way system for networking:

- The networking route with a library automation and networking through its own application software "Maitrayee" and
- The e-mail route connecting member libraries with on-line access to various databases within network and Internet access.

Calibnet established a high-tech resource base and provides the following services:

- Online/CDROM based global information search and retrieval services
- Full-text document delivery
- Database services

MALIBNET

The need for interconnecting libraries and information centres in Madras was visualized in the Indian National Scientific Documentation Centre (INSDOC) in 1991. Initially six major academic institutions were directly linked to the Malibnet host system. Two important databases have been created utilising the resources available in Madras libraries. One is a Directory Database of Current Serials in Madras covering 30 libraries, and the other is a Contents Database covering articles published in 300 journals available in Madras libraries.

Both these databases are continuously updated and also expanded. They are available for online-access to any user and the information is also supplied in diskettes and hard copy. Photocopies of articles from member libraries can be supplied within two days. Madras has about 60 important libraries besides information centres like INSDOC. About 15 of these libraries have a holding of well over 100,000 items. These libraries act as good resource centres on the network. As of December 1993, all the 60 libraries together invest about Rupees 8,000,000 on acquiring journals and books every year.

It is estimated that 40 per cent of the information acquired is redundant. With the libraries networked and resource sharing implemented, each user on the network can get access to a vast amount of literature, and redundancy can be brought down significantly. A novel and unique feature of Malibnet is that the members will be permitted to offer their own innovative information services on the network. A membership in MALIBNET is open to universities, colleges, R&D institutions, industries and individuals.

Malibnet presently offers the following information services:

- Current serials acquired in about 60 libraries
- Full journal holdings of about 60 libraries
- Contents information of about 500 important journals
- Electronic mail including internet connectivity
- Door delivery system for document photocopies
- It also offers access to about 1000 international databases

MYLIBNET

It is the first library network established in a small city. The launching of MYLIBNET in association with Mysore city library consortium (MCLC) took place on 12th June 1995. There are 16 institutional members. The holding list of Mysore city libraries has been computerised and software has been developed to enable users to access the catalogue and information on-line. Mylibnet provides e-mail facilities to its members.

BONET

The Bombay Library Network (Bonet) was setup at the National Centre for Software Technology (NCST), Bombay, on 6 November 1992. The Network is sponsored by NISSAT. The aim of Bonet is to build a low cost library information system which can possibly be used as a model for future expansion of this service even outside Bombay.

Bonet also benefits significantly from the experience gained, and facilities created, by the Education and Research Networking (ERNET) project of the Department of Electronics, Govt. of India, assisted by the United Nations Development Programme (UNDP). Bonet is aimed at promoting cooperation between libraries in Bombay.

The focus is on inter-library activities, rather than on computerizing individual libraries, which will no doubt computerize their own operations and are likely to share their experiences with each other. Bonet offers training related to library computerization and networking, and speed up computerization of Bombay libraries. Bonet membership provides for access to its centralised catalogues and for E-mail among Bonet members. However, access to library related services outside Bombay in India and abroad would require use of ERNET.

The services offered through Bonet include the following:

- Consultation on standards
- Organized training for selected staff of participating libraries
- On-line catalogue of periodicals for the region
- On-line catalogue of books for the region
- On-line catalogue of preprints/reprints
- Inter-library lending of books and periodicals
- Inter-library request for photocopying
- Computer network support for book ordering
- Information retrieval services
- On-line document delivery of items (such as technical reports) made available by participating libraries in machine readable form
- On-line access to foreign databases, subject to the user's willingness to pay the costs incurred
- E-mail interface for inter–library queries
- E-mail facilities to order reprints from abroad, when necessary
- Dissemination of information, on new books etc, using E–mail, Bulletin boards, and SDI techniques
- Courier service for inter–library exchange of materials

Under Bonet the following databases were created:

- 25,000 items in a bibliographic database on computers and software technology
- Union catalogue of journals and other periodicals in libraries in the region
- Tables of contents of 250 Indian periodicals created by the national centre for information
- A number of CDROM databases have been mounted on a Novell Server for use to members

PUNENET

Presently, 30 libraries and 15 professionals from Pune city are accessing the Punenet through modem. The users not only access Punenet data, but also use the e-mail and internet facilities.

Following databases are available on Punenet for its members:

- Catalogues of holding of all member libraries
- Union catalogue of current periodicals in Pune libraries and information centres
- Publishers and book sellers database
- Database on international grants and fellowships in the health sciences
- Hard databanks in biotechnology
- Access to NICNET and databases available on NICNET *e.g.*, MEDLANS,AIDS database, US patent database

- Access to internet and various databases available on internet
- Patent information
- Union catalogue of books available in British libraries in India

ADINET

Ahmedabad Library Network (ADINET) was formally inaugurated in February 1995 when a memorandum of under-standing was signed between NISSAT and ADINET at Ahmedabad. ADINET has ten institutional members, five associate institutional members and two professional members. A centralized database has been created at ADINET which contains institute master, journal master and book databases. It also organized six work and training programmes. ADINET provided e-mail connectivity to 30 libraries of Ahmedabad.

INFLIBNET

Information and Library Network (INFLIBNET), a programme of the University Grants Commission, was launched in May 1991. The main aim of INFLIBNET is to establish a national computer-communication network to link libraries and information centres in universities, colleges, universities, UGC information centres, institutions of national importance, R&D institutions, etc., and thereby improve capability in information handling and services.

It is a programme for academic excellence to be achieved through establishment of a mechanism for information transfer and access to support scholarship and academic work. It facilitates pooling, sharing and optimization of scarce library resources in the country. As a major programme it helps modernize libraries and information centres in the country through application of information technology.

The National Centre of INFLIBNET is located in Gujarat University campus at Ahmedabad. At present, INFLIBNET aims at computerizing and networking of university/college libraries. Every year, INFLIBNET programme is identifying a number of university libraries for automation depending on the budget allocation. The selected institutions are given funds for procuring computer systems, retroconversion and networking. Application software for data entry and other library functions, library standards and formats, etc., are provided by INFLIBNET to the participating libraries.

Manpower development is an important part of the programme. Training courses for core library staff engaged in computerised library operations, have been conducted since 1992-93.

Development of suitable software, standards for various library operations and communication based services (*e.g.*, e-mail, bulletin boards) designing suitable network architecture and preparation of union catalogues of serials, books, non-book materials, and cooperation with other networking organisations like NISSAT, NICNET, etc., are other important activities.

Objectives of Inflibnet

Inflibnet is an autonomous institution and aims to provide a channel to the academicians and researchers for exchange of information from sources within the country and abroad:

- Modernize libraries/information centres in India
- Mechanization for information transfer and access
- Facilitate pooling, sharing and optimization of library resources
- Organize library services at macro level
- Speedy and efficient services to end users
- Promoting equity

The ultimate aim is to provide the end-users a mechanism for sharing and using information resources and for exploiting modern information technology.

Functions of Inflibnet

- Aims to establish a nation-wide network for computer communication linking academic libraries and information
- Aims to establish a mechanism for information transfer and access to support scholarship and academic work
- Aims to organize library services at macro levels at affordable cost and maximise benefits providing speedy and efficient services to end users.
- Will include participants from colleges, universities, R&D institutes, institutes of higher learning, informa-tion centres, institutes of national importance and document resource centres
- Covers all disciplines such as science, technology, medicine, agriculture, fine arts, humanities, social science
- Will provide networking to members using available communication infrastructure in the country.

BASICS OF NETWORKING AND SECURITY

COMPUTER NETWORKS

A computer network is an interconnection of various computer systems located at different places. In computer network two or more computers are linked together with a medium and data communication devices for the purpose of communicating data and sharing resources. The computer that provides resources to other computers on a network is known as server. In the network the individual computers, which access shared network resources, are known as workstations or nodes. Computer Networks may be classified on the basis of geographical area in three broad categories.

- Local Area Network
- Metropolitan Area Network
- Wide Area Network

Local Area Network

Networks used to interconnect computers in a single room, rooms within a building or buildings on one site are called Local Area Network. LAN transmits data with a speed of several megabits per second. The transmission medium is normally coaxial cables.

LAN links computers, , *i.e.,* software and hardware, in the same area for the purpose of sharing information. Usually LAN links computers within a limited geographical area because they must be connected by a cable, which is quite expensive. People working in LAN get more capabilities in data processing, work processing and other information exchange compared to stand-alone computers. Because of this information exchange most of the business and government organisations are using LAN.

Major Characteristics of LAN:

- Every computer has the potential to communicate with any other computers of the network
- High degree of interconnection between computers
- Easy physical connection of computers in a network
- Inexpensive medium of data transmission
- High data transmission rate

Advantages:

- The reliability of network is high because the failure of one computer in the network does not effect the functioning for other computers.
- Addition of new computer to network is easy.
- High rate of data transmission is possible.
- Peripheral devices like magnetic disk and printer can be shared by other computers.

Disadvantages:

If the communication line fails, the entire network system breaks down.

Use of LAN:

- Followings are the major areas where LAN is normally used:
  - — File transfers and Access
  - — Word and text processing
  - — Electronic message handling
  - — Remote database access
  - — Personal computing
  - — Digital voice transmission and storage

Metropolitan Area Network

Networks used to interconnect computers in a city or a town are called Metropolitan Area Networks. Generally telephone lines are used to connect these computers. Alternatively, wireless mode also is used for this purpose. Computers are connected to the telephone lines through devices called Modems.

Modems

The word modem is a contraction of the words modulator-demodulator. A modem is typically used to send digital data over a phone line. The sending modem modulates the data into a signal that is compatible with the phone line, and the receiving modem demodulates the signal back into digital data. Wireless modems are also frequently seen converting data into radio signals and back.

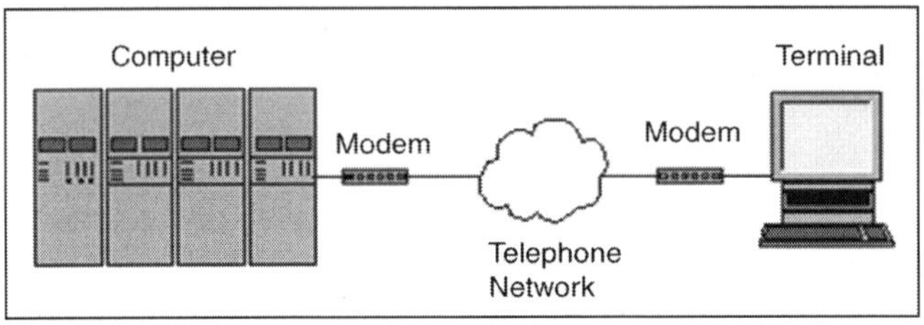

Fig. The Modem.

Wide Area Network

The term Wide Area Network is used to describe a computer network spanning a regional, national or global area. For example, for a large company the head quarters might be at Delhi and regional branches at Bombay, Madras, Bangalore and Calcutta. Here regional centers are connected to head quarters through WAN. The distance between computers connected to WAN is larger. Therefore the transmission medium used are normally telephone lines, microwaves and satellite links.

CHARACTERISTICS OF WAN

Followings are the major characteristics of WAN:

- *Communication Facility*: For a big company spanning over different parts of the country the employees can save long distance phone calls and it overcomes the time lag in overseas communications. Computer conferencing is another use of WAN where users communicate with each other through their computer system.
- *Remote Data Entry*: Remote data entry is possible in WAN. It means sitting at any location you can enter data, update data and query other information of any computer attached to the WAN but located in other cities. For example, suppose you are sitting at Madras and want to see some data of a computer located at Delhi, you can do it through WAN.
- *Centralised Information*: In modern computerised environment you will find that big organisations go for centralised data storage. This means if the organisation is spread over many cities, they keep their important business data in a single place. As the data are generated

at different sites, WAN permits collection of this data from different sites and save at a single site.

Difference between LAN and WAN:

- LAN is restricted to limited geographical area of few kilometers. But WAN covers great distance and operate nationwide or even worldwide.
- In LAN, the computer terminals and peripheral devices are connected with wires and coaxial cables. In WAN there is no physical connection. Communication is done through telephone lines and satellite links.
- Cost of data transmission in LAN is less because the transmission medium is owned by a single organisation. In case of WAN the cost of data transmission is very high because the transmission medium used are hired, either telephone lines or sate llite links.
- The speed of data transmission is much higher in LAN than in WAN. The transmission speed in LAN varies from 0.1 to 100 megabits per second. In case of WAN the speed ranges from 1800 to 9600 bits per second.
- Few data transmission errors occur in LAN compared to WAN. It is because in LAN the distance covered is negligible.

NETWORK TOPOLOGY

The term topology in the context of communication network refers to the way the computers or workstations in the network are linked together. According to the physical arrangements of workstations and nature of work, there are three major types of network topology. They are star topology, bus topology and ring topology.

Star topology

In star topology a number of workstations are directly linked to a central node. Any communication between stations on a star LAN must pass through the central node. There is bi-directional communication between various nodes. The central node controls all the activities of the nodes. The advantages of the star topology are:

- It offers flexibility of adding or deleting of workstations from the network.
- Breakdown of one station does not affect any other device on the network.

The major disadvantage of star topology is that failure of the central node disables communication throughout the whole network.

Bus Topology

In bus topology all workstations are connected to a single communication line called bus. In this type of network topology there is no central node as in star topology. Transmission from any station travels the length of the bus in both directions and can be received by all workstations. The advantage of the bus topology is that:

- It is quite easy to set up.
- If one station of the topology fails it does not affect the entire system.

The disadvantage of bus topology is that any break in the bus is difficult to identify.

Ring Topology

In ring topology each station is attached nearby stations on a point to point basis so that the entire system is in the form of a ring. In this topology data is transmitted in one direction only. Thus the data packets circulate along the ring in either clockwise or anti-clockwise direction. The advantage of this topology is that any signal transmitted on the network passes through all the LAN stations. The disadvantage of ring network is that the breakdown of any one station on the ring can disable the entire system.

Communication Devices

Major Communication Devices Used Today

- *Wire Pairs*: Wire pairs are commonly used in local telephone communication and for short distance digital data communication. They are usually made up of copper and the pair of wires is twisted together. Data transmission speed is normally 9600 bits per second in a distance of 100 meter.
- *Coaxial Cables*: Coaxial cable is groups of specially wrapped and insulted wires that are able to transfer data at higher rate. They consist of a central copper wire surrounded by an insulation over which copper mesh is placed. They are used for long distance telephone lines and local area network for their noise immunity and faster data transfer.
- *Microwave*: Microwave system uses very high frequency radio signals to transmit data through space. The transmitter and receiver of a microwave system should be in line-of-sight because the radio signal cannot bend. With microwave very long distance transmission is not possible. In order to overcome the problem of line of sight and power amplification of weak signal, repeaters are used at intervals of 25 to 30 kilometers between the transmitting and receiving end.
- *Communication Satellite*: The problem of line-sight and repeaters are overcome by using satellites, which are the most widely used data transmission media in modern days. A communication satellite is a microwave relay station placed in outer space. INSAT-1B is such a

satellite that can be accessible from anywhere in India. In satellite communication, microwave signal is transmitted from a transmitter on earth to the satellite at space. The satellite amplifies the weak signal and transmits it back to the receiver. The main advantage of satellite communication is that it is a single microwave relay station visible from any point of a very large area. In microwave the data transmission rate is 16 Giga bits per second. They are mostly used to link big metropolitan cities.

Information Security

Information security is characterised as the preservation of:

- *Confidentiality* – ensuring that information is accessible only to those authorised to have access.
- *Integrity* – safeguarding the accuracy and completeness of information and processing methods
- *Availability* – ensuring that authorised users have access to information and relating assets when required.

Information security is achieved by implementing a suitable set of controls, which could be policies, practices, procedures, organisational practices and software functions

Information systems are prone to potential expensive security risk and threats leading to high client concerns for IPR (Intellectual property rights) protection.

According to the '2000 Information Security Industry Survey' published by ICSA (International Computer Security Association), the top 3 IT security concerns are

- Malicious Code (includes viruses, Trojans, worms, and hostile ActiveX and Java)
- Loss of Privacy/Confidentiality (includes abuse/misuse of data) and
- Electronic Exploits/Tools (includes cracking, eavesdropping, spoofing and toolkits).

If information assets are not suitable protected, it can be:

- Given away or stolen without depriving you of it.
- Modified without your knowledge to make it worthless.
- List without trace or hope of recovery
- Violation of IPR leading to lawsuits/ loss of customer confidence.
- Corruption/ loss of integrity of importance date, *e.g.,* software codes
- Loss of business due to leakage/ theft of company intellectual property
- Mobile workforce not able to access internal IT systems
- Unanticipated disruption in off-site work due to break down of communication links.
- Leak and unauthorised use of confidential information, business strategy.

- Physical damages/ theft of critical IT infrastructure component.

Information Security Through Network Access Control

What is Network access control:

- Imposition of certain controls to restrict access to a shared network based on the access control policy.
- The controls can be implemented by putting firewall at the network perimeter.
- The firewall filters traffic by means of predefined tables or set of rules.

Firewall

Firewall is an intermediate system plugged between two networks, which can act as a security wall. The main purpose of a firewall is to control access to or from a protected/trusted network.

It implements a network access policy by forcing connections to pass through the firewall, where they can be examined and evaluated. Without firewall a site is more exposed to inherently insecure host operating systems, TCP/IP vulnerabilities and attacks from the Internet. It is also very difficult to maintain same level of security for all the hosts in a network.

Benefits of firewall:

- Protection from vulnerable services, e.g. NIS, NFS, source routed packets
- Controlled access'
  — Help to control access to and from a network.
- Concentrated security
  — Additional security measures, *e.g.,* one time password system ,etc., can be implemented in single place at the firewall instead of in individual host.
- Enhanced privacy
  — Blocking of services like finger, DNS helps to hide information, which could otherwise be useful to the attackers.
- Logging and statistic s of network use and misuse
  — Help to monitor usage of network services and detection of potential intrusion.
- Policy enforcement
  — Helps to implement organisation network access control policy.

Firewall Components

There are three basic components of firewall

- Firewall Policy

- Packet filters
- Application gateways

Firewall Policy

The policy directly influences the design, installation and use of firewall system. The higher-level policy addresses the services that will be allowed or explicitly denied from/ to the restricted network (including exception). The lower level policy describes how the firewall will actually go about restricting the access and filtering the services that are defined in the higher-level policy.

Packet Filter or Packet Filtering Gateways

Packet filters uses routers with packet filtering rules to grant or deny access based on source IP address, destination IP address, source port and Destination port information of an IP packet. Adding TCP or UDP port filtering to IP address filtering results in great deal of flexibility.

In general the packet filters operates on the each packet in individual and Hence, stateless but Stateful packet filters use some of the state information derived from the past communication.

It can be applied on outbound interface as well as on inbound interface. When IP packets arrive at a network interface of a packet filter and are examined against the rule of filtering. Selection criteria uses information found in packet header and related to the network interfaces, the packets appear.

Application Gateway

Gateways interconnect one network to another for a specific application. Its major function is application specific and used as proxy. If an application Gateway contains proxies for FTP and TELNET, then only that traffic will be allowed and other services are completely blocked.

Packet filter and application gateways are usually combined in a firewall configuration to implement the firewall policy.

Dual – homed Firewall

It is a host with two network cards, one connected to the external or untrusted network and other is to the internal or trusted network.

The key security principle is not to allow traffic coming in from an untrusted network to be directed routed to the trusted network. IP source routing and IP forwarding services are disabled in this host.

CONCLUSION

Following the launching of Delnet and Calibnet, the library automation and networking movement in India is surely catching on.

The objectives which are:

- Better utilization of funds through sharing of resources by creation of commonly usable data-bases and communication between libraries.

- Automating the functions of individual libraries at a local level for effective and efficient services to the users.

A number of benefits are being offered to member libraries of the particular networks. First, one gets access to a very large volume of literature without increase in the library budget because of the sharing of resources among the members. Secondly, the library budget can now be diverted to acquire the most important (even if expensive) information required by an institution, the other peripheral information being available on the network.

Third, one gets near real time access to about 1000 international databases apart from the electronic mail and remote log in facilities. There are plans of these networks to connect and share the resources in the near future. Nevertheless, the growth of these networks is slow. It is taking a long time to create and provide bibliographic databases of recognisable size, *e.g.*, DELNET took already ten years in creating bibliographic databases of reasonably good size. Without the databases neither could networks be made effective to achieve the goals nor could resource sharing be effective.

Finally it appears that prospects are quite favourable for development of networks for better information services and resource sharing in India. In this direction lot of work has to be done. Some of the problems faced by other developing countries are common to India too, including financial constraints, inadequate communication, non-availability of equipments, less awareness of the value of information, reluctance to development and non-coordination of various kind of activities, resource building, resource sharing and exchange of information and ideas, non-standardization operational procedure, lack of dedication, motivation and knowledge on the part of available manpower.

10

Resource Sharing and Resource Sharing Networks in Library

ELECTRONIC RESOURCES

Electronic resources can be defined as resources in electronic format or computerprocessible format that provide information or an indicator to the information and are generally accessible over the Internet or stored on media like CD ROM/ DVD ROM or other storage devices.

The emergence of Internet and the World Wide Web (WWW) in early 1990s, as a new media of information storage and delivery, came as a real boon for evolution of electronic resources. While searching bibliographic databases became popular, it created demand for actual content in full-text that became difficult for libraries to obtain. Coincided with evolution of World Wide Web (WWW), display technology evolved, cost of storage came down drastically and networks became faster. It became possible for publishers to deliver content, either as a bitmap page images or other structured formats such as HTML, PDF or RTF. Increasingly larger number of publishers started using the Internet as a global way to offer their publications to the international community of scientists and technologists given the fact that technology is in a position to deliver more content to more users at a significantly lower cost per user.

Electronic resources on the Internet manifest themselves in numerous flavours and categories, although most of them emulate the traditional publishing while others are revolutionary in their design and approach. While the present trend to imitate and emulate the traditional models of scholarly communication may continue for some time, eventually the capabilities added by the new media would be used in more innovative ways. Some of the important types of e-resources are described here.

ELECTRONIC DATABASES

An electronic database consists of electronic resources integrated in highly organised fashion so as to provide controlled access to it by their commercial providers. The first databases were bibliographic in nature and were online version of existing indexing and abstracting services such as Biological Abstracts, Index Medicus, Chemical Abstracts, ,etc.

By the year 1988, only half of all databases were bibliographic in nature. With introduction of a number of online databases containing textual information, news, statistics, commodity prices, ,etc.,, a third type of databases holding text of full-length documents started appearing. Several full-text of encyclopaedia, directories and articles from journals are now available online.

Most of the publishers now provide access to their full-text journals through their web site or through other electronic publishing platforms.

While there are a number of public-domain databases, most online databases require annual subscription for accessing them. Thousands of databases are now available on compact discs (CD-ROM) as well as on the Web.

ELECTRONIC JOURNALS

Electronic journals, or 'e-journals', are used for those journals and newsletters that are prepared and distributed electronically. Electronic journals may be defined very broadly as any journal, magazine, e-zine, webzine, newsletter or type of electronic serial publication which is available over the Internet and can be accessed using different technologies such as WWW, Gopher, ftp, telnet, e-mail or listserv. Several traditional journals are now being published both on the Web and in print.

Content lists for most of the journals are available on the Web or distributed to subscribers as an e-mail text messages or through technologies like RSS and Atom. Internet-based electronic journals started to appear in the beginning of 1990. These journals were mostly delivered as an attachment to e-mail while their back issues were mounted on anonymous ftp sites and users were required to download them from these ftp sites. The libraries and information centres made them accessible through their gopher site.

1995 witnessed peak of Gopher technology which then dropped suddenly and dramatically by 1997. With advent of WWW technology in 1993, electronic publishing became more than a novelty, the web as a means of delivery of electronic information has grown steadily Since, then. As publishers experiment with different publication modes and models, the very definition of a journal is undergoing change in the electronic environment.

New journals have evolved based on the graphic capabilities of the Internet that are available only in electronic form. Like print journals, current and archival issues of electronic journals can be browsed through their content pages. Moreover, e-journals can also be searched not only on their metadata but also in full-text through sophisticated search interface. Currently, there are more than 50,000 peer-reviewed, scholarly electronic journals that are available on the Internet.

ELECTRONIC BOOKS

An electronic book is digital reading material that a user can view on a desktop or Personal Digital Assistant (PDA), laptop or on a dedicated, portable device with a large storage capacity and the ability to download new titles via a network connection.

More and more traditional book publishers, as well as those catering to the professional and business communities, are launching their e-book collections. The electronic books market consists of two distinct components , *i.e.,* i) electronic books consisting of digital material or contents; and ii) electronic book hardware including ebook reading appliance, PCs, laptop or PDA.

The digital material or content that make an electronic book are simply textual and graphical files consisting of bits that can be transported any digital storage media or delivered over a network connection. It is designed to be viewed on some combination of hardware and software ranging from dumb terminals to web browsers, on personal computers to the new reading appliances. More and more books are now being released on the web through enhanced interfaces that offer features such as increased search capacity within a book or entire collection of books, ability to highlight and flag a page, ability to make notes on text without damaging the book, ability to e-mail quotes from the books to other colleagues, etc.

Most publishers like Springer, Wiley InterScience, Taylor and Francis, Cambridge University Press, Oxford University Press, etc., offer their e-book collections on subscription/ one-time purchase basis. Besides, there are a number of e-books aggregators that make thousands of books available online for libraries and individuals at relatively lower cost. Three major ebooks aggregators are Questia, Ebrary and NetLibrary. However, just like other e-resources, e-books come with restrictions such as limit on downloads, in terms of number of pages, *i.e.,* one page at a time or one chapter at a time or no download at all.

ELECTRONIC THESES AND DISSERTATIONS

Theses submitted to the universities as requirement for the award of Ph.D. degree constitute a useful source of information for the new and ongoing research. Doctoral dissertations submitted to universities and academic institutions are originally created in digital format using one of the word processing software packages like MSWord, LaTex, Word Perfect, Word Pro, etc.,

or one of the desktop publishing packages like Page Maker, Ventura, etc. These documents are undisputedly highly valuable collection especially in digital format that qualify to be an important component of a digital library. The documents composed on word processing packages/ desktop publishing packages can be easily converted into PDF, Post Script or XML using appropriate software tools so as to host them on the web. Several universities and institutions have already implemented electronic submission of doctoral dissertations under the overall umbrella of an international digital library initiative called 'Networked Digital Library of Theses and Dissertations' (NDLTD).

AUDIO, VIDEO AND STREAMING MEDIA

Streaming multimedia is sequential delivery of multimedia content, including video, audio or some other learning objects, over a computer network that is displayed (or played back) to the end-user as it is being delivered by the provider.

The advent of the MP3 players and the iPod resulted in a greater effort to deliver downloadable media. Moreover, web documents are now coming with greater integration of text with media. Encyclopaedia now have articles with audio files, video clips and animation to illustrate a given topic. Media can broadly be categorised into three category, namely.

- Commercial movies that have greater copyright restrictions,
- Educational media typically are lesser controlled and many a time are made available free-of-cost; and
- Media targeted for individual users, such as movies and songs, that comes with restrictions in terms of copying and distributions.

SUBJECT GATEWAYS OR LIBRARY PORTALS

The web, being a hypermedia-based system, allows linking amongst electronic resources stored on servers dispersed geographically on distant locations.

The portal sites or gateways redirect a user to the holders of the original digital material. The librarians, being the earliest users of the web, started to gather and organise link to important web-based resources on various subjects. A subject gateway can be defined as facilities that allow easier access to web-based resources in a defined subject area.

The simplest types of subject gateways are sets of web pages containing list of links to resources. Some gateways index their lists of links and provide a simple search facility. More advanced gateways offer a muchenhanced service via a system consisting of a resource database and various indexes, which can be searched and/ or browse throughout a web-based interface.

Subject gateways are also known as Subject-based Information Gateways (SBIGs), subject-based gateways, subject index gateways, virtual libraries, clearing houses, subject trees, pathfinders, ,etc. Subject gateway is an important component of a library web site designed for the library users so as to help them discover high-quality information on the Internet in a quick and effective way. In the traditional information environment human intermediaries, such as publishers and librarians, filter and process information so that users can search catalogues and indexes of organised knowledge as opposed to raw data and information. Subject gateways work on the same principle, , *i.e.,* they employ subject experts and information professionals to select, classify and catalogue Internet resources to aid search and retrieval for the users. Users are offered access to a database of Internet resources descriptions which they can search by keywords or browse by subject area. A description of each resource is provided to help users assess very quickly its origin, content and nature, enabling them to decide if it is worth investigating further.

In the process users get benefited from the expertise of librarians and subject experts with subject gateways rather than having to locate, evaluate, filter and organise the resources themselves. Specialised software are available as freeware or as priced software to create and maintain professionally developed subject gateways.

RESOURCE SHARING

The sharing is a need-based activity framed around the age-old concept of give and take. In general it is as old as the civilization. In "the field of libraries we might trace the history of resource sharing since their inception in various forms *viz.*, shared cataloguing, library cooperation, interlibrary loan and union catalogue etc.

The term library resources include any and all of the materials, functions and services, which constitute a modern library system. It is amalgamation of people, processes, ideas, materials and money which forms the substance of a library and can be described as its resources.

Resource sharing is a sort of implied agreement amongst participating libraries wherein each participant willing to share its resource to other members and in turn are privileged to share the resources of its partners as and when the need arises. At present time when the Computer and Communication Technology has gained the central role in all walks of life and drastically changed the way people think, communicate and do business, it became indispensable to computerise and network the libraries just to survive.

The entrance of these new technologies in library premises rescheduled the functioning of libraries and provided a new dynamic shape to the age-old concept of resource sharing. Lack of effective and efficient technology has been a major hurdle for resource sharing in India, besides the lack of co-operation among the participating libraries.

Now by the use of Information Technology, it became possible to create co-operative functional resource sharing library-network which is the—most important requirement at this juncture where the economic consideration, information explosion and specialized users needs are forcing the libraries to co-operate.

RESOURCE SHARING: NEED OF THE TIME

The increased growth, use and value of information generated the concept of information society or information oriented society. If we analyse the situation from invention of printing press to Internet, we find that the complete civilization is moving from generalisation to specialisation, whether it is growth and nature of subject, commodities or services. In this era of specialization, the efficiency and efficacy of libraries will be measured by the services provided by them not by the physical collection they have. In this situation the sharing of the resources only may provide the variety of new information services, because in this era it is not possible for any library to accommodate the universe of knowledge physically within the library boundaries. So the resource sharing became the need of the time to fulfill the ever-specialized user's information needs in cost effective manner as the main objectives of resource sharing are:

- Reduction in all round cast.
- Avoidance of unnecessary duplication of information materials and efforts.
- Possibility of developing specialised activities specifi-cally concentrating on some particular area. Maximum accessibility to information without losing the individual identity of libraries.

At present, specifically in case of Indian academic libraries, which are planning and going to adopt the Information Technology, the resource sharing is needed for:

- Retrospective conversion of their bibliographical data to electronic form.
  - To help less equipped libraries.
  - To reudce the cataloguing cost.
  - To share the valuable resources
  - Documents and information.
  - Technical expertise.
  - To decentralise information.
  - To boost the distance learning and more.

PROBLEMS, PROSPECTS AND PREREQUISITES

If we look at the usefulness and strength of resource sharing among libraries, we find a very enthusiastic picture, but on the other hand when we analyse the ground realities of the present situation of our academic institutions and libraries, it seems worthless to talk about these services and activities. We have to accept the realities to reform them as soon as possible, because the growth of IT will not leave space to do anything after some years.

The major problems to be eliminated before may be identified as:

- The required technology and needed organisational structures are not presently available to provide the required level of service, comparable to that available today without the concept of resource sharing.

- Resource sharing will effect the economics of publishing by increasing unit pricing as library orders decline. A substantial part of the prospective saving from resource sharing will thus evaporate.
- A large library may become more and more of a lender of materials, causing resource sharing to be a drain rather than a source of additional material.
- If all libraries turn to resource sharing, none will acquire sufficiently and have books to lend.

In spite of these lacunae we have started to move in the direction. At this stage it is essential to develop some sort arrangements to stream line the movement. Followings might be recognized the prerequisites of a functional resource sharing system.,

Infrastructure

It includes the installation of required hardware and software to create bibliographical, contents pages, abstracts and full text electronic databases and their networking. It is also needed to create various union catalogues and to develop efficient software to handle on-line users query. In addition to these a sound document delivery system could also be needed to send the required information to its end user.

In nut shelta library wants to be part of resource sharing network should have to have computers, printers, modem, scanners, database creation and networking software of specified standards, telephone connectivity, network access, photocopying machines, fax and a reliable postal system. The cost effectiveness of resource sharing is diminished at the present, because it has to run in parallel with other running system.

Common Code of Conduct

Apart from similar software and networking protocols the participating libraries have to evolve a common code of conduct regarding the collection development and resource sharing. There are several basic agreements among libraries that must be developed to operate a co-operative resource-sharing network.

It includes:

- Agreement to share currently owned materials will protocols, limitations and priorities.
- Financial agreement, to safeguard the individual recognition of the libraries.
- Agreement on acquisition policies to ensure consistent development of holdings and to avoid redundancy.

- Agreement of record keeping to streamline and to ensure the smooth operations from acquisition to borrowing and lending.

Legal Copyright and Photo Copying Laws

It is noticeable that the resource sharing activities should violate the copyright and photocopying laws.

Trained Manpower

The establishment and organisation of resource sharing activities are not possible with out the competent, trained and dedicated manpower. At present it is needed to organise massive education and training programmes via different modes to fulfil the required need.

Aware Users

The user is the most important component of any system. Keeping in view this fact, participating libraries and nodal agency simultaneously have to develop and organise user education/orientation programmes in changing context, to ensure the maximum utilizations of the resource sharing activities.

In addition to above said prerequisites it is essential to adopt some professional ethics to run the system smoothly. There is no procedure to impose this idea on participating libraries, but it is worth noticeable that in future only those libraries will survive whose professionals will be guided by this idea.

CHARACTERISTICS OF A NETWORKED LIBRARY RESOURCE SHARING SYSTEM

Where there is a system there must be its users. The satisfaction of users should be the criteria to measure the effectiveness of the system. A sound library resource sharing system, whether it is automatic or manual should have following characteristics. These characteristics should be kept in mind to establish or remodel the networked system.

These checkpoints are also useful to measure the effectiveness of the existing resource sharing system:

- *Speed*: The resource sharing system should be speedy. It should be based on the latest means of data communication systems and programmes. It should be able to judge tile timeliness and urgency of user's information need, because the use of information depends on whether it is provided at right time or not.
- *Accuracy*: The resource sharing system should be able to locate and provide the accurate information. It should be reliable and error free.
- *Cost/Fee:* The information provided should be cost effective. It must be less than the original cost of document.
- *Staff Courtesy/Knowledge/Assistance:* The professionals engaged in the resource sharing activities should be knowledgeable and prompt to

handle the queries. The speed and accuracy of manual resource sharing system depends on these professionals.

- *Consistency of Service and Reliability:* It must be consistent and reliable. The resource sharing activity should be adopted as an important component of present library system.
- *Communication (Provision for Status Reports):* The union catalogues should be able to provide the status report regarding availability of the document.
- *Delivery and Request Options:* The resource center should be able to deliver the needed document! information through required mode of delivery *i.e.* via e-mail, fax, courier or by post.
- *Self-service Options:* It will be easy to use, so that user can handle it without any problem. These character-istics should be considered as guiding principals to establish a new resource sharing system and to measure the efficiency and efficacy of existing one.

THE LANDSCAPE OF LIBRARY RESOURCES

Technology offers opportunities to be innovative, as the following discussion of electronic resources and services demonstrates, but it is important to bear in mind that not all e-learners are equal when it comes to access to computing equipment; the availability, speed, and stability of Internet connections; or the information skills that are needed to make optimum use of virtual libraries. Access to print-based library materials continues to be important, because not all of the information resources that elearners need are available in electronic format: many of our most valuable research materials are still print-based.

The Digital Library Federation and the Council on Library and Information Resources commissioned a survey of the use of print and electronic scholarly information resources at institutions of higher education across the United States. The survey found that, although almost half of undergraduates report using electronic resources all or most of the time for their coursework, this was the case for only 35.2 per cent of graduate students. Only 34.7 per cent of faculty indicated that they use electronic resources all or most of the time for their research, and just 22.7 per cent said this of their teaching. Although there has been a shift away from purchasing print materials to be housed in a physical building and towards providing access to licensed digital resources made available over a computer network, librarians continue to work to resolve issues pertaining to distance delivery of resources that are unavailable in digital format.

Online catalogues and indexing and abstracting systems provide elearners with convenient access to bibliographic information about valuable scholarly documents. When those documents are not available in full-text form online, a demand is generated for delivery from a library's print collection or from the collections of other libraries through interlibrary loans.Typical solutions for delivery of non-digital formats include the use of mail and courier services, the establishment of collections at designated sites, and the negotiation of agreements with other libraries through consortia. Given that a growing number of learners are accessing library collections online, librarians are working to develop an integrated approach to providing access to electronic resources that facilitates retrieval and reduces confusion.

A library Web site can function as an information gateway, an entry point to a range of online resources, with key components being the library catalogue and journal databases. Most online catalogues permit the integration of electronic books and electronic journals, enabling learners to locate items from digital and physical collections with one search. User services—such as the ability to check due dates, renew materials, and request materials online—are also provided. Gateways may also organise collections and incorporate directories like that provided by Athabasca University's Journal Databases: List Databases by Subject page. Librarians have become increasingly creative in enhancing their Web sites. Because not all e-learners have physical access to reference tools—the quick fact-finding tools that are the staple of library collections—libraries can perform a valuable service by providing pointers to online versions. Athabasca University Library's Digital Reference Centre, for example, offers a digital version of an academic library's reference collection, including almanacs and directories, atlases and maps, data and statistics, and dictionaries and encyclopaedias. Librarians select quality Internet resources to help e-learners navigate the Web. For example, the British Open University Library's ROUTES database contains quality-assessed, courserelated Internet resources "selected by course teams and the Library's Information Specialists". As libraries work to enhance their presence on the Web, a growing number are investigating the potential of electronic course reserves. The traditional course reserves desk of an academic library, with its limited copies, short loan periods, and high late fines, can be a considerable source of frustration for students.

In the e-reserves model, the library makes available, through the World Wide Web, items that faculty have selected and "placed on reserve" for students in a particular course. San Diego State University (SDSU) pioneered e-reserves in the early 1990s. SDSU uses Docutek's ERes, a system that provides access to course readings, chat rooms, and bulletin boards. Many other libraries have initiated their own projects. Electronic delivery of course reserve material has become a hot topic in the library literature.

The Association of Research Libraries (ARL) maintains the Electronic Reserves Listserv, and an archive of the discussion can be accessed on the Web. Most e-reserves operate on a password-protected model: one must be affiliated with the institution, or even registered in the course, to view course reserves. A typical e-reserve solution is to employ an electronic course reserve module that permits full integration with the library's online catalogue.

Content in ereserves databases varies. Scanning and mounting readings in portable document format (PDF) is time-consuming and requires copyright clearance. Other options for content include incorporating institution-produced materials (*e.g.,* lecture notes and video or audio clips), using licensed digital resources through direct linking to items by means of a persistent URL, and including selected resources freely available through the World Wide Web. Librarians can take a creative, pro-active approach to e-reserves. Athabasca University Library has developed a platform for ereserves that operates on a somewhat different model than do other e-reserves systems. The Digital Reading Room offers a digital solution for course readings and supplementary materials.

An in-house storage and retrieval system was developed for the DRR using open source software. The model operates along the principle of open access to collection creation tools, thus permitting course content creators, educational media developers, and librarians to develop a multidisciplinary knowledge database.

Each course in the Digital Reading Room has a Digital Reading File (DRF). The licensed contents, such as journal database articles, require authentication through the Library's proxy server, permitting only the Athabasca University community of users to access them; non-licensed resources, such as Web sites, are freely available to the public. A search engine permits e-learners to search across the DRFs, providing a multidisciplinary aspect to course reserves that is not typically encountered.

By encouraging the inclusion of resources in a variety of formats, including text, graphics, video, audio, simulations, and games, the DRR supports a wide range of learning objectives and styles. The DRR accommodates the inclusion of non-digital resources by providing e-learners with a means to request them from the Library.

The DRR is being developed using metatags that conform to the IEEE LOM standards and use the CanCore implementation guidelines to insure consistency and search capability across database collections such as MERLOT. Managing the remote access and authentication issues involved in making digital resources available has become a significant area of support to users of the electronic library.

Librarians may be called upon to respond to questions concerning log-in and password information, browser configuration, software installation, and a range of troubleshooting needs. Access problems are hugely frustrating for e-learners, and must be resolved quickly. Ensuring that front-line library staff are adequately trained, providing clear instructions on the library's Web site, and coordinating support activities with computing services personnel can contribute to effective technical support.

E-learners also benefit from having a variety of means of contacting the library, including e-mail, Web forms, and a toll-free telephone number.

LIBRARY RESOURCE SHARING AND NETWORKING

The term resource applies to a thing, person or action to which one resorts to in times of need and sharing indicates allotting, apportioning or contributing something that is owned, to benefit others. Resource sharing, therefore, refers to reciprocity, implying a partnership where each member has something useful to contribute to others and which each is willing and able to make available when needed.

Resource sharing is an empty concept, but for the approach permitting resource sharing to work is that which:

- Entails having resources to share
- Having a willingness to share them, and
- Having a plan for accomplishing resource sharing

Resource Sharing is an integral part of modern library services. In the developed countries, no library services can be thought without sharing of resources. In the past, ₹ was limited to the interlibrary loan system. In the modern age, with the development of science and technology and innovations of techniques and devices, resource sharing has become easier and fruitful due to the availability of databases, information network, and online sharing facilities. Thus, the resourcesharing system helps one library to access to resources of other libraries.

When resource sharing is agreed upon by participating institutions, then the following aspects must be planned:

- Identify and locate major collections, sources and materials
- Assemble, publish and distribute collective information for all participating bodies
- Workout the basis for sharing, reference service, lending service, copying service, access to materials, delivery service, and lists of holdings
- Establish means of sharing ideas, development and problems in the form of a newsletter
- Plan for new developments in the knowledge of what others are doing
- Developing a National Information Policy

The following are the most important benefits of resource sharing to participating institutions:

- Easy access to materials
- Enables co-operating institutions to extend limited resources
- Allow greater staff specialization
- Improve services to users
- Avoids unnecessary duplication

- Reduces the number of places which will need to go for services
- Improves working relationships between cooperating libraries.

Resource sharing refers to a joint use of resources available on a system or a network by user or peripherals. In the language of information management, when we talk about resource sharing we simply mean collective use of information of all types by various end users from a control coordinating unit or from within a network component at a reduced cost with easy accessibility.

Library cooperation and resource-sharing activity can take place in several forms and can happen at many levels, which include:

- Interlibrary loans/reciprocal borrowing privileges
- Exchange or sharing of expertise, resources, and facilities
- Exchange of publications and photocopies and other reprographic services
- Sharing of bibliographic information
- Cooperative acquisition, cooperative cataloguing, and cooperative collection development preparation of union list of holdings
- Cooperative relationship and network development

The implementation of resource sharing is largely depends on library networking. It gives an easy and wider access to information as members have an expanded information-base and service. A network is a form of arrangement or an administrative structure that links a group of individuals or organizations who have agreed to work together and/or share resources. Information networking entails the sharing of resources so that the information needs of both actual and potential users of information—from the local to national level—of all network participants are met. The network enables the participating bodies to facilitate and expand their users' access to literature and information without corresponding investment in purchase, and processing of information is exchanged through the network on a formal basis. The network may be responsible for coordinating, organizing and providing information and literature support at the national and international level.

The main activities and functions of the network are as follows:

Acquisition of materials:

- Joint purchasing of materials
- Assignment of specialization in material acquisition
- Coordinated subscription
- Exchange of duplicate holdings

Technical services:

- Co-operative cataloguing
- Abstracting and indexing services
- Interlibrary loan
- Reciprocal borrowing privileges
- Reference and/or referral services

Publication programme/repackaging information:

- Union catalogue/list of periodicals
- Mutual notification of purchase through lists of new arrivals or acquisition list
- Bibliography development
- Newsletters
- Joint directories of personnel, projects, consultants, resource persons, etc.
- Manuals

Coordination services:

- Clearing house functions
- Retrieval and storage function
- Referral center

Delivery/mailing service:

- Research, training and other special services
  - User interest surveys
  - Joint research projects
  - In-service personnel training
  - Workshops and meetings
  - Translation services

PUBLIC LIBRARY INFORMATION NETWORK

HISTORY

The Ohio Public Library Information Network (OPLIN) began to take shape in 1994 when a small group of librarians from a suburban library system discussed the need for a statewide public library network similar to the networks used by academic libraries (OhioLink) and K-12 libraries (INFOhio). This group of librarians reached out to the Ohio Library Council (OLC, then known as the Ohio Library Association), which helped to develop a plan to create the network and lobbied state legislators for the funding to build it.

Fran Haley, who had recently joined the OLC, was instrumental in bringing together experienced individuals to develop the network plan and in inviting the entire library community to participate in the process. Greg Byerly, was hired by the OLC to draft the initial plan for OPLIN.

He also worked to allow the state's public libraries to purchase telecommunications services from the statewide SOMACS (State of Ohio Multi-Agency Communications System) contract. The SOMACS contract provides postalised rates for its telecommunications circuits, so that the monthly price remains the same regardless of the length of the circuit or the location of the library.

OPLIN was created by state law in 1995. With the persistence of the OLC and the support of the legislature and then-Governor Voinovich, OPLIN was initially allocated $4.85 million. Before the state budget was passed in 1995, an additional $8 million was added to fund startup costs to network public libraries. The OPLIN board decided to provide funds for the initial installation connecting branch libraries to the network, but not to support recurring costs for these connections.

The board also decided to provide a telecommunications line for one library site (usually the main library) and to support its recurring costs in addition to purchasing computers so that each library would have two public workstations with which to access OPLIN. All but one of the 251 main library systems in Ohio joined OPLIN immediately.

Local boards passed a resolution for each library system to join, and each established its own Internet access policy for the network. The library system pursued funding for the project at the right time, as the state budget was flush, and the overall economic situation in the state was favorable. Funds remained even after OPLIN had been built, allowing the libraries to purchase subscriptions to databases and other electronic materials.

SERVICES

OPLIN provides both broadband Internet connections and information services to Ohio public libraries. Its mission is to ensure that all Ohio residents have fast, free public Internet access through the state's local public library systems, as well as the use of highquality research and reference databases not available free of charge on the World Wide Web.

OPLIN provides these services at no cost to the libraries. Unlike the situation in many other states, OPLIN coordinates the acquisition and installation of the physical telecommunications circuits that connect the main libraries to the network's hub in Columbus. (Most other library networks deliver content and services primarily via a physical network provided by some other organisation.) OPLIN leases circuits for the main libraries under two contracts the state has with telecommunications service providers.

Branch libraries, however, must obtain their own local broadband telecommunications connection to their main library. OPLIN also serves as the Internet service provider (ISP) for all public libraries in Ohio. It manages mail servers and provides the libraries with e-mail services. In addition, OPLIN provides web hosting services for those libraries with their own web site.

User Support and Communications

The OPLIN Support Center serves as the first line of defence for database problems and network troubleshooting. The center received 2,304 library technical service requests in fiscal year 2008, the majority of which related to e-mail issues. The OPLIN Support Center is open only during the workweek; after-hours and weekend calls are directed to the State of Ohio's Network Operations Center. OPLIN communicates with its members in a number of ways. It operates three e-mail lists: one for non-technical topics, one for the OPLIN office to announce new services and important changes to existing services, and one for technical topics. OPLIN also publishes a quarterly newsletter, participates on social networking web sites, publishes three blogs, and has a web site.

Telecommunications and Broadband Services

OPLIN obtains the local telecommunications circuits for all but one of the main libraries in the State of Ohio. These circuits connect the main library to the OPLIN hub in Columbus. As part of a state agency, OPLIN is authorised to lease these circuits under two state contracts: the SOMACS contract, serviced largely by AT&T and used to lease traditional T1 circuits that provide a capacity of 1.5 megabits per second (Mbps), and a separate contract for fibre-based Ethernet services.

OPLIN often transitions main libraries that need upgraded capacity to an Ethernet connection, but these Ethernet services are not available statewide. OPLIN also provides its members with continuous monitoring of broadband traffic.

Every quarter, traffic statistics for each main library are reviewed to see whether traffic patterns warrant an upgrade to a fibre based Ethernet circuit (or DS1 or DS3 if Ethernet is not available). The additional bandwidth and coordination for implementation are handled by OPLIN at no charge to the main library.

NETWORK STRUCTURE

In addition to the local circuits that connect the main libraries to the OPLIN hub, OPLIN maintains a high-capacity connection from its hub to the Internet over a shared, channelised DS3 connection that is managed by the Ohio Office of Information Technology (OIT). The OIT router manages traffic to OPLIN-provided resources, to the Internet, or back to other OPLIN member libraries.

The bandwidth charge for this connection to the Internet is the fastest-growing expense for OPLIN. As figure indicates, each main library receives a router provided by OPLIN to connect its circuit to the OPLIN hub. Management of this router is carried out collaboratively between OPLIN staff and the engineering group within OIT. The router represents the demarcation point between OPLIN services and the main library's local area network (LAN).

Each main library is responsible for its own LAN management services. OPLIN offers each main library a subnet of 32 publicly routable Internet Protocol (IP) addresses. Each main library administers these addresses following its own policies.

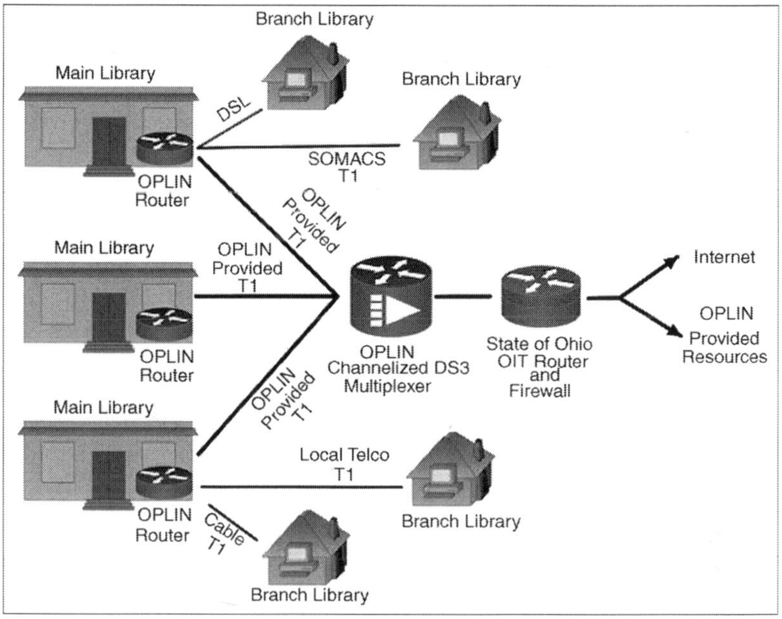

Fig. Structure of OPLIN.

As noted, OPLIN does not provide the local broadband connections for branch libraries. The branch libraries associated with each main library system can use a variety of options for connecting to the main library. In many cases, the SOMACS contract allows libraries to pay for a postalised T1, which is available statewide for only $400 per month. Figure shows this option in green.

While the SOMACS contract is available to any branch library, occasionally less expensive options exist. Some branches choose to purchase a digital subscriber line (DSL) circuit to connect virtually to the main library through a virtual private network (VPN). On other occasions, the branch library is located close enough to the main library that a local telephone company can connect both locations with a DS1 for less than the $400 per month under the SOMACS contract. The line in figure highlights this option. Finally, in some communities, cable TV companies offering telecommunications services can provide a branch library with either a DS1 or an Ethernet connection. Fibre is another option that is gaining popularity among libraries in Ohio. The State of Ohio has signed a separate contract that includes AT&T's Optical Ethernet Metropolitan Area Network (OPT-E-MAN). OPT-E-MAN is typically provisioned via a fibre connection with bandwidth increments as low as 5 Mbps and scalable to 100 Mbps.

Libraries that can purchase fibre-based service are ideally positioned to add bandwidth quickly and less expensively than is the case with traditional telephone company services (*e.g.*, T1/DS1, T3/DS3). Pricing for Ethernet services can vary significantly from location to location. The price for a 10 Mbps circuit can range from $600 per month to about $1,000 per month, not including router management fees and Internet access bandwidth.

GOVERNANCE

OPLIN is an independent state agency within the State Library of Ohio. It is governed by a board of eleven members selected by the State Library Board from the staffs of member public libraries and current or past trustees. The OPLIN Executive Director and the State Librarian or his/her designees serve as ex officio board members. Stephen Hedges has served as OPLIN's Executive Director since, 2006 and supervises four staff members.

OPLIN receives fiscal and logistical support services from the State Library of Ohio and contracts with OIT for assistance with network management. OPLIN is now defined in the Ohio Revised Code. Until recently, it was a line item in the State Library budget, meaning that it technically ceased to exist every 2 years. OPLIN is now part of the permanent law, which allows it to take advantage of longer service contracts.

FINANCE

The majority of OPLIN's budget—58 per cent—is spent on purchasing Internet connections to public libraries, which it regards as its most important role. Another 30 percent is spent on databases, which make up about a third of the total cost of the Ohio Web Library database collection. About 2 per cent of OPLIN's budget is allocated by the legislature for grant subsidies to local libraries to help defray the cost of filtering Internet content; another 1 per cent funds conferences and other training for public librarians.

The remaining 9 per cent of the budget is used for all other costs—rent, salaries and benefits (for five staff), supplies, postage, office equipment, etc. Thus more than 90 percent of the OPLIN budget is spent on direct services to public libraries, and less than 10 per cent on administrative costs. From the network's inception in the fiscal year (FY) 1995 budget bill through FY 2007, annual funding for OPLIN varied between $5 million and $8 million each year. Because of the state's recent fiscal problems, OPLIN's budget was reduced in 2008 and 2009, and additional reductions may occur in 2010.

To make up for the loss of state revenue, OPLIN has entered into an agreement with eTech Ohio to manage its E-rate applications this year. OPLIN expects that eTech Ohio's E-rate expertise will lead to more federal E-rate discounts than in the past. Libraries can call on eTech Ohio for E-rate consulting, and eTech Ohio will also be conducting E-rate workshops.

LIBRARY AND INFORMATION NETWORKS IN INDIA

The explosion in the amount of literature that is available, increases among the number of users and their different needs, and the application of electronic media are forcing libraries to construct and participate in networks. Magnetic tapes, floppy disks, and CD-ROMs provide enough data storage capacity. Retrieval through telecommunications networks and access to international databases are available for searching for information on various subjects. With the advent of networks, remote transmission of texts and graphics, video clips and animated clips are also possible.

DEFINITIONS

- A library network is broadly described as a group of libraries coming together with some agreement of understanding to help each other with a view to satisfying the information needs of their clientele.
- UNISIST II working document defines Information Network as
  - A set of inter-related information systems associated with communication facilities, which are cooperating through more or less formal agreements in order to implement information handling operations to offer better services to the users.
- The National Commission on Libraries and Infor-mation Science in its National Programme Document defines a network as
  - Two or more libraries engaged in a common pattern of information exchange, through commu-nications for some functional purpose.

OBJECTIVES

- To promote and support adoption of standards in library operations.
- To create databases for projects, specialists and institutions to provide online information services
- To improve the efficiency of housekeeping operations
- To coordinate with other regional, national and international network for exchange of information and documents
- To generate new services and to improve the efficiency of existing ones

NETWORK DEVELOPMENT IN INDIA

Some factors that are responsible for the development of library and information networks in India are:

- The report of the working group of the planning commission on modernization of library services and informatics for the seventh five year plan, 1985-90
- The National Policy on Library and Information systems document accepted by the ministry of HRD, Government of India.
- The report on national policy on university libraries prepared by the Association of Indian Universities

- The UGC report on information systems for science and technology under the Department of Science and Industrial Research (DSIR) Government of India has been vigourously promoting an integrated approach to library automation and networking.

LIMITATIONS IN NETWORK DEVELOPMENT

A network may fail in the early stages if there is not proper planning or if adequate funds are not available. Moreover, a common memorandum of agreement signed by the partici-pating libraries at the institutional level is essential for the success of a network venture. On a more practical level, catalogue data must be in a standard, machine readable form for it to be shared and exchanged. And, finally, a continuous flow of external assistance is crucial for the network's survival.

TYPES OF NETWORKS

Presently, there are three types of computer networks:

- LAN;
- MAN and
- WAN.

Local Area Network (LAN)

A LAN is a number of related computers and electronic devices that share information over a transmission media. A typical use of LAN is to tie together personal computers in an office so that they can all use a single printer and a file server. The LAN can be within a building or a campus wide network.

Metropolitan Area Network (MAN)

Attempts are being made to develop this type of network in metropolitan areas such Delhi, Calcutta, Bangalore, Madras, etc.

Wide Area Network (WAN)

A large-scale network, involving offices in different cities and countries is referred to as WAN, which is specially designed to interconnect data transmission devices over wide geographical areas.

CATEGORIES OF NETWORK

Library networks have been divided into two categories: general network and specialized network. The latter can further be divided into metropolitan network and countrywide network.

GENERAL NETWORKS IN INDIA

Nicnet:

- *Title:* National Information Center Network

- *Sponsor:* Planning Commission, Govt. of India.
- *Membership:* Four national and regional nodes, 32 state and union territory nodes; seventy cities and towns
- *Services:* Bulk file transfer; teleconferencing; full text and bibliographic retrieval services
- *Application:* ICMRNIC Center; MEDLARS in India; Chemical Abstracts database

Indonet:

- *Title:* INDONET data Network
- *Sponsor:* CMC Ltd = Informatics India Ltd
- *Membership:* Commercial computer network
- *Services:* Database services such as DIALOG, COMPUSERVE; IP; SHARP
- *Applications:* ACME; file transfer; international gateway

I–NET (VIKRAM):

- *Title:* I–NET
- Sponsor: Dept. of Telecommunications, Govt. of India
- *Connectivity:* Packet switched public data network covering nine cities
- *Services:* Information exchange through e-mail/FTP; Bibliographic databases

SPECIALIZED NETWORKS

Metropolitan Networks

CALIBNET:

- *Title:* Calcutta Libraries Network
- *Sponsor:* NISSAT–Govt. of India
- *Applications:* Cataloguing; serials control; acquisitions; circulation
- *Services:* CAS; SDI; union catalogue; partial database; editing and retrieval of records;
- Global information; search; full-text document delivery; library automation; CALIBNET INFO Services

Bonet:

- *Title:* Bombay Library Network
- *Sponsor:* NISSAT and NCST
- *Objective:* To promote cooperation among libraries in Bombay
- *Services:* online catalogue; online document delivery; IRS; interlibrary loan; dissemination of information

Delnet:

- *Title:* Developing Library Network
- *Sponsor:* NISSAT and NIC
- *Objective:* To promote resource sharing; develop a network of libraries; collect, store, disseminate information

- *Members:* 165 Institutions, 600 Libraries, 15 States in India, 5 from outside India
- *Services:* resource sharing; free Software; ICE online facility; books database; thesis database; Indian specialists; database

Adinet:

- *Title:* Ahmedabad Library Network
- *Sponsor:* NISSAT, DSIR and INFLIBNET
- *Objective:* To bring cooperation among its regional libraries; to develop databases; to integrate scientific and technical information systems
- Members: nine libraries
- *Services:* library automation; library holdings; database in progress

Mylibnet:

- *Title:* Mysore Library Network
- *Sponsor:* NISSAT
- *Objective:* Developing software tools; conducting seminar; workshops/ training programmes; conduct surveys
- *Host Site:* CFTRI, Mysore
- *Members:* 116 Institutions
- *Services:* MYLIB Database; E-journals; food patents; CFTRI Library Bulletin; public services.

Countrywide Area Network

Desinet:

- *Title:* Defence Science Information Network
- *Sponsor:* DESIDOC, Delhi
- *Activity:* Focus on scientific, research and defence communities

Ernet:

- *Title:* Educational and Research Network
- *Sponsor:* Dept. of Electronics, Govt. of India; UNESCO
- *Members:* eight institutions
- *Services:* Communication services such as e-mail, file transfer, remote log on, database access, bulletin board etc.,

Sirnet:

- *Title:* Scientific and Industrial Research Network
- *Sponsor:* CSIR (Commissioned Agency-NCST, Bombay)
- *Members:* 40 labs and R&D Institutions
- *Applications:* scientific communication; leather technology; natural products; food technology; medicinal Plants

Vidyanet:

- *Title:* Vidyanet (Dedicated Communication Computer Net)
- *Sponsor:* TATA Institute of Fundamental Research, Bombay

- *Objectives:* To provide rapid means of communi-cations by linking computers at various institutions in India to similar networks outside the country; to stimulate corporate research, the day-to-day exchange of research information and the execution of joint projects and publications
- *Services:* File transfer facility; sharing of computer resourccs and access to remote applications, data-bases, libraries, etc.

Btisnet:

- *Title:* Btisnet (Specialized Information Network)
- *Sponsor:* Dept. of Biotechnology, Govt. of India.
- *Connectivity:* 10 Specialized Information Centres in genetic engineering, plant tissue culture; photosynthesis and plant molecular biology; cell transformation; bio-process engineering.
- *Services:* Data processing using applications software; online communication access; facsimile facility

Inflibnet:

- *Title:* Information Library Network
- *Sponsor:* UGC
- *Connectivity:* computer communication network of universities and R&D; libraries and bibliographic information centers throughout the country
- *Members:* 200 Universities; 400 College libraries; 200 R&D libraries
- *Services:* catalogue service; database Services; document supply services; e-mail; BBS: audio and video conferencing, etc.

Balnet:

- *Title:* Bangalore Library Network
- *Sponsor:* JRD;. Tata Memorial Library
- *Members:* 100 Libraries

Malibnet:

- *Title:* Madras Library Network
- *Sponsor:* INSDOC and NISSAT
- *Members:* 15 Libraries
- *Activity:* Two important databases, a directory database of current serials in Madras and a contents database covering articles published in 300 journals available in Madras libraries.

11

Academic Libraries in India: A Present-Day Scenario

Education aims to impart knowledge and makes good citizens. Libraries are the repositories of knowledge and form an integral part of education. Libraries have a long history, starting with the chained and closed-access libraries of earlier times to the present-day hybrid, digital, and virtual libraries that use the latest technology for provision of information through various services. Librarians have also changed from storekeepers who were concerned with protection of books against theft, mutilation, and pilferage, to that of information officers, navigators, and cybrarians who find themselves in the vast ocean of reading material and are busy in satisfying their clients who want anytime and anywhere information.

With the advent of computers, the nature of libraries has changed dramatically. Computers are being used in libraries to process, store, retrieve and disseminate information. As a result, the traditional concept of library is being redefined from a place to access books to one which houses the most advanced media including CD-ROM, Internet, and remote access to a wide range of resources. Libraries have now metamorphosed into digital institutions. Gone are the days when a library was judged by its quantitative resources. Today, libraries are surrounded by networked data that is connected to a vast ocean of Internet-based services. Moreover, electronic resources relevant to the professions are developing at an unprecedented pace.

Academic libraries are considered to be the nerve centres of academic institutions, and must support teaching, research, and other academic programmes. The situation in academic libraries of India is the same as that of academic libraries the world over; however, Indian libraries must provide maximum information with limited resources.

ACADEMIC AND RESEARCH LIBRARIES

The application of computing to library work in India has a history of at least three decades because since the time the computer entered premier academic institutions and selected R & D facilities, it has been explored for improving information processing and management routines. *Information technology* (IT) enriched library services arrived initially for *science and technology* (S&T) information handling and for the special libraries attached to *research and development* (R&D) centres and academic libraries in higher education institutions. In comparison to other libraries, academic and research libraries have better infrastructure and skilled manpower in greater numbers, making them able to offer information services comparable to advanced countries. Like qualified teaching and research personnel and well-equipped laboratories, the right information service is another vital element in the trinity which completes a fruitful academic or research environment.

MARKET-DRIVEN COLLABORATION

Academic and research libraries, especially in developing countries, are passing through a very challenging phase in their existence due to unfriendly trends in the emerging information market. On the one hand, these libraries are still left with many of the old problems such as poor budgetary support and weak infrastructure, as well as staff in fewer numbers and often with less expertise. But the new information marketing techniques, like the possibilities of delivering and accessing electronic information in diverse channels, force these libraries to be very vigilant and cautious in their approach towards information acquisition and services. Libraries and professionals in India were quick to understand the emerging information environment was forcing their users to depend largely on those resources, which are becoming more expensive day by day due to the rise in production costs, fall in subscriptions and inflationary trends of Indian currency.

When individual libraries found that alone they are not in a position to satisfy the information requirements of their clients, they formulated various collaborative arrangements with other libraries such as,

- *Interlibrary loan* (ILL) services,
- *Document delivery services* (DDS),
- Resource-sharing, and
- Consortia-based subscriptions.

PRESENT PRACTICES AND EMERGING GOALS

The special libraries attached to research and higher education were lucky enough to garner resources to automate their in-house routine operations and for hosting online public access catalogues (OPACs); some of them also set up facilities to search electronic databases. A few of them evolved the desired infrastructure for Internet surfing, for hosting of full-text database access, and for setting up digital libraries. The major advantage of the progress in computerization is a considerable increase in the amount of information available online. We have experienced that at the start of computer applications only the surrogates (metadata) existed online, but some full-text content has been made accessible online in recent years.

These libraries are experiencing the virtues of electronic information in different forms such as e-journals, e-books, bibliographic/full-text electronic databases on CD-ROMs and through Web access. Due to publishers' 'electronic plus' policies, libraries are able to access electronic versions of printed sources such as journals either for free or by paying an additional fee. However the goal these libraries in specialized research and academic centres should have set for themselves is to enhance their information facilities to fully functional digital libraries, comparable with similar facilities in the developed countries.

CULTURES AND CONFLICTS FACED BY LIBRARIES

The fixed roles suggested by Levy for researchers, publishers and libraries are either overlapping or changing in the electronic scene. There are cases where an author or a library is acting as electronic publisher, and there are publishers providing a wide variety of information packages beyond the contents of printed journals.

The real question is: has the library really lost ground in the emerging information scene? Even the critics will not say so. The concerns expressed are only to revitalize the professional skills of librarians, rejuvenate the style of working and reorient the library towards its rightful place in effective dissemination of information. Maybe the common feeling that the library is a central place in the institution visited everyday by large numbers of users, like any public utility, has lost some ground in the electronic scene. Non-etheless, apart the continuing provision of information services for print sources, the electronic revolution has reaffirmed the library more as an information service and access centre than as an information storehouse.

THE EDUCATIONAL SYSTEM OF INDIA

India has a large higher education system. The growth rate of educational institutions in India was very slow before independence in 1947.

Today there are a total of 237 universities, including 116 general universities, 12 science and technology universities, 7 open universities, 33 agricultural universities, 5 women's universities, 1 language universities and 11 medical universities along with 12,600 colleges that provide education in all disciplines. The number of teachers is 3.1 million, and 7.8 million students are enrolled in higher education.

University Grants Commission (UGC)

UGC, established by an act of parliament in 1956, coordinates and monitors the higher education system in India and provides grants to the universities and colleges. Two hundred ninety four universities/institutions in the country are directly under the purview of UGC.

It also advises the union and state governments on measures to university education. It frames rules and regulations for overall teaching and research at higher education. As a result, it also looks after the academic libraries, *i.e.*, sets various standards for library education, library staff, library services, etc. A number of committees have been set up by the UGC for the support of higher education in general and the library services in academic libraries in particular.

UGC has also set up three information centres covering different disciplines—the *National Centre for Science Information* (NCSI) at Indian Institute of Science Bangalore, SNDT Women's University Mumbai, and National Social Science Information Centre at M.S. University at Baroda, to provide the document delivery services to students, teachers, and researchers.

Information and Library Network

The University Grants Commission has set up an autonomous Inter-University Centre in 1991 called INFLIBNET. It is involved in modernizing university libraries in India and connects them through a nation-wide high-speed data network. It promotes automation of libraries, develops standards, creates union catalogues of serials, theses, books, monographs and non-book materials; provides access to bibliographic information sources; creates database of projects, institutions, specialists; provides training, etc.

Almost all academic libraries, especially university libraries, are members of INFLIBNET. It has also developed library automation software called SOUL *(Software for University Libraries)* and has distributed the same free of cost to its member libraries.

Other Networks

Besides Inflibnet, a number of other national networks and various library networks have also been developed including:

- Nicnet (National Informatic Center's network),
- Indonet,
- Ernet,
- Calibnet,
- Delnet:
  - Adinet is associated with Inflibnet,
  - Delnet with NIC and
  - Malibnet with CFTRI.

A number of educational institutions are members of such networks. These networks, especially DELNET are engaged in compiling union catalogs, creating various databases of experts, providing training to library staff, ILL, online facilities, reference service, assistance in retrospective conversion, etc.

Library Consortia

Due to a financial crunch and the rising costs of journals, many Indian university and college libraries cannot subscribe to all the required journals and databases. To overcome this problem, libraries are forming consortia.

Some special libraries and organizations like the Indian Institute of Astrophysics Library, Inter-university Centre for Astronomy and Astrophysics Library, *National Centre for Radio Astrophysics* (NCRA) Library, Physical Research Laboratory (PRL) Library, Raman Research Institute (RRI) Library, Tata Institute of Fundamental Research (TIFR) Library, Council of Scientific and Industrial Research, Department of Atomic Energy, etc., have established consortia to share electronic access to journal literature.

NISCAIR (formed by the merger of INSDOC and NISCOM) is developing a consortium for CSIR labs for accessing e-journals. Consortia in India are still a new concept that requires proper guidelines and methodologies. In a survey by UGC in 2001, it was noted that although 142 university libraries had computer and Internet facilities and were interlinked to INFLIBNET, they were subscribing to printed journals only.In order to solve this problem, UGC launched a major initiative called UGC-INFONET that provides high speed Internet connections so as to have electronic access to professional literature including research journals, abstracts, review publications, and databases from all areas in science and technology, as well as in social sciences and humanities.

Today, a number of professional journals are available over UGC-INFONET to all universities. The e-subscription initiative under UGC-Infonet is an important portal for sharing print as well as electronic resources amongst university libraries. INFLIBNET functions as a resource center with an aim to cater to the needs of its members for resources not accessible to them in electronic media or are available in print media.

SCHOOL LIBRARY

A school library is a library within a school where students, staff, and often, parents of a public or private school have access to a variety of resources. The goal of the school library media center is to ensure that all members of the school community have equitable access "to books and reading, to information, and to information technology."

A school library media center "uses all types of media... is automated, and utilizes the Internet for information gathering." School libraries are distinct from public libraries because they serve as "learner-oriented laboratories which support, extend, and individualize the school's curriculum... A school library serves as the center and coordinating agency for all material used in the school."

Researchers have demonstrated that school libraries have a positive impact on student achievement. More than 60 studies have been conducted in 19 U.S. states and one Canadian province. The major finding of these studies is that students with access to a well-supported school library media programme with a qualified school library media specialist, scored higher on reading assessments regardless of their socio-economic statuses.

In addition, a study conducted in Ohio revealed that 99.4 per cent of students surveyed believed that their school librarians and school library media programmes helped them succeed in school. A report that reported similar conclusions was compiled by Michele Lonsdale in Australia in 2003.

HISTORY OF SCHOOL LIBRARIES

The later part of the 19th century marked the beginning of the modern American library movement with the creation of the American Library Association (ALA) in 1876 by a group of librarians led by Melvil Dewey. At these beginning stages of development, the school libraries were primarily made up of small collections with the school librarian playing primarily a clerical role. 1920 marked the first effort by the library and education communities to evaluate school libraries with the publication of the *Certain Report*, which provided the first yardstick for evaluating school libraries.

School libraries experienced another major push following the launch of *Sputnik* in 1957, which forced the United States to re-evaluate its priorities for math and science education. As a result, the 1960s were one of the greatest periods of growth and development for school libraries due to an increased flow of money and support from the private sector and public funding for education. Most notable during this time was the *Knapp School Libraries Project* which established model school library media centers across the country.

Hundreds of new school libraries were expanded and renovated during this time. Most recently, school libraries have been defined by three major guidelines documents: *Information Power* and *Information Power II*. Globally important mission statement is the Unesco School library Manifesto.

THE PURPOSE OF THE SCHOOL LIBRARY

The school library exists to provide a range of learning opportunities for both large and small groups as well as individuals with a focus on intellectual content, information literacy, and the learner. In addition to classroom visits with collaborating teachers, the school library also serves as a place for students to do independent work, use computers, equipment and research materials; to host special events such as author visits and book clubs; and for tutoring and testing. The school library media center programme is a collaborative venture in which school library media specialists, teachers, and administrators work together to provide opportunities for the social, cultural, and educational growth of students. Activities that are part of the school library media programme can take place in the school library media centre, the laboratory classroom, through the school, and via the school library's online resources.

THE SCHOOL LIBRARY COLLECTION

School libraries are similar to public libraries in that they contain books, films, recorded sound, periodicals, realia, and digital media. These items are not only for the education, enjoyment, and entertainment of the all members of the school community, but also to enhance and expand the school's curriculum.

STAFFING OF THE SCHOOL LIBRARY

In many schools, school libraries are staffed by librarians, teacher-librarians, or school library media specialists who hold a specific library science degree. In some jurisdictions, school librarians are required to have specific certification and/or a teaching certificate.

The school librarian performs four leadership main roles: teacher, instructional partner, information specialist, and programme administrator. In the teacher role, the school librarian develops and implements curricula relating to information literacy and enquiry. School librarians may read to children, assist them in selecting books, and assist with schoolwork. Some school librarians see classes on a "flexible schedule". A flexible schedule means that rather than having students come to the library for instruction at a fixed time every week, the classroom teacher schedules library time when library skills or materials are needed as part of the classroom learning experience.

In the instructional partner role, school librarians collaborate with classroom teachers to create independent learners by fostering students' research, information literacy, technology, and critical thinking skills.

As information specialists, school librarians develop a resource base for the school by using the curriculum and student interests to identify and obtain library materials, organize and maintain the library collection in order to promote independent reading and lifelong learning. Materials in the library collection can be located using an *Online Public Access Catalog* (OPAC).

This role also encompasses many activities relating to technology including the integration of resources in a variety of formats: periodical databases; Web sites; digital video segments; podcasts; blog and wiki content; digital images; virtual classrooms, etc. School librarians are often responsible for audio-visual equipment and are sometimes in charge of school computers and computer networks. Many school librarians also perform clerical duties. They handle the circulating and cataloging of materials, facilitate interlibrary loans, shelve materials, perform inventory, etc.

ACADEMIC LIBRARIES' EXTERNAL ENVIRONMENT AND ENVIRONMENTAL SCANNING BY MANAGERS

Academic libraries just like other libraries, information centers and similar organisations operate within the context of two environments - internal and external. Both of these environments are interconnected. Whilst, the library's internal context consists of organisational structure and of its functions and the way they are configured in pursuit of specified organisational objectives; each library operates in complex and changing external environments, which frequently produce new challenges which must be controlled to ensure the library's future survival and success. Their impact is a twoway process. Changes in the external environment affect the organisation's internal environment, whilst decisions made at managerial level will impact upon both the external and internal environment. Finally, one of the major and important tasks of a manager is the environmental scanning to acquire information and use it to determine the role of the library in its environment, its influence and image, and the services it provides. The external environment of an organisation may be viewed as a source of information, resources, or variation. External environment is not a collection of other systems and organisations, but it is an active environment. Changes, events and trends in the environment continually create signals and messages. Organisations detect or receive these cues and use the information to adapt to new conditions. Dill views the environment as a source of information, and suggests that the best way for analysing the environment is to treat the environment as information which becomes available to the organisation, or the organisation may get access via search activity.

Because information allows management to improve its strategic planning, tactical implementation of programme and it's monitoring and control; in messy environments, having access to timely and relevant information can give a firm competitive advantage. Information perspective indicates that, when managers suppose that. the environment is unpredictable, they feel uncertainty, and this situation occurs, when they feel that they have no information for accurate decision-making. Another perspective views the environment as a source of resources upon which the organisation is dependent. Munificence; concentration, and interconnectedness are three structural characteristics of the environment that affect resource dependence. Organisations require resources to survive. Typically, acquiring resources means that the organisation must interact with others who control those resources. The third perspective, based on ecological view in organisation studies, developed principally by Hannan and Freeman, and Aldrich. This point of view tries to explain why certain forms of organisations survive and thrive, while others languish and perish by using evolutionary biology rules. A firm's competitive position, financial success, and even survival depend on its ability to scan, understand and adapt to environmental conditions. In many of related studies, the external environment serves as a great source of strategic information. In order to succeed in formulating the strategy for future, managers and decision-makers need to collect, interpret and utilize information from the external environment. A manager achieves this factor of importance by environmental scanning.

Environmental scanning is the activity of gaining information about events and relationships in the organisation's environment, the knowledge of which would assist management in planning future courses of action; and has been the subject of extensive research. Hosseini define environmental scanning as monitoring, evaluation and dissemination of information about environment of organisation to important personnel of organisation.

CONCEPTUAL FRAMEWORK AND RESEARCH QUESTIONS

In the most general sense, an environment can be defined as everything which surrounds a system. Duncan, defines the environment as "the totality of physical and social factors that are taken directly into consideration in the decision-making behaviour of individuals in the organisation". The external environment comprises all of those forces and events outside the organisation that impinge on its activities. One of the research found that perceived importance is itself the most important predictor of scanning activity. Kefalas and Schoderbek found that executives in a dynamic environment did more scanning than those in a stable environment; and they concluded that executives' hierarchical level was not related to the focus of scanning and there was considerable scanning of the market sector by executives of all functional specialties. Burns and Stalker indicated that when the external environment was stable, the internal environment of the organisation was generally characterized rules, procedures and clear hierarchy of authority - a typical bureaucratic structure. Uncertainty is inherent in the environment and Duncan found that the level of perceived uncertainty increases with the complexity and the rate of environment change. The amount of scanning measured was based on Hambrick's study, by analysing the manager's level of interest in keeping abreast of trends; the frequency with which information comes to the manager's attention. In this study we measured the perceived importance (PI), variability or rate of changes (PV) and complexity of academic libraries environment from the managers' viewpoints. Then Daft, Sormunen and Parks' definition of environmental sectors was accepted, and thus the external environment of academic libraries at IAU were divided into six sectors as was applied by Choo: Customer, Competitor, Technological, Regulatory, Economic, and Socio-cultural.

RESEARCH OBJECTIVES

This study attempts to achieve the following objectives:

- To determine "important, variable and complex" sectors in the external environments of libraries as perceived by managers.
- To determine the amount of scanning that managers do on each of the environmental sectors of the target libraries.
- To determine the PSU and PEU of each of the environmental sectors and their relation with the amount of scanning.

RESEARCH QUESTIONS

- Q1: Which sectors of the external environment of academic libraries of IAU are perceived to be important by respondents?
- Q2: Which sectors of the external environment of academic libraries of IAU are perceived to be variable by respondents?
- Q3: Which sectors of the external environment of academic libraries of IAU are perceived to be complex by respondents?
- Q4: Which sectors of the external environment of academic libraries of IAU are scanned mostly by respondents?
- Q5: What is the rank of each sector of the external environment of academic libraries of IAU by applying perceived strategic uncertainty (PSU)?
- Q6: What is the rank of each sector of the external environment of academic libraries of IAU by applying perceived environmental uncertainty (PEU)?

RESEARCH HYPOTHESIS

The perceived strategic uncertainty (PSU) for each sector was calculated by adding the perceived variability (PV) and perceived complexity (PC) values of each environmental sector and multiplying the sum by the perceived importance value of that sector for formulating the hypothesis. This study hypothesized that:

- H1: Perceived strategic uncertainty (PSU) of an environmental sector positively correlates with the amount of scanning (AMS) in that sector.

Then, perceived environmental uncertainty (PEU) was measured by summing the variability and complexity values across the six environmental sectors and the second hypothesis was formulated as follows:

- H2: Perceived uncertainty (PEU) of an environmental sector positively correlates with the amount of scanning (AMS) in that sector.

METHODOLOGY

In the context of this research, the following analytical survey method and face to face interview is used to explore the relationship between variables and recognize the managers' point of view.

POPULATION AND DATA COLLECTION

The study population consists of managers of library and information centers of large and very large units of IAU*. The units of IAU are located in different groups based on. All units of IAU are more than 232 units in total. Foe homogeneous of research population and delete impact of organisation size we select the large and very large units as populations of this study.

Of the 94 selected units, 33 were large and 61 very large, where library and information center managers composed the population of this study.

DATA COLLECTION INSTRUMENT

Data were collected by mail questionnaires which were sent to the managers of libraries and information center of study populations; and personal interviews were performed via telephone to check validity of results from the mail questionnaires. From the population of 94 managers, 85 returned questionnaires, giving a response rate of 90.42per cent. Chronbach's alpha was accounted for examining the reliability of questionnaire, that was equal to.922, and therefore the reliability of the questionnaire was confirmed.

Based on Saaty and Shih approaches, it was confirmed that "no matter how a structure is validated, group participation with knowledgeable people is a good way to ensure its logicality and completeness". Thus, the questionnaires were reviewed by fifteen experts in the field of Library and Information Science and Management. In order to prepare the items in the questionnaires, the items in the previous researches were used as a valid pattern.

MEASUREMENT OF VARIABLES

Environmental Sectors

In order to measure perceived environmental uncertainty, the external environment is divided to six sectors, as defined by Daft, Sormunen and Parks, and Choo. Customer, Competition, Technology, Regulatory, Economic, and Socio-cultural Sectors.

- Customer sector refers to those companies or individuals that use the services offered by the respondent's library and information center, and include companies that acquire information materials and products of library.
- Competition sector includes the companies, products and services, and competitive tactics: companies that offer substitute services and compete with respondent's library, and competitive actions between the respondent's library and other organisations in the same industry.
- Technological sector includes the development of new techniques, innovation and methods in offering information services to customers, and general trends in research and science relevant to the respondent's library.
- Regulatory sector includes governmental legislation and regulations, community policies and political developments at all levels of government.
- Economic sector includes economic factors such as rate of income for individuals, rate of inflation, unemployment rate, and economic growth rate.

- Socio-cultural sector comprises social values in the general population, work ethics, Islamic-based ethics, and other demographic and cultural trends.

Environmental Uncertainty

In organisational research, perceived environmental uncertainty is often analyzed using Duncan's two dimensions of environmental complexity and variability. A complex environment requires that numerous environmental factors be taken into account in decision-making.

A variable environment is one in which these factors change frequently and rapidly. In this study the measurement of perceived environmental uncertainty is based on Duncan's two dimensional model: The Simple complex dimension is the number of environmental factors taken into consideration in decision-making; the static-dynamic dimension is the degree to which these factors remain the same or change continually over time.

Following Duncan's model, Daft, Sormunen and Parks, and also Choo used complexity and variability and Revilla, Prieto, and Prado, used dynamism and complexity to measure the perceived environmental uncertainty of chief executives. The perceived importance of environmental sectors were used to formulate the perceived strategic uncertainty. Finally, the perceived environmental uncertainty and perceived strategic uncertainty were measured by the following formulas:

- PEU= PV+PC
- PSU= PI* (PV+PC)

The following questions are asked for taking respondent approach about perceived importance, perceived variability and perceived complexity: Respondents assessed the relative importance, variability and complexity of each of the six defined environmental sectors by answering the following questions:

- Q1: How important to your organisations (libraries) are trends and events in each environmental sectors?
- Q2: What is the rate of change taking place in each environmental sector?
- Q3: What is the complexity level of each environmental sector?

By using a five-point likert scale labeled from 1= Not important to 5= Very important, for Q1; using a five-point scale labeled from 1= Low to 5= High, for Q2; and using a fivepoint scale labeled from 1= Low to 5= High, for Q3 respondents answered.

Amount of Scanning

Although Hambrick measured environmental scanning using frequency, level of interest, and hours spent scanning, this study similar to Choo used only frequency and level of interest such as: How frequently does information about each environmental sector come to your attention? To what extant do you keep yourself informed about developments in each environmental sector?

RESULTS

Both descriptive profiles of respondent managers' statistics were applied to reach valid findings. The nature and application of these statistical tests and methods are detailed out where results are offered. Data collected were analyzed using the statistical software package Statistical Product and Service Solutions (SPSS). Of the 94 managers of Library and Information Centers of IAU, 85 managers returned completed questionnaires. The distribution of respondents is similar to that of the study population: 30 respondents from large units and 55 from very large units. As for their educational backgrounds, approximately 40 per cent have bachelor, 40 per cent master, and 10 per cent have Ph.D. degrees. On the whole, 85 per cent of respondents' educational field was library and information science and 15 per cent was in other fields.

THE ACADEMIC LIBRARY DIRECTOR

Many library boards and local governments across the country will be going through a search process for a library director over the next five to ten years-some more than once. Some boards and local government officials will be putting their heads in the sand to avoid thinking about this issue; others will peek up slowly, until they willingly engage in the process. It is, after all, their most important function. Why is it so difficult? It is not hard to answer this question.

It is about change, it is about real work, it is about risk, challenge, and uncertainly. It is also about evaluation and assessment. There will be more meetings, more dialogue, and a need to talk honestly and look at yourselves-as leaders-and at your organisation-as an important entity in your community or educational institution. It is hard: change is hard, and costly, and frightening-and it the most important activity the members of a board will undertake. While fraught with challenge, this period is also filled with opportunity if you take the time to pause and reflect before rushing to fill the vacancy. This chapter helps you navigate the white water of both.

This one is written and directed first to those library boards of trustees that hire library directors, second to library directors, and third to everyone else-staff, consultants, students, and faculty. Our values are reflected in our belief that the board's role is to set policy and that the library director, with staff, is responsible for implementing policy. Further, research and our experience have taught us that trustees should steer far away from micromanaging the library; the most important task of the board is to recruit, retain, evaluate, provide feedback to, engage in dialogue with, and support the library director-as well as to terminate the library director if warranted. There is no more important function. The library board, to support your efforts in director succession planning. If your library does not have a governing board-if, for example, a university search committee or city or county hires the director-many of the principles that follow still hold true. We hope you are reading this before you have to hire a new library director, because the most effective boards are thinking and planning ahead in order to stay ahead. They are looking at ways to capitalize on the inevitable opportunity they will have to shape the library and search for the new. They may even be working with retiring directors to create new models for succession, like those envisioned in the e-mail that opens this chapter, that could bring the library new benefits and create a win for everyone.

There will be many retirements in the next five to ten years as baby boomers leave our libraries. It will be a very competitive time. We are not seeing a plethora of members of the Generation X community ready and waiting in the wings-and that is why we are writing this chapter to help libraries, their boards, or other governing bodies plan for the inevitable, be proactive, rise to their fiduciary responsibility, and continue to meet community needs. But if you find yourselves with a hiring emergency, this chapter can still help you. It offers a step-by-step emergency plan for succession that you, your departing director, HR department, and city or county leadership should become very familiar with.

WHY PLAN?

The primary purpose of an effective succession plan for a library director is to facilitate a seamless transition to the new director. A commitment from the board of trustees or other governing body to a timely planning process ensures that the library makes this transition most effectively and successfully, so that the transition appears seamless to the library's community stakeholders. There are many decisions to make, prompted by many questions, outlined below. These questions are about time lines, responsibilities, and desired outcomes- all of which guide the planning process. To be most effective, the process must be systematic and suited to your library's specific needs. In other words, what follows is not in and of itself a succession plan for your library director. There is no one single cookie-cutter plan.

Rather, to be effective, the board of trustees, with staff support, must engage in a dialogue that responds to key questions. There is no one right answer to these very delicate questions. What is important to note is that the process is a critical aspect and can make or break a succession. The other crucial and often neglected aspect of a leadership change is that it is a transition and needs to be considered holistically, not as a one-day or one-time event. The questions and issues we build into the following outline for succession planning address both of these aspects of recruiting a library director, helping to make the transition a smooth and successful one. Our outlined plan is broken into three major phases: preparation, recruitment, and transition.

EMERGENCY SUCCESSION PLAN

Sometimes a surprise happens: the director lets you know, with little or no warning, that she is leaving the job for another opportunity, family issues, health, or other reasons. In the worst case, she has been struck by a bus or challenged by a major illness, and there is little time to prepare. That is why it is important to have in place, at a minimum, an emergency plan. The trustees of one of our academic library clients made the mistake of not worrying about succession planning since, the library director, who was 60 years old, said that he was planning to stay for another five years, at least until age 65. They did not want to upset the director, whom they valued highly, by raising the issue of succession planning before he was ready for it. And what happened? They were surprised-and so was he! His daughter had triplets, and he and his wife decided to move cross-country to help her. The moral is clear: every library should have at least an emergency plan for library director succession at all times. An emergency succession plan ensures the continuous coverage of executive and administrative duties critical to the ongoing operations of the library and its services to its customers or patrons and fenders, political officials, and others by outlining policies and procedures for the temporary appointment of an acting executive director. There are several key components to such a plan. It should identify the priority functions of the library director, both the general functions of a library (or any) leader as well as tasks that are exclusive to your library. Second, the plan should specify what happens in the event of a short- or long-term absence of the library director. This includes notification of trustees, the process that the board or board president begins once notified, the compensation and authority of an acting director and provisions for recruiting a new director.

Another component of the emergency succession plan should be the identification of one or two senior staff members capable of appointment to the position of acting or interim director. If the board decides to divide the functions of the director, these should be clearly delineated in writing. If necessary, any provisions for cross-training staff to help them fulfill priority director functions should be made. Such cross-training should begin with the adoption of the plan. Finally, a communications plan and protocol should be outlined, including categories of constituents (*e.g.*, public officials, customers) who should be personally notified, how (in writing, personally, by phone) and by whom (the board, interim director, other), and in what time frame. If the succession plan has to be implemented in an emergency, the board should ensure that the following are in place:

- Board members who have experience in search/transition

- Senior staff member(s) or others who can serve as interim director
- An up-to-date job description for the position of interim or acting library director
- A key contact list to notify individuals and communicate plans/status
- Written procedures for conducting a search (with and without a search firm) and for the selection process
- Identification of a key spokesperson for the library board

PREPARATION

During this first phase the library has an opportunity to take stock, reflect on the past, anticipate and plan for the future, and identify the competencies needed by the incoming library director. Keep in mind that each library needs different competencies of its director at different points in its life cycle as well as in accordance with changing community, staff, governance, or other needs.

Libraries facing a union drive, major fund-raising or bond challenge, building projects or construction difficulties, technology overhaul, political upheaval or contentious board relations, low staff morale, or other challenges require unique skills sets of their director. Be very honest, first to yourselves and then to your candidates, about your needs and the knowledge, skills, abilities, and competencies required of the director entering your system. Do not skip over the preparation aspects of this process.

When a library hears that its director is leaving, it is too easy to just rush into the hiring phase. Do that at your own peril. Remember: sometimes you have to go slow to go fast. The work you do in the preparation phase provides a foundation that enhances the success of the library and its incoming director. If you are open, you will see many opportunities in this time of transition. Not rushing, and taking the time to look forward, will help you hire the right leader, one who has the competencies to bring the library to new phases of growth in line with its strategy.

GETTING STARTED: SHOULD YOU USE A CONSULTANT?

In recent times many libraries, large and small, have been engaging search consultants or transition consultants. Some consultants generally focus their attention on helping the library recruit a new director. Some assist the board of trustees to ascertain the needs and expectations of the library or to prepare for the arrival of the new director. Some help the library build internal and board capacity so that it is in stronger shape before welcoming the new director. Others recommend working through the roles of the board and director so there is an easier transition and both can hit the ground running in an effective and healthy manner (yes, this includes eliminating practices of micromanagement, promoting open communications, creating a performance plan, and other forms of open feedback and dialogue). In a few cases, "houses are cleaned," with ineffective or inattentive staff and board members being retired early or otherwise asked to leave prior to the new director coming on board. There are pros and cons to retaining the services of a consultant.

Why retain a consultant:

- Unlike library staff, the consultant is an expert experienced in the search or transition process. She can also provide an unbiased perspective, and the library is the beneficiary of best practices learned from her research and experience with other organisations. A consultant who specializes in libraries (academic or public) knows, and has connections with, many of the most effective leaders in the country-some of whom may never consider applying for a position advertised in a journal but would respond to a phone call from a respected colleague.
- A consultant can help provide an objective assessment of a library's situation and help identify issues library leadership may not have been able to articulate effectively.
- The board of trustees may desire a fresh look at the library's strategy, its structure, and the nature and scope of the position of library director.
- You may recognize the need for external help with the transition, because you do not have the time to devote to a search or for other reasons.

Why conduct the search in-house:

- Members of the board of trustees and staff have the expertise and time to conduct the search and design a transition process.
- Consultants are an extra expense.
- Board members may see every candidate fresh by not having relationships with potential candidates.
- Your staff or board members have been active in the state and national library associations and personally know or are aware of potential candidates.
- An external consultant cannot know the details of your situation as well as you do.

PRIMARY TASKS OF THE PREPARATION PHASE

In this phase, you begin looking at yourself and your library. Taking the time to assess the library's strategy, culture, and governance honestly supports and guides the succession planning process. It also helps your library board's capacity building and development process.

Solidify the Management Team

This is also a time to think about staffing in light of what is required to achieve the strategic direction. For example, suppose there is a gap in marketing competencies at the staff and leadership levels, and strategies to move the library forward indicate a need for marketing expertise. In that case it would be appropriate to establish a plan to develop these competencies in the senior staff, agree to hire a senior staff person with these competencies, or retain the services of a marketing consultant. You may realize some salary savings in the turnover of the director position, and now is the time to use whatever financial flexibility is associated with her departure. But whether the changes you need cost money or not, consider what changes should be made in leadership, systems, staffing, or structure to ease the director's transition into your library and her ability to hit the ground running. Also at this time, the board should ensure that there is staff or board backup for key director functions. It is also critical that administrative systems (especially financial and human resources) are in order, so that the library can operate effectively during the transition to a new director, which often involves a period when the library must function with interim leadership.

Identify Library Vulnerabilities

This is an excellent time to take a realistic look at the state of the library and to design and implement strategies where they are needed. For example, this might be the time to create a position of deputy or assistant director-perhaps a step the director had been avoiding. Or it might be a good time to create an advisory board for marketing, or fund-raising-if the assessment identifies these as areas of weakness. Ensure that the library's financial and HR systems are in order, so that the library's daily operations can run smoothly during any period of interim leadership.

Assess Staff for Leadership Potential

Whether or not you have a succession plan in place, you should ask:

- Are there current employees who have the potential to fill any given position? Now? After a formal training and development process?
- Are these employees interested and motivated to pursue this growth opportunity?
- Will the succession planning process in which your library is engaging put in place a formal training and development process to cultivate these new leaders?

Build the Board's Leadership Abilities

Is your board operating at an optimal level? Is there a job description for the trustees? Does the board have trouble making decisions or working through conflict? Is there agreement about the kind of authority you are prepared to give the next director and what kind of accountability mechanisms you should consider to ensure responsible board oversight? Assess board governance practices and organisational health, looking at mission, vision, and strategic and operational planning processes. This is an ideal time to build the leadership capacity of the board and its members. A board member with organisational or board development skills can do this, although you might prefer to use an objective outsider to help you address these often complex, difficult, and very human issues. Using a consultant to interview the departing director as well as individual board members in confidence can really assist the process of moving ahead quickly. The consultant can use this information to help move the board forward in its thinking about roles, relationships, and how board members can individually and collectively support the library and its director.

Identify the Library's Broad Strategic Directions

Where are you in implementing the strategic plan? How are your customers and partners responding? Is the annual performance evaluation for the director tied to progress measured against your strategic initiatives? Is there a process for the new director to provide input to the plan?

Back Up the Library Director's Key Relationships

Too often we find that the library director is the only person who knows key elected and appointed government officials, important community leaders, grantors, and executive directors of other partners. This is the time to make sure that staff and board members also know and have connections with these leaders.

Set Financial Parameters

Discuss possible financial and budgetary issues for the succession (hiring costs, severance package costs for the exiting director, training and development and compensation package for the new director, fee for a search or transition consultant if used).

Prepare a Communications Plan

This is one of the most important steps. Communications to all key stakeholders (city/county officials, higher education leadership, board of trustees, Friends of the Library, library foundation, community leaders, and staff) should be ongoing, sincere, and transparent. Updates at each step in the process are critical. Connect with stakeholders (internal and in the community); talk to them about their needs and expectations for a new director in your community. Determine by whom and how communication will be handled. Board members may develop the plan or assign communication responsibilities to a board committee or staff member to be coordinated. The communications plan you prepare now will be used regularly and often with staff, board members, and all stakeholders is to keep them up to date on the status of the search and transition. It should utilize all of your library's communication channels, such as your web site and intranet, newsletter, and news releases. Ultimately, it will

- Announce why the director is leaving and highlight her many accomplishments.
- Announce the formation of a search committee.
- Invite community input regarding possible attributes for success, candidates, and organisational priorities.
- Circulate the profile and encourage applicants to apply.
- Provide status reports.
- Announce selection of the new director and let the community know how they can meet her.

At every milestone in the process, your communications plan should answer these questions: who needs to know what is happening, and how do we tell them?

Deal with the Personal and Professional Barriers for the Departing Director

Issues might be the degree to which the director is emotionally and financially prepared for retirement or the best exit strategy to make all parties feel good about the ending. You will want to help make the departing director's transition as easy as possible, especially if she is appreciated throughout the community and has served for a long time. Set a fixed departure date. Everyone needs to be able to move forward, and there is much work to do. Or, you may even decide to continue some new kind of working arrangement with the departing director, redefining what retirement means. In that case, all parties want and need clarity about what the new arrangements and roles are-and are not. Make plans now for when and how you will say good-bye, publicly and graciously, to the departing director. Celebrate her successes and contributions.

PRIMARY TASKS OF THE RECRUITMENT AND SELECTION PHASE

As soon as the library director announces her intention to leave the system and sets a date for so doing, the recruitment and selection process begins.

Appoint a Selection Committee

Such a task force, appointed by the board, might be composed of members of the board as well as key constituents such as county elected or appointed officials, the school system superintendent, the director of the county's literacy group, the head of the United Way, a teenager, and a representative from the chamber of commerce. The library's HR director staffs the committee process. The charge for this group is very specific: identify and prioritize the key competencies, knowledge, skills, and abilities that the next library director should possess before advertising the position. Input from the library's key constituencies is important to this process. Ultimately, the full board will interview the final two or three candidates. When finalists are brought in for interviews, the selection committee members will attend public presentations or meet and- greet sessions and provide feedback to the board, to help them make a better decision.

Should you use staff in the recruitment process? There are differences of opinion about how and to what extent staff should be involved in the leadership selection and transition process. We believe, again, that staff should be kept informed and that ongoing communication is important to staff at all levels, but that they should not play a deciding role in selection. We strongly support Tom Gilmore's thoughtful perspective: "The only universally wrong step a board can take (and many do) is not to have thought through how the staff will be involved and be kept informed at all stages of the process." Gilmore suggests that staff should be very involved in assessing the library's strategic challenges and identifying the characteristics needed of the director as well as in recommending candidates and resources for recruitment. Staff should also be invited to meet the final candidates, often as part of an interview process, and provide their advice and input. However, the final selection should not be made by staff; that is a decision to be made by the board of trustees. In general, we agree that staff should not serve on the search committee.

If your library has an HR director, it would be appropriate to ask her to staff the process and work directly with the members of the search committee. If not working with a search or transition consultant the HR director should, at a minimum, support the search committee by engaging in the following tasks:

- Work closely with the committee chair throughout the process in a support capacity.
- Issue invitations to serve on the search committee, prepare agendas (with committee chair), and arrange for meeting room space, refreshments, and so forth.
- Take notes at meetings; send to committee members.
- After search committee conversations, draft the job description and other collateral public relations materials.
- Help prepare the communications plan for staff and community.
- Advertise the job opening as appropriate, for example, in Library Journal, Library Hotline.

- Determine how and when candidates will receive communications throughout the process, and who will communicate with candidates.
- Screen résumés against established criteria.
- Prepare summaries of highly qualified candidates for the search committee.
- Provide sample interview questions and any other preparation needed by interviewers.
- Schedule telephone screening interviews on behalf of the search committee.
- Schedule and arrange interviews for finalists.
- Check references.
- Suggest, based on data, a fair and equitable compensation and benefits package for the person selected. Determine who will handle the offer and salary negotiations.

Thc HR dircctor must act with the highest integrity and utmost confidentiality throughout this process. You may wonder if another staff member could take on this role. The answer is possibly, and probably not. In our experience, general staff are accustomed to and respect the barrier of silence from HR staff about all personnel issues. They do not have the same expectations of other staff, nor are other staff members accustomed to this level of confidentiality. Keep in mind that the confidentiality extends beyond your library. Many applying for the position will not make their interest known at their present workplace. Recruiting at this level must be handled delicately and with the utmost confidence. Many high-potential and highly visible candidates working in other libraries will not apply unless confidentially can be guaranteed unless and until they are named as a finalist.

There are other considerations as well. Consider the plight of one system that did not have a full-time HR manager. With the resignation of the library director, the library's four senior managers were asked to function as a team in an "interim director" role. We worked with this team to help them clarify roles, responsibilities, and expectations. The group worked together rather effectively-until a shift in roles occurred. One of the team members was assigned by the board to work with the search consultant and staff the search committee. Although this individual was capable, other team members became jealous and insecure because they were not privy to the same information as their colleague. This made for a less than effective process and also affected the team's longer-term working relationships.

Develop an Up-to-Date Job Description

Although your inclination may be to reach for the departing director's job description, resist the temptation. Instead of looking to the past and what was, focus on the future. Look forward towards the library's aspirations and then shape the job, and job description, around your current and future leadership needs. What are the core values, beliefs, and assumptions about how the library operates that are important for the new director to understand? What are the "non-negotiable" behaviours that the director should uphold and nurture? What current processes and activities create the most frustration, confusion, or dysfunctional behaviour within the library that the board wants the director to change? Does the new director need to fit the current culture, or is she expected to change it? How? Completing a profile of the ideal candidate helps you update the library director's job description as well as recruitment materials such as job postings. Craft a profile by answering these questions.

- What are the desired experiences and qualifications of the director?
- How are your library's values and needs matched to the director?
- What is exceptional about your library and why is this job a wonderful opportunity?
- What leadership skills and competencies are unique to the library's needs and challenges?
- What are the key attributes needed (*e.g.*, visionary, seasoned manager who provides stability and structure, turnaround expert, transformational change agent, entrepreneur, community builder, strategic thinker/actor)?
- Does the new director have to be a librarian?
- Does she need to be politically astute?
- Does she need to have skills in fund development?
- Does she need to be skilled in working with a union?
- How does the director attend to the board's feelings and needs?
- How does the director envision changes in organisational functioning?
- How does the director communicate and interact with the board?

It is tailored to one library's specific situation and goes so far as to indicate by weighted values how the board of trustees wants the new director to spend her time. Your board might ask the library's HR director to gather some examples from other libraries that should be suitable models.

A MOBILE FUTURE FOR ACADEMIC LIBRARIES

In the past few decades, some technological changes have appeared gradually and their impact on higher education has been incremental. In other cases, over relatively short periods of time, technological changes, such as the introduction of Web browsers, have had a major, and some would say revolutionary, impact on higher education as well as the broader society. Which will it be for mobile devices? Will their impact be gradual and incremental or sudden and revolutionary? There is a case for both points of view. Since individuals have been using devices such as laptops and mobile phones for decades, one might argue that the impact of the use of mobile devices on peoples' behaviour in general and on higher education in particular has been relatively gradual.

On the other hand, as devices with compelling new features emerge and wireless connectivity is almost ubiquitously available, we may be on the verge of a revolutionary phase of mobile device impact on higher education and libraries. This stage will examine trends and developments for mobile devices and will discuss what impact they may have on the future of academic library services. The stage focuses on a few types of mobile devices (particularly smartphones and e-book readers), selected applications for mobile devices, and provides some thoughts on the implications for library information and services. While many academic libraries are experimenting with various types of reference services for users of mobile devices, fewer are thinking of the potentially dramatic changes that the uptake of devices with sophisticated capabilities may have on their user community and more specifically on the use of digital information resources.

Keeping abreast of this rapidly changing arena can be challenging, and this stage attempts to provide an overview of developments of significance to academic libraries. The 2010 edition of the annual and influential Horizon Report, sponsored by the New Media Consortium and the EDUCAUSE Learning Initiative, came out at the time of the writing of this stage. Mobile computing was the first trend they identified, with an adoption timeframe of one year or less. The 2010 report marks the fourth appearance of mobile computing on this annual list of key technology trends for higher education. The report is compiled through a process to first identify a wide array of current and emerging technologies, which are then ranked in importance by an international advisory board using a modified Delphi process.

Therefore, many individuals around the world who are involved in developing, using, and monitoring technologies in higher education believe that mobile computing has great significance for our education institutions. Last year's report commented, "Over the past several years, we have watched mobiles become ever more capable and more common. The rapid pace of innovation in this arena continues to increase the potential of these little devices, challenging our ideas of how they should be used and presenting additional options with each new generation of mobiles". The students that we serve in higher education often own a variety of mobile devices, including laptop computers, cell phones, and MP3 players or other audio player devices.

The annual EDUCAUSE survey of undergraduates' use of technology stopped asking about student ownership of cell phones because they are so ubiquitous. However, they have been asking about ownership of Internet-capable handheld devices for the past few years so that they can monitor this emerging trend. In another survey, about half of students reported owning an Internet capable handheld device and around 12 per cent said they plan to purchase one in the next year. Many students do not use the internet capabilities of their devices at present, primarily due to cost considerations. In order to better understand how students might want to use internet-capable cell phones, the survey asked this year about potential uses.

Only 14.8 per cent selected "library services" as one of the top three institutional services they would most likely use from a smartphone. While librarians might feel discouraged by this number, I think it is likely that students do not yet understand the full range of library content and services that they might potentially reach via a smartphone.

DEVICES

Mobile devices include laptops, netbooks, notebook computers, cell phones, audio players such as MP3 players, cameras, and other items. This stage will focus on smartphones (and assumes the inclusion of the iPod Touch, which has the features of a smartphone minus traditional telephone capabilities) and on e-book readers. The array of names used for telephone handheld devices can be confusing, *e.g.* cell phone, mobile phone, handheld device, smartphone, etc. The use of the term "smartphone" has become popular to identify devices that have Internet capability and functionalities that are similar to computers, although there is no industry-wide standard definition of the term. The capabilities and uses of smartphones have gone well beyond the simple cell phones of 20 years ago.

When Americans first bought cell phones, they used them for communication on-the-go and the communication was solely via voice phone calls. While Europeans, Asians, and Africans have long used their mobile phones for text messaging, many Americans were much slower to move into this different mode of communication via the phone device. Only when the service became more predictably affordable and teenagers in households quickly adopted the mode of communication did texting begin to take off in the US. The third way that individuals use some cell phones – smartphones – for communication is e-mail; internet-capable models such as Blackberries and iPhones make checking and writing e-mail from many venues possible and more convenient than carrying a laptop computer in all travel situations.

In a period of around twenty years, mobile phone devices have become much more versatile, allowing communication between and among individuals in at least three ways that are now considered mainstream, *e.g.* voice, texting, and e-mail. In addition, other modes of communication, such as the use of Twitter or communicating updates on a Facebook page, are becoming popular activities on cell phones. While this range of communication capabilities has significance for libraries, especially in the provision of reference service, it is possible that it will actually be the use of smartphones for reading, watching, listening to, and producing digital content that will have the most impact on libraries. The lightning pace of development of new applications, or apps, for smartphones such as the iPhone, is enhancing the ability to use a wide range of information resources in various formats on handheld devices.

At MIT, with the introduction of the iPhone in spring, 2007, they found that the functionalities "spurred mobile web access on the MIT campus, especially among students. For many users, the mobile device was no longer just a telephone; rather, it was quickly evolving into a handheld information retrieval device." The 2010 Horizon Report states, "Third party applications for all kinds of tasks can now be developed once and ported to a variety of mobile platforms... It is these applications that are making mobiles such an indispensable part of our lives. Tools for study, productivity, task management, and more have been integrated into a single device that we grab along with car keys and wallet." It is truly remarkable to consider the kinds of activities one can engage in today using a single handheld device, including:

- Voice and video calling.
- Sending and receiving e-mail.
- SMS text messaging.
- Searching the internet.
- Searching databases of scholarly information.
- Organising citations.
- Accessing a course management system.
- Reading or listening to books and articles.
- Taking photos.
- Playing videos.
- Making videos.
- Setting an alarm clock.
- Using a GPS navigation system.
- Playing games.

In effect, the smartphone can provide capabilities that are very similar to laptop computers. One of the questions for the future is whether individuals will prefer to own one device that has many functions but may not perform all of them well or own a number of devices. It is likely that individuals will vary in their reliance on a smartphone for various functions. For example, a serious photographer will likely own and use a separate camera, and someone who writes lengthy documents (*e.g.* college students and faculty) will likely continue to have some type of computer that has a larger monitor and keyboard. Another question is what other types of devices will emerge and win popularity. Roy Tennant reports on prototype wearable technology devices that include cameras that can record information and use it to find information related to an item and then project that information onto a surface. A library user could aim the camera to a code on a book in the stacks, software could connect the code to information or reviews about the book, and then project that information onto a surface. We may see more use of codes on labels, similar to bar codes that will link physical objects to information on the internet. Lorcan Dempsey reports that the University of Bath in the UK is already using codes – specifically a type called QR codes in its catalogue. A user can scan the code into his or her phone and go into the stacks to find it with the call number readily available on the phone. In addition, the user can save the information provided by the code to begin compiling a bibliography. Libraries have traditionally served as a public good, providing resources and services to all, including those who could not afford to purchase some types of content or services on their own. While it is unlikely that libraries will provide smartphones, either for use within the library or for loan because most would agree that provision of telephone service is outside the scope of library service, many libraries are already loaning a wide variety of mobile devices.

For example, laptops are one type of mobile device, and many academic libraries have laptop loan programmes. Some libraries also loan cameras, video cameras, MP3 or similar audio player devices, headphones, etc. A small number of libraries are loaning Internet-capable devices such as the iPod Touch. It is also possible that more departments or institutions will begin to require that students have a mobile device that can be used for a variety of purposes in their coursework. The library will want to be part of campus discussions on such decisions so that they can ensure that library content and services will be able to interoperate with the device and platform selected. The proliferation of mobile devices will have implications for library space configuration and services. For example, libraries may want to offer large monitors and keyboards that students can use with their personal mobile devices. They may want to install lockers with electrical outlets so that students can recharge their devices while they go to class or take a break.

And, they may want to change the ratio of desktop computers to open tables as more students rely on their own devices. Currently, many students who own laptops do not bring them to campus, but students almost always bring their cell phones wherever they go. In fact, this is true of people of all ages and nationalities. In an international survey, three quarters of respondents said they never leave home without their mobile phones. A market researcher affiliated with the survey commented, "... the mobile is part remote control, part security blanket. Mobiles give us safety, security and instant access to information. They are the number one tool of communication for us... They are our connections to our lives." As smartphones become our users' key information devices, libraries will want to have a significant presence in offering content and services suitable for those devices.

E-BOOKS AND E-BOOK READERS

E-books, or books in digital form, may be purchased or freely downloaded in formats that will enable individuals to read them on standard computers, or they may be configured in proprietary formats for particular devices. Most academic libraries already offer e-book content that users can download and read on standard computers. Amazon's Kindle device and SONY's e-book reader will soon be joined by the nook from Barnes and Noble; these are purpose-specific handheld mobile devices. These devices are linked to content purchase programmes that limit what may be put on the device and in some cases, what may be shared with others. Both companies that produce e-books for computers and companies that produce e-books for their proprietary systems are now offering or promising to offer content configured for Smartphones. Some academic libraries are already experimenting with lending e-book readers loaded with content or providing specific content to fulfil interlibrary loan requests on an e-book reader. It is difficult to predict whether such devices will grow in popularity or will cede their market share to smartphones. The larger screen makes these devices more acceptable for some users to read online materials they might have formerly preferred to have in print. However, the current limited functionality, for example inability or poor capability for annotation or note taking, has made them less acceptable in some areas of higher education, particularly as textbook substitutes. The app for smartphones, released by Eucalyptus in fall, 2009 may be a harbinger of some trends. First, it has a page-turning function that gives the feeling that one has when turning the pages of a physical book; readers may like this feature.

Second, it makes available books from Project Gutenberg, one of the earliest projects to digitise books and make them available to the public; all books are out of copyright. The Eucalyptus homepage even advertises one of its functions as "Search like a librarian", a positive attribute of their system. The availability of a large collection of digitised books, Project Gutenberg, also brings to mind the potential impact that the Google Book Settlement may have on the availability of e-book content. Will collections of content be marketed through the e-book reader producers? Will the content, either public domain or in-copyright, be repackaged in collections and made available to libraries or the general public in formats for various devices or with enhanced functionalities for particular devices? E-books may be seen as a mechanism to promote environmentally friendly practices.

Princeton University has launched a small experiment in which around 50 students enrolled in three courses have been given Kindles in order to determine whether the use of the device reduces the amount of printing by students. The university estimates that 10 million pages were printed by students in computer labs in a year, and they believe that much of that printing was of materials on electronic reserve from the library. The experiment will help the university determine whether e-book readers reduce the cost of printing and conserve resources. While the experiment was developed primarily for financial and environmental reasons, at least one of the professors whose course is included is also interested in whether the e-book reader can enhance student learning. The library, computer center, and faculty are collaborating on this project.

MAKING PAYMENTS VIA DEVICES

Another trend that may have an impact on libraries and other areas in higher education is the capability to use mobile phones for payments for goods and services. In particular, there is an emergence of applications for contactless mobile payments that use radio frequency identification technology (RFID) to enable mobile subscribers to make payment by waving their device directly in front of a terminal or automated device, such as a vending machine. Globally, the payments made via these systems have exploded, from $3 billion in 2007 to $10 billion in 2009. Libraries will want to keep abreast of any campus initiatives to move to this type of technology for vending machines, printers, etc. so that their needs can be taken into account. This will be yet one more activity that mobile phones may be used for by our community.

MOBILE DEVICES, STUDENTS, AND LEARNING

As librarians work with students as part of information literacy classes, at service desks, and in cyberspace, it is important to realise that for students, the mobile device will increasingly become an instrument for creation of digital content, and not just a device for access to content. Students can use smartphones to create short videos, to type a blog entry for a class assignment, to "tweet" in response to a question posed by a professor or to create a group poem, or to take photos or record audio to embed in a Powerpoint presentation or text document. Some of this content creation may be in connection with independent assignments and some may be developed as part of coordinated class field work.

In describing the potential use of mobile devices for elementary students on field trips, the researchers wrote, "Mobile devices can capture authentic educational multimedia data, in context, that have previously been unavailable. Data captured in context allows for sharing and remembering experiences upon return to the classroom. Using multiple forms of data capture, for example, supporting photographs with audio recordings and student notes can assist students and teachers in seeing the whole picture of a learning experience." Librarians can teach students about the availability of access to information from their mobile devices in the field, to support research. They can assist students in learning about software to organise their information on their smartphones or how to develop mash-ups using geographic applications and other information resources.

They can support students' creative work with mobile devices. This requires an awareness of innovative assignments, outreach to faculty, and the skills to teach these technologies. In one application developed for students with laptops and targeted for science classes, LectureTools allows students more functionality than a typical personal response system or "clicker." The professor can ask students questions beyond multiple-choice, enabling them to work with images or respond to more complex questions. In addition, a student has developed some applications for LectureTools, including one that enables students to connect with others, finding which students may live in the same dorm or share particular interests.

While LectureTools is employed on laptop computers, these types of functionalities may be adapted for smartphones in future. The incorporation of active learning functions along with social networking capabilities makes this a particularly interesting tool. One can imagine librarians incorporating the use of such tools in information literacy classes. Another model is the Hotseat application, which allows students to use either their laptop or their mobile phone to comment or ask questions during class. Faculty involved in pilot classes using Hotseat have found that the application encourages participation by more students when controversial issues are discussed, enables students to share information among themselves and to set up ad-hoc study groups, and encourages more interaction between professor and students.

As more and more students buy internet-capable phones and when phone plans that include internet access become more affordable, students will seek streamlined ways to locate the kinds of information they need. Campus information portals for mobile devices are one emerging model, and some academic libraries are already represented in these venues. Another model will be the development of applications, sometimes by members of the university community, including students. At Stanford University, two undergraduates along with friends built an iPhone app "iStanford" that provides some of the features of standard university portals, *e.g.* access to the course catalogue. In addition, they are releasing features that will allow students to access grades, add and drop courses, and perform other activities usually restricted to the secure campus network.

The students have worked with the Stanford information technology unit to integrate, with university approval, their application into core computer systems at Stanford. Librarians should seek faculty on their campuses who are developing or using innovative tools like those described here and begin experimenting with them in partnership with faculty and students. Mobile devices can offer more opportunities for students to be actively engaged in their learning and to fully participate in the social nature of learning. Librarians might encourage, through contests or other means, student development of apps that make library content and services more useful for specific groups of users.

INTERNET TRAINING FOR ACADEMIC LIBRARY STAFF

Educational institutions are being encouraged by the Government and other organizations to upgrade their resources for research and education. Consequently the academic libraries of the higher education institutions are also being upgraded. Internet has proved to be boon in this endeavor. Internet has helped these libraries to be interconnected and share their resources and also to access resources in remote locations. Internet connections have been growing in the recent years with good connectivity and access.

But are these libraries fully geared up especially in terms of their employees' skills to be able to fully utilize the Internet for the benefit of the academic community? It has already been widely discussed that training is essential for the staffs to work in a network and automated environment. The Library Association Working Party on Training cites in its Policy Statement that training "is of fundamental importance to all levels of staffs working in all types of library", contributing to "greater efficiency and continuity, with real cost benefits". Since technology keeps on changing it becomes even more necessary for the staff to be trained in Internet.

OBJECTIVES

The present study aims to understand the status of Internet training for the academic library staff within greater Guwahati. Since the importance of Internet is growing in today's academic environment therefore the issue of training the academic library staff in handling Internet is becoming important. So this study will investigate the various training methods used in the academic libraries, the content of such training, problems encountered and whether any evaluation is undertaken for such training. The investigation will also try to reveal the attitudes of the library managers with regard to training their staff on Internet. In order to understand the status of Internet training for the staffs of the academic libraries a sample of six academic libraries was taken. A questionnaire-based survey of the sample was conducted. The questionnaire contained both close-ended questions and open-ended questions.

The questionnaire was prepared based on some existing studies already done on understanding the Internet training of academic library staff. Comprehending the importance of the study the author personally went to the respective libraries to collect the data.

INTERNET AND ITS USE IN ACADEMIC LIBRARIES

Many of us by now are familiar with Internet especially those working in the academic libraries. This is because the academic libraries have been the pioneer in the field of automation and Internet. Internet has become essential for today's education and research in the academic institutions. Library being a hub of research and academic activities are therefore being provided with Internet connections. The Internet is a unique information resource, bringing a wide range of material from around the world to a local machine. One of the earliest usages of the Internet was to access the OPAC *i.e.* the Online Public Access Catalogues of different libraries or within a campus. The union catalogues which lists the holdings of several libraries was another important tool accessible through net.

Another area of growing importance for academic libraries is that of electronic journals. Big publishing houses like Elsevier, Springer, ACM etc. are providing packages of their journals to libraries in electronic form via Internet. So at nominal subscription the libraries can access to these costly journals, which are becoming increasingly popular with the users.

Thus grew consortia based subscription in India. INDEST, INFONET and CSIR Consortium are the examples of library consortia for sharing journals and bibliographic information. These consortia based journal subscription are available through the Internet. The Indian National Digital Library in Engineering Science and Technology *i.e.* INDEST was set up by the Ministry of Human resource Development (MHRD) for subscription to electronic resources for 38 institutions including IISc, IITs, NITs, IIMs, etc. Over 6000 e-journals are accessible through this consortium, which has its headquarters in IIT Delhi. Infonet Contortia is set up by UGC and operated through its INFLIBNET Centre, Ahmedabad. Over 100 Universities are its members. It covers disciplines like Arts, Sciences, Mathematics and statistics etc. About 4000 full text electronic journals from 25 publishers are currently accessible. CSIR e-journal Consortia provides access to 3300+ e-journals from 11 publishers to all CSIR S&T staff of different CSIR institutions located around India.

These consortia not only provide full text access but they also give access to bibliographic databases like COMPENDEX, INSPEC SciFinder Scholar, and Web of Science etc. Many open access materials important for education and research are available on the Internet. They are very useful in the context that they are not fee based and also don't have restricted access and are thus becoming very popular with students and researchers. Communicating with users is very important in academic libraries.

Widespread access to the Internet has also created new means of communicating with users. In some cases, Internet technologies (e.g. email and publishing on Web pages) are used to reproduce an existing service in another medium, such as online "suggestion boxes". However, there is "added value" to such a service as users can mail in their suggestions from terminals on or off campus at a time convenient to them. Email enquiry or reference services also represent an extension of mainstream library activity - although some academic librarians initially had concerns about being able to meet the demand of such a service. Reference and enquiry services in academic libraries in the main seek to teach their users how to search for information themselves, rather than answering the enquiries themselves, as is more likely to be the case in a special library.

A significant number of British academic libraries have adopted electronic mail enquiry or information services - at the University of Hull the "email help line" is treated as an extension of the Enquiry Desk service. Anecdotal evidence suggests that electronic enquiry services are not overwhelmed, and most users do stay within the parameters of the service. The most successful email enquiry services have developed their procedures and boundaries prior to the service going live.

As many enquiries fall into the category of Frequently Asked Questions, these can thus be answered by existing position statements. Electronic mail also has great potential to cut down on the mountain of paperwork involved in sending out recall notices, notifying readers that items can be collected etc. Some library systems allow students to renew loans (provided no other reader is waiting for the book) directly via the OPAC or to request a renewal via email. Similarly, weblogs or simply blogs are now becoming very popular on the Internet as a communication medium. A library weblog can be used to:

- Providing news information for users
- Providing links to recommend internet sources
- Book reviews, information about new books
- Providing entertainment or amusement for users
- Providing news or information for librarians
- Book discussions
- Provide news or information for the trustees
- Provide research tips
- Communication among the librarians (in a library system).

The library can make good use of the electronic mail system of Internet *i.e.* Email to communicate reservation alert, current awareness services like SDI, new arrivals of books and journals, receiving interlibrary loan request and sending overdue notices to the users. In addition to these specialist services academic librarians also make use of the Internet information that is available to all users. Much bibliographical and price information can be found from online bookstores and Web sites for professional organizations and publishers. A wide range of factual information from government and NGO sources is available too.

Although librarians have more skepticism about the well-publicized Web search tools than most users, such services can be valuable, particularly for easily defined topics (such as names or abbreviations) and the sheer range of material indexed, subjects covered and the speed with which they search can make them useful when a clear starting point is not obvious. They may not always retrieve a full answer, but may give helpful clues.

Internet resources are just another information medium academic librarians are extending their skills to encompass it. So they may offer a current awareness service to teaching and research staff to inform them of new Web sites and discussion lists; they will apply established criteria to assessing the content of information sources or the effectiveness of secondary services like search tools.

The hypertext nature of the Web makes it easy to make additional explanation or instruction for a resource as an optional choice. This concept of instruction at the point and time of use is harder to achieve in the physical library.

WHY INTERNET TRAINING IS NECESSARY

In the Internet age there is acute need of Internet specialists. These specialists will be armed with the necessary skills and training to help the users to locate their information pin pointedly and efficiently on the net. Libraries specially the academic libraries would have a great demand for these specialists.

Internet connectivity in the academic libraries is growing day by day. So, the present administration of the academic institutions should take necessary steps to equip the library staff with the required skills and training on Internet. Training can help to understand many essential aspects of the Internet such as follows:

- Are we using the right type of Internet connection for our needs? Are we getting a good deal?
- How quickly can we find what we looking for on the Internet? We should be able to find useful information about virtually any topic in less than a minute. If you're taking longer, you're doing something wrong.
- How do we know if we are safe? Most people who contract viruses or other nastiest thought they were protected.
- Are we using email correctly? Or are we really annoying we our colleagues and they are too polite to tell us? We might be unpleasantly surprised to learn the truth.
- How do we avoid those terrible pop-up windows?
- How do we know if information is real or a hoax?
- How can we make surfing faster?
- How can we get the maximum satisfaction without spending more time on net?

As noted by Paula L. Matthews while employing Internet in academic libraries one of the important issues for the administrator is the implementation library staff training. "A lack of training can result in:

- Poor staff performance;
- Lack of motivation;
- High staff turnover;
- Resistance to change;
- Costly errors or accidents;
- Unfulfilled objectives;
- Undesirable low standards of service.

Academic librarians may well draw on training materials available on the Internet for the higher education community. Recently the issue of whether librarians should learn HTML (Hyper-Text Markup Language) was debated on a North American discussion list. The conclusion was that knowledge of basic HTML was necessary in order to prepare presentations and information guides, which are an integral part of the librarian's professional role. As an increasing number of academic libraries experience some measure of "convergence" with other academic support services, library staff has many opportunities to augment their IT skills and collaborate with colleagues in other services. The combination of technical knowledge and the ability to evaluate information sources is a powerful argument for the continued need for LIS professionals in higher education.

The users of the Academic libraries including some faculty member do not have net skills. In such cases the academic library staff has to come forward to help them. For readiness the staff should have some kind of net skills. The transition of traditional library resources to technology based library resources has put a lot of pressure on the academic library staff. Unless the staff is kept up to date on Internet skills he will face more pressure to work in such conditions. So training of staff has become a necessity in today's context

Bibliography

Anderson, B.: *Library Management Styles and Structures: A Need to Rethink*, Toronto: Thomson Nelson, 2008.

Arora Kanu : *University Library System : Centralization and Decentralization*, Regal, Delhi, 2008.

Balkus, R.: *Writing Abstracts for Free-text Searching*, Washington: Social Security Administration, 2009.

Ballabh, Anand : *New Approaches to Library Administration,* Rajat, Delhi, 2002.

Brian, R.: *Documentary Abstracting: Toward a Methodological Model*, London: Macmillan, 2004.

Buckland Michael : *Book Availability and the Library Users,* New York: Perga-mon Press, 1975.

Burnette, D.: *Library Patrons and the Law*, Alexandria: Council on Library Science Education, 2003.

Cohen, M.: *Maintaining the Privacy of Library Records*, London: Waverly Book Company, 2003.

Dasmann, J.: *Using Qualitative Data Analysis Software: Merits and Hazards*, New York: Computers in Human Services, 2001.

George, R.: *String Indexing*, Expanded, Baltimore, MD: Johns Hopkins University Press, 2003.

Glaser, B.: *Confidentiality in the Use of Library Materials*, Mill Valley: Sociology Press, 2001.

Guba, E.: *RSS for Non-Techie Librarians*, San Francisco: Jossey Bass Press, 2003.

Hollingsworth, J.: *Information Representation and Retrieval in the Digital Age*, Philadelphia: University of Pennsylvania Press 2005.

Jackson, Sideny L. : *Libraries and Librarianship in the West: A Brief History,* New Yokr: McGraw-Hill Book Company, 1974.

Jeffreys, S.: *Effective Library and Information Centre Management,* Toronto: Thomson Nelson, 2006.

LeCompte, M.: *Computers in Libraries*, San Diego: Academic Press, 2004.

Mackenzie, A.G.: *Academic Libraries in Contraction: Facts, Theories and Fancies*, USA: Aslib Proceedings, 1996.

Madhusudana, B.: *Management Information and Decision Support Systems in Libraries*, London: Weekly Press, 2002.

Meyers, William P.: *Indexing Books: Lessons in Language Computations*, UK: British Library, 2005.

Mishler, E.: *Accessibility in the Virtual Library*: London: Harvard University Press, 2002.

Payne, P. and Willers, J.M.: *Using Management Information in a Polytechnic Library.* NJ: Journal of Librarianship, 1999.

Sparrow, E.: *Management Information in the British Library Humanities and Social Sciences Division*, UK: Journal of Librarianship, 2002.

Strauss, A.: *Assistive Technology in Special Libraries*, San Francisco: Harper Bowling Green State University, 2000.

Van Maanen, J.: *Library Assistive Technology: Predictions and Trends*, Chicago: The Hotel Monthly Press, 2006.

Vygotsky, L.: *Adaptive Technology Equipment for the Library*, New York: Columbia Press, 2001.

Index

M

N

O

P

Q

R

S

T

U

V

W